THE RELIGION OF DOSTOEVSKY

A. Boyce Gibson

THE RELIGION OF DOSTOEVSKY

THE WESTMINSTER PRESS
PHILADELPHIA

PUBLISHED BY THE WESTMINSTER PRESS ®
PHILADELPHIA, PENNSYLVANIA

PRINTED IN THE UNITED STATES OF AMERICA

Library of Congress Cataloging in Publication Data

Gibson, Alexander Boyce, 1900–1972.
  The religion of Dostoevsky.

  Bibliography: p.
  1. Dostoevskiĭ, Fedor Mikhaĭlovich, 1821–1881—
Religion and ethics. I. Title.
PG3328.Z7R424   891.7′3′3   73–9956
ISBN 0–664–20989–0

CONTENTS

PREFACE

This work is the repayment of a debt incurred fifty years ago. It was the novels of Dostoevsky which, by excluding the 'natural' and 'rational' religion in which I was reared, started me off as a Christian-in-process. They have been to me not only surpassingly great literature, but the inspiration of a lifetime. Not least, they have shown me that religious faith and philosophic doubt in a sense belong together, and have helped me to see that the practice of my religion and my scruples as a professional philosopher, so far from compromising, actually enhance each other.

My first guide on these paths was A. D. Lindsay, my tutor at Balliol College, Oxford, and the professor under whom I served as assistant at the University of Glasgow – later to be Master of Balliol, and to be ennobled as the first Lord Lindsay of Birker. The inspiration of this delayed reaction goes back to him; and it is devotedly dedicated to his memory.

I wish to thank Mrs Nina Christesen, head of the Department of Russian Studies at the University of Melbourne, for her interest and advice; for the extended loan of Russian works not otherwise readily available in Australia; and for permission to use in Chapter 7 material published in *Melbourne Slavonic Studies* 4 November 1970. I wish also to thank Dr Dmitri Grishin, of the same department, well known for his work on Dostoevsky's *Diary of a Writer*, for discussing details with me, and for putting at my disposal his remarkable knowledge of personalities and problems in Russia in the latter part of the nineteenth century. Both of them have helped me on the finer points of the Russian language. Neither should be held responsible for my interpretations or my opinions. In addition I am most grateful to Mrs Jean Archer and Mrs Isobel Robin for typing from a handscript notorious to several generations of University secretaries.

I have cited from Constance Garnett's translation of the novels; it is the most widely available, and despite a smoothness notably absent from the original, is hardly ever seriously misleading. For *Stavrogin's Confession*, I have worked from the Russian text, as edited by Andrey Kozin. I have not deliberately set out to discuss the views of other critics, but have sometimes tangled with them incidentally. I received my copy of Richard Peace's *Dostoyevsky* too late for overall revision, but I have referred to it in Chapter 5 to remedy what would have been a serious defect: a failure to mention Dostoevsky's relation to Russian sectarianism.

On the vexed question of transliteration, I have been traditional where traditions are firmly established (e.g. *Dostoevsky, Turgenev, Berdyaev, Zernov*). Otherwise, I have used -ye or -yo, as pronunciation requires, for the Russian -e (e.g., *Yepanchin, Alyosha*) but have stopped short when the effect seemed too cumbrous: I cannot bring myself to write *Lyebyedyev*. In general I have returned foreign names to their native spelling: one could hardly write *Prince Garry* (for Harry!) in a reference to Shakespeare's Henry IV, Part I, any more than one could write *Gete* for Goethe, or *Yum* for Hume. But I believe I follow the usual courtesies in transliterating literally the foreign names of distinguished contemporary Russians (e.g. *Fridlender*). The final -ii I render, traditionally, with -y: this covers all names ending in -skii, and, not so happily, names like *Porfiry* and *Arkady*. In the latter cases, at least, I should have liked to align with Peace and write -iy, and we shall probably come round to it; but it is not for one who is not primarily a linguist to innovate, even in good company.

I have finally to thank the publishers.

INTRODUCTION

Of books on Dostoevsky there is no end. The only excuse for another is that everyone sees him differently. He is the sort of writer whom everyone *will* see differently. He is as far as possible from the well-organized one-piece writer with an assured direction and intention. He is, more than most, an universal writer, but his comprehensiveness is not orderly or systematic; it is shown rather in his capacity to exhibit contradictories simultaneously. Commentators with a systematic turn of mind will fasten on one or another of the conflicting elements, whether of thought or of feeling, and try to piece them together, or to explain one of them away. In doing so they recast Dostoevsky in their own image. To discern his general drift, it is necessary to hold on to the apparent contradictions and to estimate their weight in the total construction. The one thing not to do is to attempt a well-mannered compromise. In *The Light and the Dark*, C. P. Snow makes one of his characters observe that the truth lies at both extremes, but never at the middle. Dostoevsky would have applauded. If an over-all view is possible, it can only be on that assumption; not by selection, or by being reasonable.

There are three factors which make the endeavour unusually difficult. In the first place, restricting ourselves for the moment to the novels, there is Dostoevsky's disconcerting way of distributing his sentiments. That eminent critic, M. M. Bakhtin,[1]

[1] In *Problemy tvorchestvo Dostoevskogo*, 1929. It has now been absorbed into

describes his writing as 'polyphonic': that is to say, his characters speak with their own voices, each individually, rather than for the author, and these voices talk with the author, dialogically, and even across him. If that is so, we should be careful not to attribute their *obiter dicta* to Dostoevsky personally. Not only so: Dostoevsky allows them to distort, or to place in a totally different perspective, views which in his own person he expresses unambiguously. Examples are Shatov's admission of a fatal flaw in Russian nationalist religion in *The Possessed*, and, in *The Idiot*, the anti-Catholic tirade launched by Myshkin at his betrothal party, in which a favourite hero is made to look ridiculous – by expressing, inopportunely, sentiments which Dostoevsky set out at length in *The Diary of a Writer*. Those characters have taken up the author's personal opinions and have despoiled them for their own purposes.

That leads to the second complicating factor. Dostoevsky expressed himself not only as an artist through his novels, but also as a journalist and commentator in *Time*, *Epoch*, and above all in the *Diary*. What he says in these extra-curricular exercises (which took much of his time and to which he attached what seems to us to be an extravagant importance) does roughly correspond to the drift of his novels; but where the publicist declaims, the artist probes beneath the surface. That is not surprising: political and religious decisions are for the most part adopted on a balance of considerations, which, in practice, is taken as final, but which, in the suspending reflectiveness of art, may be called in question. Most people, and certainly all people with Dostoevsky's gift of self-examination, inwardly ponder over their external certainties. The public Dostoevsky was a Christian, and in his later years a Christian propagandist: Dostoevsky the artist calls so much in question that highly qualified critics have seen his public professions as a mask for his inward misgivings. At the very least, the artist gives the atheist so much rope that he confronts the believer on equal terms; and who is to say that Dostoevsky's outward decision for orthodoxy

---

Problemy poetiki Dostoevskogo, 1963. See p. 64, note 16. For full details of the references cited in this book see Bibliography.

is to override the evidence of his artistic intimations? Indeed, one would expect the reflective artist to see further than the impetuous commentator. In the case of Shakespeare, there is no such problem; all we know about his outlook is in the plays; such personal details about him as have been recovered (for example, that he seems to have had a good head for business) bear on the interpretation of the plays not at all. In the case of Dostoevsky, the two faces overlap without coinciding: which makes it difficult to arrive at a total estimate, even of the novels.[2]

The third perplexing factor is the phenomenon of 'the double'. This was the title of Dostoevsky's second published work, and he announced it as something new to the realm of fiction: 'the Double was the greatest and most important social type which I was the first to discover and proclaim'.[3] It is certainly a clue to the major novels (Nastasya Filippovna, Stavrogin, Ivan Kara-mazov); and even when the character is not doubled against himself he forms a double with some other character (Myshkin and Rogozhin, Sonya and Svidrigaylov). Simplicity in Dostoev-sky is usually doubleness minus.[4] This polarization of the emotions could be interpreted as a clinical discovery: there is more of the medical heritage in Dostoevsky than has commonly been allowed for. But it was also part of his own character; he could depict it so well because he knew it from the inside. He was vain and humble, demanding and self-sacrificing, irritable and devoted; and it is probably not too much to add that what has been called his 'cruel talent' was the reverse side of his horror of cruelty. In *The Raw Youth* Versilov is made to say: 'I am capable of experiencing in complete comfort two contradictory feelings at one and the same time – independently, of course, of my own

---

[2] Apart from his novels, in which Dostoevsky is able to distance his convictions, and his journalism, in which he is content to parade them, there is his private corres-pondence. Much of it is hasty and uninstructive and overburdened with his financial difficulties. But some letters in which he previews his projected novels, or sets out his convictions without having to adapt them to his characters or to maintain his own public stance, are among our most valuable sources.

[3] Quoted by E. H. Carr, *Dostoevsky, 1821–1881*, p. 43, from a letter written after his return from Siberia.

[4] The simplicity of Sonya, as the notebooks show, is the result of paring off suc-cessive layers of complexity. In the original draft she storms and argues.

will.'[5] In the same spirit, Dostoevsky wrote in his own person to Yekaterina Yunge:[6] 'What do you mean by complaining of your doubleness? . . . I too suffer from the same kind of doubleness, and I have done so all my life. It is a great torment, but a great delight too.' He continues: 'If you had been more limited, you would have been less conscientious and would not have suffered from that doubleness. On the contrary, you would have suffered from great conceit.' The passage throws light on Dostoevsky's notable antipathy to one-track practical minds; but it also prepares us, not only for characters exhibiting convincing contradictions of thought and behaviour, but in addition for possibly contradictory ways of presenting them on the part of the author. And this, too, is a source of perplexity for the interpreter. It may even be the central perplexity: it shows up both in the distribution of 'voices', and in the differences between the *Diary* and the novels.

These considerations apply particularly to Dostoevsky's 'Christianity', which, in this study, is the main object of review. We know what he wanted to believe, and, with the more conscious part of his mind, did believe; we can trace the growth of his mind from a Christian childhood through Utopian liberalism to the brink of atheism; we can trace the return journey through acquaintance with the 'people' and exasperation with Utopianism of any kind, especially Utilitarian, to a Christian anthropology with populist-nationalist grass-roots; and thence to the final stage of orthodoxy, when he had returned to the practice of his religion and was diligently attending church festivals and exploring monasteries, and had taken up with that brilliant young philosopher of religion, Vladimir Solovyov. That covers the whole period of preparation for *The Brothers Karamazov*; but it is just in that work that the difficulty of interpretation is greatest. Those who find Dostoevsky's presentation of Christian faith and practice unreal or unworthy of his literary genius (they

---

[5] P. 206. All the quotations in this book of writings of Dostoevsky are taken from the translations by Constance Garnett and published by William Heinemann, 1912–20, unless indicated otherwise.

[6] In a letter dated 11 April 1880, when he was in the last year of his life and at the height of his fame.

include almost all post-revolutionary Russian critics), and those who find Ivan Karamazov's case for atheism overpowering (like D. H. Lawrence and Middleton Murry), will insist that as an artist Dostoevsky breaks through his self-pretences to his own deepest sense of the way things are. Yet no account can properly represent him, even as an artist, which in any way slurs his complete devotion to Christ.

Are we then to leave these impressive incompatibles staring at each other, across the invisible barrier between art and non-art? Only, we think, as a last resort. Artists have first of all to live, and those built like Dostoevsky have to turn lives into art. It is hoped, in what follows, to contribute to a more comprehensive view first, by tracing the stages in the growth of Dostoevsky's public religion, and then by an analysis of the major novels – again, with special attention to their place in the sequence. Reference will also be made to the external events, biographical or historical, with which they were connected. As a practising journalist, Dostoevsky was sensitively responsive to contemporary happenings, and in his fiction he continually adjusted his anthropology to accommodate or to reject the latest developments.[7] He was not at all the type of thinker who matures early and spends the rest of his life variously expressing a fixed outlook. He was impetuous, premature, experimental; he reacted strongly, and then reacted against his reaction; and only at the very end does his conviction consolidate into anything like a pattern. Even so, he died before fully expressing it in artistic form; *The Brothers Karamazov* was to have a sequel, and perhaps to be the first of a series.[8]

Another way of examining the twists and turns of Dostoevsky's religion, and particularly the alleged discrepancy between his public religion and the religion of the novels, is to ask what can be reasonably expected of a Christian novelist, and in particular from a novelist in the mode of nineteenth-century Russian Orthodoxy. Much of the scepticism expressed about the religion

[7] For example, the role of N. G. Chernyshevsky in focusing his vision on disinterested evil in *Notes from Underground*.

[8] Balzac's *La comédie humaine* is a possible precedent. Dostoevsky knew his work extremely well, and admired it.

of the novels starts from the assumption that the Christian novelist will speak in his own person through a megaphone and give
the devil no chance to speak at all. It is enough to reply that
those who think like that have not studied Christian novelists
(from Bunyan to Graham Greene, they testify to the contrary)
and know nothing of the knife-edge balancing-act which is
Christian experience. The particular issue is more difficult. Some
of the problems of Western critics are due to unfamiliarity with
Dostoevsky's Russian Orthodox setting; and almost all the
difficulties of post-revolutionary Russian critics arise from their
determination to turn their backs on it. For example: Westerners
discern in it an age-long heritage of passive endurance, and as
foreigners usually take as typical of another culture that aspect
of it which least resembles their own, they have represented
Orthodoxy in its Russian form as a religion of suffering and taken
Dostoevsky to be its exponent. Post-revolutionary Russians,
with their activist preoccupations, notice the same thing, with
disdain and indignation, and condemn it in Dostoevsky as stulti-
fying his undoubted discernment of social evils. Neither of them
pause to reflect that the acceptance of suffering, while part of the
tradition, is by no means the whole of it, and that for Dostoevsky
it is only a stage on the journey and not a final therapeutic
recommendation. Dostoevsky was wholly Orthodox in sentiment and loyalty, but he had an incurable Western itch for a
better world, as more conservative Orthodox writers have themselves observed. In an article in the Australian quarterly review,
Twentieth Century,[9] Dr D. Grishin combs them over and repro-
duces the following. From Konstantin Leontyev: 'Only those
little acquainted with true orthodoxy . . . can consider *The
Brothers Karamazov* an orthodox novel': or again, 'for Dostoevsky his dreams of a heavenly Jerusalem on this earth were dearer
than the truth of life and the true morals of the Church'. From
Dmitri Merezhkovsky: 'Dostoevsky's orthodoxy was private,
personal, unhistoric, non-popular, without belief in the miraculous.' And V. V. Rozanov complains that he was unorthodox in

---

[9] Autumn 1963, pp. 257ff. It remains to be said that both Leontyev and Rozanov
were too odd to be typical, and at least as idiosyncratic as Dostoevsky.

allowing Ivan Karamazov, with Alyosha's connivance, to attribute the sufferings of children to the indifference of God rather than to the sins of their parents. They were not wholly mistaken: Dostoevsky was fascinated, to the end of his days, with the earthly paradise (after all, Christians do pray: thy will be done on earth as it is in Heaven); he demythologizes hell, and says nothing about the fear of the Lord, which for Leontyev was all-important; and he values humility not for itself but as a way of dissipating the primary evil of humiliation.[10] What attracted the attention of the Westerners and the displeasure of post-revolutionary Russians was only part of the Orthodox story, and an even smaller part of the story about Dostoevsky.

To return. We propose to record what is known from outside the novels of Dostoevsky's engagements, disengagements and re-engagements with the Christian faith, and briefly to consider, with special reference to his particular background, the purposes and predicament of a Christian novelist. These enquiries will pave the way for our main objective, which is to trace chronologically the currents and counter-currents of his thought and feeling in the novels themselves.

[10] Cf. St Basil (a Greek Father): 'He who subjects himself to his neighbour in love can never be humiliated.' The Eastern Church was concerned with this issue before Russia was heard of; it was not, as Dostoevsky thought, a Russian discovery.

✖❦ ONE ❦✖

The Public Religion of Dostoevsky

I

There is little doubt about the facts: they have come out grad-
ually, but are now recorded in all the biographies. The only
problem is how to read them.

Dostoevsky received a strictly Orthodox family education. 'I
knew Christ in the family home while still a child', he wrote; and
again, evaluating the experience, 'without something holy and
precious carried over from the memories of childhood, one cannot even live'.[1] It is not always noted that his experience was
unusual. In the best circles the church was no more than a necessary political convenience. Most of Dostoevsky's fellow-
conspirators in the Petrashevsky affair, as he himself points out,[2]
had no such reflections to fall back on. Dostoevsky, the grandson
of a priest from Volhynia and the son of a severe and cross-
grained but undoubtedly pious hospital doctor belonging only to
the minor nobility, and a mother brought up in a pious household
of Moscow merchants, came to maturity in a period of Russian
history in which formal profession and effective unbelief were
the rule in high places, and his own education shows how little
his parents counted for in the best society. But there is no reason
to doubt either their sincerity or their thoroughness. He tells us:
'In our family, we knew the Gospels from our earliest childhood.'[3] Like his Father Zosima,[4] he was brought up on Hübner's

---

[1] *Diary of a Writer*, tr. B. Brasol, I, p. 152; cf. *The Brothers Karamazov*, p. 836.
[2] Loc. cit.   [3] Ibid.   [4] *The Brothers Karamazov*, p. 306.

One Hundred and Four Stories from the Old and the New Testament.
The family received religious instruction from the deacon at the
hospital to which his father was attached.[5] Every year they paid
a holiday pilgrimage to the Troytsa monastery for the festival of
St Sergius – they stayed there two or three days, taking part in
all the services, absorbing the splendour of the ritual and sharing
the fervour of their fellow-worshippers; and we should remember
that in the Orthodox Church very young children receive the
bread and wine of the Holy Communion. Dostoevsky has himself
recorded that it all made a profound impression on him and he
was grateful for it to the end of his days. Even in his most un-
believing period in Petersburg he told his medical adviser,
Yanovsky, that 'prayer is the best therapy'.[6] Emotionally and
practically, he was well prepared for a Christian career. But in
the Dostoevsky ménage there does not appear to have been
much religious discussion: Dostoevsky *père* did not admit religious problems. There was also no philosophical theology in the
church of his time which could have given rise to them: no
Thomas Aquinas or Duns Scotus, no Descartes or Leibniz, no
Bossuet or Paley. Dostoevsky's religious education did not supply him with the means to meet an intellectual challenge. He saw
the difficulties coming: at the age of seventeen he wrote to his
brother: 'Nature, the soul, God, love – all this is understood by
the heart, not by the mind.'[7] It is one of the major problems of
interpretation to discover for how long Dostoevsky was to
shelter under this alibi, and whether, in the end of all, there may
not be something to be said for it.

In 1837 his father decided to send his two elder sons to
Petersburg to be trained as engineering cadets. Fyodor, un-
accustomed to casual social contacts, kept very much to himself.
His fellow-students at the Academy found his piety excessive.
But, as he gravitated to literature, his attitude appears to have
changed. From 1841 on there are fewer religious references in
his correspondence – except in his letters to his father, where

5 This and the following details are recorded by Pierre Pascal, *Dostoïevski*, pp. 12ff.

6 Yanovsky, who attended Dostoevsky till he was sent to Siberia, was the first of
three good Christians who helped Dostoevsky in his moral and spiritual difficulties.

7 31 October 1838 (*Pisma* I, p. 50).

they are suspiciously obtrusive. Simultaneously he seems to have
been interesting himself in the writings of French Utopian
socialists. His youth *chef-d'oeuvre*, *Poor Folk* (1846), which made
him instantaneously famous, is strongly humanitarian, with few
overtones of either politics or religion, but it is the one novel in
which poverty is not only the background of the action, but the
trigger which precipitates the events. Its most important result,
from the point of view of this essay, is that it put Dostoevsky in
touch with the eminent critic, V. I. Belinsky, whose influence on
him can be traced throughout his life.

Belinsky was far more formidable than the French romantics.
To start with (and Dostoevsky always held this in his favour),
he was fervently Russian. 'Without nationalities humanity would
be a dead logical abstraction.' On this subject he agreed with the
Slavophiles rather than the 'humanistic cosmopolitans', 'for if
the former do err they err like human beings, whereas the latter,
if they speak the truth, sound like a book of logic.'[8] The whole
sentence reads just like Dostoevsky. In the second place, though
self-taught and according to Dostoevsky uncertain in foreign
languages, he had mastered the essentials of the Hegelian left,
especially Feuerbach. *The Essence of Christianity* is a work always
to be reckoned with in the study of Dostoevsky, and whether he
had read it or not is beside the point. He was profoundly in-
fluenced by the reputation and the vehement temperament of
Belinsky, was flattered by his attention (in his early years, at
least, he was highly susceptible to flattery), and he took over
Feuerbach in the warmer Russian style which Belinsky had provided for him. That meant systematically treating statements
about God as statements about men. It did not mean denying or
discarding them, but it did mean atheism – together with the
humanitarian content with which the statements about God had
been mistakenly associated. Dostoevsky was already predisposed
to a kind of Christian socialism. He was now told that if there
was to be social reform it would have to start with the denial of God.[9]

8 V. J. Belinsky, *Selected Philosophical Works*, p. 371.
9 The assumption is that religion is subservient to political authority. In Russia
in 1845 it largely was.

In the third place, Belinsky found in Feuerbach an affirmation of human solidarity sufficient to resist the encroaching individualism of the times – expressed with a fervour almost eschatological. He wrote: 'If I did succeed in reaching the top of the evolutionary ladder, even then I would demand an account from you[10] of all the victims of the conditions of life and history, of all the victims of accident and superstition . . . otherwise I will throw myself headlong from the top rung.' This thought is basic to Dostoevsky's whole way of thinking and plays a major role in *The Brothers Karamazov*: not only in the rebellion of Ivan, where it has been identified, but also in the autobiography of Father Zosima, where it has been missed: it is one of the premisses behind 'each is responsible for all'. It is in fact the crucial link between the two sides of Dostoevsky's 'world-understanding'.

There is no doubt, on Dostoevsky's own evidence, that he swallowed Belinsky whole. In 1845 he ceased to attend Holy Communion; and though he quarrelled with him after a year's close association (mainly, it would seem, over his criticism of *The Double*), he still 'passionately embraced his teaching'.[11] But Yanovsky reports his church attendance in 1847 (the year Belinsky died, in Austria, at the age of 36) and refers to their many conversations about religion. He even describes his patient as 'a patriot and a believer'.[12] It is easy to believe that, writing thirty years later, he was allowing subsequent events to influence his recollections, and in any case to attend church with a

10 Belinsky here appears to be apostrophizing Hegel. He continues: 'I will not have happiness if you gave it to me gratis unless I feel assured of every one of my blood brothers, the bone of my bone and flesh of my flesh. Disharmony is said to be the condition of harmony: that may be very profitable and pleasant for melomaniacs, but certainly not for those whose fates are destined to express the idea of disharmony.' – Letter to V. P. Botkin, 1 March 1841 in *Selected Philosophical Works*, p. 150. Ivan Karamazov said it more clearly, but not differently, and was left unanswered. It is the one feature common to Dostoevsky the rebel and Dostoevsky the Christian.

11 *Diary of a Writer*, I, p. 9.

12 Quoted by N. Lossky, *Dostoevsky i ego khristyanskoye mïroponimanye*, p. 59. Yanovsky wrote his reminiscences in 1885, after the death of Dostoevsky, he also wrote some letters about his early acquaintance with him to his widow. He gives the impression of being reliable, but loyal almost to a fault. At any rate, his is the most detailed evidence for Dostoevsky's religious condition at the time, and unless reason can be found for rejecting it, it should be allowed to stand.

friend is no evidence for a fixed attitude, least of all in the case of a 'double' like Dostoevsky. But of one thing we can be sure: even in the midst of his Western misadventures, Dostoevsky remained devoted to the figure of Christ. That was not wholly inconsistent with his new convictions. In this age of 'Christian atheists' inside the churches, it is easier to follow the perplexities and repugnances of nineteenth-century 'Christian atheists' outside the churches. So long as Christ is delivered of his shroud of deity, he can be revered as the best man ever. If this is a way out, Dostoevsky certainly took it. And that is how he was able, with a clear conscience, to read Belinsky's famous letter to Gogol, no less than three times, to his underground societies.

The story of his association with the Petrashevsky circle, and with its more radical offshoot under Durov, is well known and need not be repeated. For what they were worth, Dostoevsky was certainly heavily involved with them. He was too ardent, and perhaps also too religious, to be satisfied with Petrashevsky, who was both a materialist and a muddler.[13] He attached himself to the activist group of Durov, who was both more Christian and more revolutionary. In that capacity and that frame of mind he repeatedly read aloud, to both circles, Belinsky's letter to Gogol.

It has been said that the letter was 'packed with atheism'; but, whether by conviction or by cunning, that was not the way Belinsky wrote it. He insinuated the atheism which we know he professed; for example, he stressed the point which Dostoevsky never quite succeeded in meeting,[14] that the Russian temperament is not at all mystical, and its religious expressions purely superstitious. He attacked the church shrewdly and venomously; but he tempered the wind to Dostoevsky by asking: 'Why have you mixed Christ up in all this?' 'He was the first to bring to people the teaching of freedom, equality and brotherhood and to set the seal of truth to that teaching by martyrdom.'[15] And his

---

[13] Later, he wrote disparagingly of 'circles in which heated discussions on matters of importance are conducted, and a few home truths are uttered, and it all peters out' (*Dostoevsky's Occasional Writings*, tr. David Magarshack, p. x).

[14] *Diary of a Writer*, I, p. 452.

[15] *Selected Philosophical Works*, p. 506.

way of admiring Voltaire was not to claim him as anti-Christian, but to affirm that 'he was more the son of Christ . . . than all your priests, bishops, metropolitans and patriarchs – and every schoolboy knows it!'[16] With the atheism concealed as sociological description, and Christ raised to the height of human excellence, everything we know of Dostoevsky at the time suggests that he could have read it with conviction and a clear conscience, and to say that he did so only because he had promised, as he did at the enquiry, while fair enough as a defendant's stratagem, was a signal understatement. As for the authorities, all they cared about was the church, which the letter certainly lampooned without mercy.

For the rest of his life, Dostoevsky felt the force of Belinsky's argument. Often he wrestled with it and tried to banish it; at such times he denounced Belinsky as an atheist and a deceiver.[17] As he grew surer within himself his recollections were more generous.[18] At the end of his life he wrote a letter which shows that the incubus was no longer riding him. He was replying to a father who wanted advice on his son's reading. Conventional for once, he commends 'only those books which produce beautiful impressions or give rise to lofty thoughts'. And to his list he admits the writings of Belinsky![19]

To return. When he confronted the authorities after his arrest, Dostoevsky was a wishful Christian convinced by Belinsky's social and philosophical analysis. In that spirit he expected to die: from those convictions, he tells us later, no one of his fellow-members, in the face of immediate execution, would have wished to withdraw.[20]

He could even, he says, have taken part in a revolution: referring to subsequent history, he could, *at that time*, have become a Nechayevist. The administration was not mistaken in thinking him one of the most conspiratorial members of his

[16] As late as 1876, Dostoevsky said the same thing about George Sand: 'Without knowing it, she was one of the staunchest confessors of Christ' (*Diary of a Writer*, I, p.340). An echo?

[17] Particularly in his correspondence from abroad, 1868–69.

[18] *Diary of a Writer*, long entry, I, pp.6–9.

[19] *Dostoevsky's Occasional Writings*, tr. David Magarshack, p.316.

[20] *Diary of a Writer*, I, p.151.

group, even if it was, as a group, not particularly conspiratorial. But there is no reason to suppose that he was not entirely sincere in his devotion for Christ, or that something in him not merely conventional (when was he ever merely conventional?) drew him to the occasional practice of public worship recorded by Yanovsky for 1847–49.

Twenty years later, when opinion about religion was more sharply polarized, the two strands of Dostoevsky's behaviour would have been incompatible. In 1849, when a sort of atheistic Christian socialism with overtones of holiness was an allowable option, they could combine in that loose consistency which admits of different convictions in different contexts. Dostoevsky revered Christ but sat loose to all theology. In fact, throughout his life it was the devil in him who talked theology, and genuine theologians of a later period had, retrospectively, some ground for their suspicions. But he differed from the convinced atheist (whose intellectual convictions he could not refute) in thinking that theology was not all that important. As he grew older he began to see how Christian action could lead into Christian conviction. But he never saw Christian theology as the condition of Christian action: the most it could be would be a hobbling attempt to give an account of it. In 1849 he was still impressed by Belinsky's refusal of the world as it stands to the extent of venerating Christ simply as an 'ideal'. It took a multiplication of antipathies (Dostoevsky had this dialectical way of thinking) to carry him further.

For the rest, two comments, to be expanded later.

1. As C. S. Lewis has reminded us, 'only a minority of religions have a theology'; for example, 'there is no series of statements which the Greeks agreed in believing about Zeus'.[21] To maintain a religious stance in the absence of what are supposed to be the appropriate beliefs is not, on the evidence of religious history, a contradiction in terms: and least of all in the Russian Orthodox Church in the mid-nineteenth century. Only towards its close did some of its best minds begin to take a philosophical survey of their beliefs, which up to that time were mainly outgrowths of

[21] 'Theology and Poetry', *They Asked for a Paper*, p. 150.

the central rituals and festivals. Thus the absence of a theology would at that place and time be less remarkable than it would have been in theologically conditioned Western Europe, and less likely to denote a loss of faith. That the absence of a theology might itself be an anti-theology would be less evident to Feuerbach's Russian readers than it was to Feuerbach himself.

2. But, secondly and principally, Dostoevsky was never particularly concerned for consistency. We have alluded to his interest in 'doubleness', his own and his characters': we may add the testimony of his friend N. N. Strakhov, on his 'capacity to take into his mind discrepant structures'. His was probably an extreme case; but don't we all? Why should one not find one's way in life, using, in different contexts, now one clue, now another? During 1847–49, Dostoevsky wanted to promote certain social reforms; his special subjects, so to speak, in the circle are said to have been judicial reform, the freedom of the press, and the abolition of serfdom – none of them inconsistent with the Christian religion, and as a matter of fact Dostoevsky held tenaciously to his opinions on them even as a 'conservative'.[22] He also wanted to express his infinite devotion to Christ, even to the extent of maintaining the formalities of church connection. If some of his fellow-conspirators were atheists, and some of his fellow-worshippers reactionary, that does not invalidate his two-eyed stance, even according to the best rational principles. But perhaps this apology would have been too rational to satisfy him. At this time he would have said that on the intellectual issue the Westernizers were in the right, but that in the constitution of man reason is one factor only; his heart must speak for itself; and if the result is discomfort, there is honesty in admitting it; most of us prefer to paper the cracks, in an exercise of Sartrian 'bad faith'. E. H. Carr[23] refers us back to Elizabethan England, 'before the orderly blight of rationalism had descended and before human nature had been obscured beneath a specious

---

[22] If the official church was against them it should be remembered that the church was under strict imperial supervision. Literary critics sometimes refer to the procurator of the Holy Synod as if he had been a sort of archbishop. In fact he was an imperial officer planted on the Synod to keep ecclesiastics in order.

[23] *Dostoevsky, 1821–1881*, p. 318.

surface of coherence and consistency'. Few of us would survive a searching enquiry into the 'coherence and consistency' of our beliefs and activities; Dostoevsky differed only in that he was better aware of it, and less reticent.

But, even so, the conflict was there, and, looking back, Dostoevsky saw it as a conflict. Recalling this stage of his development at the end of his life, he wrote: 'From the people I received again into my soul Christ, whom I had known in the family home when still a child, and nearly lost when in my turn I was transformed into an European liberal.'[24] Even if the loss was never complete,[25] even if he maintained a formal tie with the church, even if he continued to venerate Christ, there was something which, later, he felt to have been wrong. If we look to the Western contacts to which the passage draws attention, we may hazard a guess as to what it was. One thing is certain: it was not simple or straightforward. Unlike Tolstoy's, which proceed through a series of clean breaks, Dostoevsky's phases overlap, and reappear in unexpected combinations.

There are two ways in which he could claim his faith had been in danger. The first 'near loss' stands out at once from his practical concerns. He did not exactly forget Christ, but he allowed him to be crowded out by his own derivatives. We have noted how Belinsky praised Voltaire as a 'son of Christ', and how even as late as 1876 Dostoevsky himself paid a similar curious homage to George Sand. He also called Dickens a 'great Christian',[26] and, unlike Tolstoy, he was not merely referring to *A Christmas Carol*. In that sense, any broadly humanitarian enterprise might be called Christian; and in that sense Dostoevsky's interest in reform could be so described. The danger that way is being so immersed in the process as to forget what started it up. The Christianity in it is 'nearly lost' by dilution.

The second aspect of the 'near loss' is the representing of

[24] *Diary of a Writer* (1880), II, p. 984.
[25] Dostoevsky writes 'nearly lost', or 'was about to lose'; in Russian, *utratil bylo*. Pierre Pascal, who translates simply, *je perdis*, misses the point of the Russian idiom. (*Dostoïevsky*, p. 17). Other writers who translate correctly, incorrectly proceed to the same conclusion.
[26] *Diary of a Writer*, I, p. 350.

Christ as an 'ideal'. An 'ideal', in Dostoevsky's language, is sharply distinguished from a 'presence'; to depict Christ as an ideal is to declare him incomparable, and therefore out of reach. Now in the literature at his disposal, French-Utopian and German-philosophical alike, presence was rarefied into ideals; but in that literature it was naïvely assumed that ideals could be quickly realized. It took Dostoevsky years of suffering and disillusion to find that they can not, even when their content is distinctively Christian.[27] But even before his exile, there was something in Dostoevsky's experience which forbade over-expectation. That was the phenomenon of 'doubleness', which, as has been noted, played a large part in Dostoevsky's life, and a still larger part in the development of the novels. A simple case is to be found in his confession to his brother Mikhail, in 1847: 'I could give my life for you and yours; but even when my heart is warm with love, people often can't get so much as one friendly word out of me.'[28]

Now 'ideals' are suited to 'doubles', and 'doubles' feed on 'ideals'. 'Ideals' easily become a high-minded imaginative substitute for action. They split the will from the deed. They are the moral expression of the self-centred post-romanticism which prided itself on attaining, at the expense of action, to more refined or exalted states of consciousness. They create a polarity between themselves and the impulses they are supposed to govern. Because they are alienated from the evil in the world. they cannot control it. In all these respects Christian concern operates in precisely the opposite fashion. That is why Christianity infected with doubleness is 'nearly lost'. That is why, later on, Dostoevsky laid so much stress on incarnation.[29] He saw ideals and doubles in the same bracket; and as he matured

[27] Later he was to call this simple-minded optimism, 'Schillerism': with some injustice to Schiller, but with a sure insight into the shallowness of his romantic-reformist aspirations. He was not alone. While he was still under the spell, Marx and Engels were jeering at the Utopian socialists and their 'duodecimo editions of the new Jerusalem' (*Communist Manifesto*, 1848).

[28] *Letters of F. H. Dostoevsky to his Family and Friends,* tr. E. C. Mayne, p. 42.

[29] 'Christ came to us so that humanity should find out that the nature of the

he drove the point mercilessly home. In the long short story *The Eternal Husband* (1870), Velchaninov became afflicted with 'higher ideas'. 'In his own mind and in his own conscience he called "higher" all ideas at which (he found to his surprise) he could not laugh in his heart – there had never been such hitherto . . . He knew very well that if only the occasion were to arise he would the very next day, in spite of all the mysterious and reverent resolutions of his conscience, with perfect composure disavow all these "higher ideas", and be the first to turn them into ridicule, without, of course, admitting anything.'[30] In short, what is too solemn to evoke laughter one day will evoke it the next day as a matter of course, without any intervening deliberation. All moral aloofness generates its opposite. Only Christian concern can grasp and grapple with it. 'Higher ideas', 'ideals', or whatever, are merely entertained, and there is a gap in which souls are lost between entertainment and embodiment. The irony of it is that the two defects which Dostoevsky saw in his earlier faith, if explored dialectically, appear as excellences, and as complementary. The dissipation of faith into projects, and the attenuation of faith into unattainable ideals, are removed at one stroke when the projects receive a commission, and the ideals a fulfilment, in a living presence.

Of the two deviations, concern with the earthly paradise, stunned for a period by his experience of the power and malignancy of evil, played little part in Dostoevsky's literary production till his orthodoxy was well established, and then he could handle it;[31] but his concern with doubleness was pressing and immediate. It is the main theme of *The Idiot*, *The Raw Youth*, and, among minor works, *The Eternal Husband*; it enters largely into *The Possessed*, and, as Ivan assumes a major role, almost captures *The Brothers Karamazov*. When, later, he deplored his near loss of Christ in the face of Western Liberalism, he may

---

human spirit can appear in such a heavenly splendour, in actual fact and in the flesh, and not only *in a kind of dream, or as an ideal*' (Notebooks for *The Possessed*, original text, p. 155. Italics ours).

[30] *The Eternal Husband*, p. 1.
[31] See Chapter 6 below.

have been thinking of the evolution of his Christianity into social reform, but he was certainly disconcerted by his discovery of doubleness in himself and as he observed it in others, and he embodied it in an immortal succession of characters, half in anguish and half in excitement. It was only late in his career that he learnt what the hypocrisies of a state-controlled church effectively concealed, that religion and doubles do not go together. Yet, almost at the start, he foresaw it, and put his premonition, symbolically and characteristically, in the mouth of an uneducated servant. In *The Double*, commenting on the two Golyadkins, Petrushka remarks: 'Good folks live honestly, good folks live without falsity, and they never have doubles . . . Yes, they never have doubles. God doesn't afflict honest folk.'[32] Between this discernment and its working out lay the Siberian exile, two marriages, and four of the world's greatest novels.

II

It has been customary to say that Dostoevsky re-learnt Christianity in Siberia, at the hands of 'the people'. At both ends, this is an over-simplification. On the one hand, his attitude when he left Russia was at least formally Christian. On the other, he did not emerge a changed man, nor had he shed his devastating doubts. At the very least, the result of the Siberian experience was considerably delayed. It did not save him from becoming, for a time, a compulsive gambler, nor from being not a little disloyal to his first wife; nor did it remove the traces of Belinsky's intellectual mastery over him. But Siberia did leave its mark; it did something, though superficially not a great deal, to strengthen his Christian conviction; but above all, it wrecked the alternatives and supplied the experiences from which Christian conviction could grow.

In the first place, it brought him face to face with evil – not the metaphysical principle but daily personal demonstrations. He noted in *The House of the Dead* that the convict shows no sign of repentance: to preserve his self-respect against the pressure of

[32] *The Eternal Husband and Other Stories*, p. 225.

his environment he has to have been right.[33] On the other hand, 'humane treatment may humanize even one in whom the image of God has long been obscured'.[34] Reform in these regions is extremely difficult, not quite impossible, but above all piecemeal and personal: so different from the over-all push-button reform planned by intellectuals from an ideological nowhere. The first casualty in Siberia was 'Schillerism'.[35] It was long before Dostoevsky could look Utopia in the face again.

His close-up observation of spiritual deformities in Siberia had a lasting effect on his fiction, and helps us greatly in our enquiry into his approach to religion. Each of the four greatest novels centres round a murder; and even when abroad in 1867–71 he studied the crime reports in Russian newspapers and made notes for future reference. A writer makes the most of his social opportunities: it was Dostoevsky's unusual opportunity to live at close quarters with criminals, because, officially, he was a criminal himself. In the end, he developed a sense of oneness with them, and came to regard them clinically rather than morally; all the more so because he identified in himself the traits which made them what they were. He saw, in particular, how crime follows the pattern of hurt pride; the hardest thing in the world to cure, for it is so often all that the victim has left to him, and to remove it (by forgiveness, for example) would be to extinguish with it his whole being. It is the most serious of all challenges to the 'idealist' version of Christianity, and indeed to Christianity as such, because it will not yield to the standard Christian treatment. In his fiction, Dostoevsky spent the best part of his career hunting it down, and only towards the end is there any sign of a

---

33 *The House of the Dead*, p. 13.   34 Ibid, p. 107.
35 In a letter to E. I. Todleben, 24 March 1856, referring to his involvement in the Petrashevsky circle, he confesses 'I was blind: I believed in theory and Utopia' (*Pisma* I, p.178). If it is urged that in a letter written to a prominent personage to facilitate his rehabilitation he had every reason to represent his role as airier-fairier than it really was, it may be replied that, he admits the intention, though 'no more than the intention', of 'acting against the government'. He certainly stresses the airy-fairiness, but this is precisely what he regrets: that he should have gone so far on an irresponsibly theoretical and Utopian basis. 'Long experience' has taught him better. His reaction against 'ideals' is quite genuine. – Todleben was the military engineer who master-minded the defence of Sebastopol in the Crimean War; he was also the brother of a fellow-cadet of Dostoevsky's at the Engineering Academy.

THE PUBLIC RELIGION OF DOSTOEVSKY 21

breakthrough. In that way, his Siberian experience only added to his spiritual difficulties. But, by closing the door on all evasion, it enabled him to come to terms with them at a higher level.

In the second place, Siberia brought him face to face with the 'people'. This confrontation which Dostoevsky experienced the hard way, from the inside, and with extreme cases, was something which the Westernizing intellectuals, sons for the most part of priests and officials, and sometimes (e.g. Bakunin) of aristocrats, had never experienced at all. Later, in the 1860's, they made a determined effort to 'get among' the people to whom they did not belong: the result was cruelly but not unrealistically caricatured by Dostoevsky in *The Possessed*. Dostoevsky himself would never have come to know them in Petersburg, where he certainly met and felt for the poor and frustrated, but mostly from his own social group. The transition in his point of view was not quick or easy. He was less well prepared than most men for the continuous society of others; and it was one of the worst inflictions of his days as a convict that he was never alone for even a minute. Moreover, he found the prisoners from the 'people' united against the 'nobles'; and according to one of his Polish fellow-political-prisoners did not make things easier when he said 'I am a noble' on unsuitable occasions.[36] The resistance of Raskolnikov to the socialities of prison life is undoubtedly autobiographical; and Dostoevsky had no Sonya to help him on the way. But slowly he appears to have got on terms with his fellow-prisoners and, at the very least, succeeded in understanding them. 'I have learnt to know the Russian people as few know them', he wrote to his brother. 'I hope that such vanity is pardonable.'[37] (He learnt, among other things, that their condition was 'wretched'.) This understanding he treasured through out his life; and it was partly his discovery of the people that led him to the people's God. It was because he was so deeply 'populist' (*narodnik*) that he fell out for good and all with Westernizing liberals with no popular connections – the sort

---

[36] Nobility was hereditary and social, not functional, and Dostoevsky belonged to the eleventh of Peter the Great's twelve grades.

[37] Quoted by Miriam T. Šajković, *F. M. Dostoevsky: his Image of Man*, p. 67.

who sell their peasant serfs and go off to Paris to write for socialist magazines. 'Do the people have to follow us, or do we have to follow the people?'[38] The people had no feeling for institutional democracy, but was bound together in an immemorial fellowship, not based on the Roman concept of rights, and therefore not excluding the transgressor, but rooted in the soil and growing imperceptibly into religion. It was through this natural unanimity leading into a relation to God that Dostoevsky finally recovered the feeling for God himself.

Thus in Siberia Dostoevsky encountered and appropriated factors in life which passed over into Christian feeling, and at the same time made him acutely aware of the practical as well as the intellectual difficulties. It is in this context that we must situate his famous letter to the Christian lady N. A. Fonvizina of 20 February 1854.[39] 'I am a child of the age, a child of unbelief and doubt, up till now, and till the grave shall cover me.' He goes on to speak of 'this longing for faith, which is all the stronger for the proofs I have against it'. And he thanks God for the moments in which he can love, and believe he is loved. 'In such moments I have formulated my creed, in which all is precious and holy to me . . . there is nothing lovelier, deeper, more appealing, more rational, more human and more perfect than the Saviour . . . not only is there no one else like him, there never could be . . . If anyone could prove to me that Christ is outside the truth, and if the truth really did exclude Christ, I should stay with Christ rather than with the truth.'

One knows what the critics (John Middleton Murry is a good example)[40] have made of this. They have fastened on a stage in the journey and treated it as final. It is true that Dostoevsky never ceased to entertain doubts: no Christian of education and intelligence can or should do otherwise; they are a necessary religious exercise. It is true, also, that in this letter the doubts

[38] *Diary of a Writer*, I, p. 204.

[39] She was the widow of a former political exile and stayed on in Siberia after his death. The letter was written after Dostoevsky's liberation from prison and at the beginning of his compulsory service in the army. The passage is quoted in English by John Middleton Murry, *Fyodor Dostoevsky*, pp. 77–8, and by other commentators. The reference in the Russian text is *Pisma*, I, p. 142.

[40] *Fyodor Dostoevsky: a Critical Study*, p. 79.

ch he had recently become, drawing inspiration from
e wisdom of a tradition originally Christian, could
in any way sympathize with either of the fashionable
h at the time of his return were just beginning to
nto articles of faith. What antagonized him was the
t assumption which was common to them, and which
elieved to be anti-Christian. He may not always have
d clearly between them; he slashed out now at one of
f the hydra, now at another; and he certainly did not
between the excesses of individualism and the
empt to correct them: the socialists too were alienated
d he saw no reason to prefer the public to the private
he Golden Calf. But it is true that he reacted strongly
individualism of the Westernizing liberals, and that
l Russian populism as an available alternative. He was
dapted to the capitalist ethic; not only as a young
t as a conservative elder statesman, he always pre-
attered and unsuccessful.

ame, when he returned to journalism, his first articles
iatory. He called on the Westernizing liberals to go
le, not as teachers but as learners; that, he thought,
wn unique experience behind him, was the way to
1 the barrier between their un-Russian education and
1 un-education (packed, none the less, with popular
the broad mass of the peasantry. But he soon found
vere incapable of the necessary humility, and not least
their contempt for the people's religion. Moreover,
enture into Europe[47] in 1862, covering Germany,
a week in London, convinced him that the much ad-
stern model was on the point of running down. Sur-
supremacy of money values in the France of Napoleon
g translated *Eugénie Grandet* as a young man, he
ve been well prepared for it); noting the noise of
and the air-pollution in London, and the contrast
he Crystal Palace and the 'half-naked, uncouth and
opulation of Whitechapel: he recalled Baal, Babylon,
like the British, talk about 'going to Europe'.

are more than merely entertained; intellectually, they hold the
field, and only the affections and an act of will weigh in on the
other side. But the last sentence is hypothetical; it remains to be
seen whether the intellectual difficulties are insuperable. He will
always have his doubts: as his Underground Man tells us, that is
the price to be paid for mind and sensibility in the mid-nineteenth
century. But doubts need not make you give up. If you are a
philosopher[41] you work at them and perhaps begin to erode
them. If you are not, the test is in the living, and, as Dostoevsky
was to discover, in the loving. The letter is a significant item in
a progress report; it reveals a sharpening of the conflict, brought
on by a growing Christian concern; it shows at least how much
Dostoevsky disliked his unbelief; and it keeps the issue open.

One feature of it, however, must be noted for future reference.
In the letter, Dostoevsky accepts the ordinary Western view
about truth, and then opposes it to his vision of what is best.
Unlike some of his near-contemporaries, notably the Slavophil
A. S. Khomyakov on the right, and the revolutionary populist
N. K. Mikhaylovsky on the left, he did not re-define truth to
include righteousness. Khomyakov wrote: 'Truth was not revealed to any one of man's faculties of cognition (reason, sentiment, aesthetic sense, etc.), but to all of them acting together,
inspired and illuminated by faith in the depth of man's soul.[42]
Mikhaylovsky particularly rejoiced in the Russian word *pravda*:
'Only in Russian, it seems, are truth and justice designated by
the same word and fused, as it were, into one great whole.'[43] It
has in fact been noted[44] that it is characteristic of Russian philosophy to seek, not *pravda* reduced to *istina*, a word technically
specified to denote theoretical truth, but *pravda-spravedlivost'*,
truth as righteousness (or vice versa), either including and subordinating, or rejecting outright, *pravda-istina*, theoretical truth
only. But at this stage Dostoevsky was intellectually drawing on

[41] Dostoevsky was not, and knew it: 'I am weak in philosophy, though strong in
my love of it' (letter to N. N. Strakhov, 28 May 1870, *Pisma* II, p. 271).
[42] Peter K. Cristoff, *An Introduction to Nineteenth-Century Russian Slavophilism: a
Study in Ideas* I, p. 135.
[43] *Russian Philosophy*, ed. James M. Edie and others, II, p. 175.
[44] Ibid. p. xi. In the letter to Fonvizina, Dostoevsky uses the word *istina* throughout.

pre-1849 resources: he did not know Khomyakov, who circulated only privately (his attempt to make religion come alive seems to have alarmed the authorities as much as atheism), and at the date of the letter Mikhaylovsky was only fourteen years old. The concept of truth with which he was operating was the unadulterated Western concept. Hence his agony at the time, and his slow recovery of whole-mindedness thereafter.

For the rest, we have from Siberia the testimony of Baron Vrangel (the second good Christian whom Dostoevsky encountered at a crisis of his fortunes), who befriended him when he was released into the army, and gave him the intellectual companionship which he so desperately needed. Vrangel speaks of his 'spiritual revival' and links it with his Bible-reading during his period as a convict. But he also observes: 'He was rather pious, but did not often go to church, and disliked priests, especially Siberian ones.'[45] We have also what may be taken as semi-autobiographical testimony from Siberia in *Memoirs from the House of the Dead*, relating to the official formalities of religion. We have noted that integration with the people, which came to Dostoevsky with great difficulty, was an inclining force in their favour. The references in the *Memoirs* are slight, but significant. Every time a Christian festival is mentioned it is shown to be an equalizing factor – and precisely because it is a *festival*; a celebration *in common*, available to convicts on the same terms as to the world outside. 'Apart from their innate reverence for the great day, the convicts felt unconsciously that by the observance of Christmas they were, as it were, in touch with the whole of the world, that they were not altogether outcasts and lost men, not altogether cut off; that it was the same in prison as amongst other people.'[46] Christmas, just for the moment, gets behind the tough integument of pride. These glimpses should not be underestimated: they prepare us for a

[45] Quoted by N. Lossky, *Dostoevsky i ego khristiyanskoye miroponimaniye*, p.66.
[46] *Memoirs from the House of the Dead*, p.124. So during the Lenten services, as recorded ibid. p.214: 'The convicts prayed very earnestly and every one of them brought his poor farthing to the church every time to buy a candle, or to put in the collection. "I, too, am a man", he thought, and perhaps felt as he gave it, "in God's eyes we are all equal".'

point that is sometimes overlooke
when it finally flowered, was a sh
church religion. But they are g
Goryanchikov (one can fairly rea
does not describe his spiritual
intelligent observations. He is lear

III

The Russia to which Dostoevsky r
older. There was a new Tsar, repu
predecessor (he could hardly have
to be abolished; capitalist enterpr
the structure of the feudal order. I
was reflected in two different way:
Dostoevsky's intellectual develop
distinguish between them, and to
common. The first is the Utilit
Chernyshevsky in his rationalist fa
second may be called the volition
Max Stirner in *The Ego and his O*
an apprehensive public in Turgenev
ing to the first, human beings are s
and necessarily, their own individ
allowed to do so, without being p
tion, families, religion, or the stat
what it ought to be. According to t
and my own standard, totally non-r
and, literally speaking, the creato
meet and collide on the subject of fr
right, the second affirms it crude
happens that a strong social mover
bining incompatibles; it thus enlist
a wider range of ideas and poli
Utilitarian-determinist trend, and
can be found contributing to the e
Neither as the idealizing socialis

[47] Russi

populi
the co
Dosto
trends
crystal
individ
he alw
disting
the hea
disting
socialis
atheists
version
against
he rega
wholly
radical,
ferred t
All th
were co
to the p
with his
break d
the Rus
culture)
that the
because
his first
Paris, a
mired V
veying t
III (ha
should
machine
between
starving

and the Apocalypse, and gave up hope. The rich English, he added, were extremely religious, but their religion was for the rich only; it ignored the poor at hand and was mesmerized by foreign missions; and it was 'typically gloomy and sullen'.[48] He came back convinced that Protestantism was sliding into atheism by way of fragmentation, and Catholicism by way of socialism. Even in his exile, he had felt himself to be profoundly Russian;[49] now he felt it more strongly than ever, and partly because he thought that Russians were universal men, not polarized by standing conflicts, able to admit more into their minds without contradiction, and destined to take over from an Europe exhausted by national and social conflicts. Whether this all-roundness and tolerance of contradiction is Russian, or just Dostoevsky, may be left for Russians to decide. At all events, his trip westward consolidated his nationalism; he turned to the native resources of his country, including its Orthodoxy. Through the Russian people he was slowly making his way back to the Russian Church.

In his discerning work, *Dostoievski*, Pierre Pascal fixes on 1862 as the crucial year in Dostoevsky's development – *la mue*, as he puts it: whether with reference to 'moulting', or to the 'breaking' of an adolescent's voice, is not clear, but either analogy is instructive.[50] It is therefore pertinent to glance at the full-scale novel published in the preceding year, 1861: *The Insulted and the Injured*. It is not vintage Dostoevsky: it is full of artificial contrivances: but its best moments are a grim foretaste of what is to come. It is a compassionate and rebellious work, in which the simple and sincere characters go to the wall, and the course is dominated by the towering super-egoist, matching his will against the world: Prince Valkovsky. It is a formidable tribute to the power and malignity of evil, and a final farewell to the futile decencies of 'Schillerism'. It did not take Stirner or any other Westerner to start Dostoevsky on this course: behind his

---

[48] *Winter Notes on Summer Impressions*, published in *Vremya*, February–March 1863.

[49] Letter to Maykov, 18 January 1856 (*Pisma* I, p. 165).

[50] P. 32. Changes in Dostoevsky's outlook were never clean-cut, but if one has to fix a date, 1862 is as right as any can be.

fastidious aristocratic cynicism, Valkovsky borrows from the convict Orlov in *The House of the Dead*. He is not in the least an enlightened Utilitarian: his urbanity is merely a mask for Lucifer. His congeners are Svidrigaylov and Stavrogin. For this study in home-grown diabolism, the revelations of social injustice, though persistent and poignant, are no more than a background. Thus we see that before his final breach with the Westernizers, Dostoevsky had pronounced his own verdict on volitional anarchism. It was to remain his principal concern, pressing heavily on his major fiction and outweighing his more theoretical concern with determinist Utilitarianism.

None the less, it was with determinist Utilitarianism that Dostoevsky, in his new role of spokesman for the people, was first to join issue. He took it to mean that by pursuing their own advantage unimpeded, men could somehow build an earthly paradise, and at the same time conform to the latest findings of science. Rightly or wrongly, that was the impression he gained from Chernyshevsky who translated John Stuart Mill but quite failed to transmit his overtones and qualifications.[51] He disliked the facile 'Crystal Palace' optimism (Victorian architecture seems to blend in his mind with Russian folklore); rightly, seeing that in Russia at the time individualist enterprise had no in-built safeguards against itself. In its native English setting it worked, and still works, insofar as it does, because of an inherited system of constitutional understandings and an underlying Puritan ethic. There was nothing remotely resembling these things in Russia in the 1860's. The social consequences are unsparingly depicted in *Crime and Punishment* and *The Idiot*. The self-interest of each could not be trusted to produce the best interest of all.

But what principally exasperated Dostoevsky was not the results of individualism, but its psychology. He found it simple-minded to the point of being infantile, and he set out in three ways to counter it. In the first place, and quite conclusively, he drew on his Siberian experience to demonstrate the sinister

---

[51] The work he translated was *The Principles of Political Economy*. Compare the reported statement of Lebezyatnikov in *Crime and Punishment*: 'Pity is now actually prohibited by science, and that is already what happens in England where there is political economy' (Part I, Ch. 2).

potency of an evil which so far from being self-interested was
wholly self-injurious – the vicious circle of pride and hurt has no
Utilitarian point at all. In the second place, he pointed out that
anyone more concerned within the complex of self-interest with
self than with interest, and relentless enough to carry self-will to
its logical limitless conclusion, will end by being a law unto himself, and the Crystal Palace will fly off into fragments. In the
third place, he was convinced that there is freedom, and where
there is freedom, there has to be evil. These are the issues canvassed in that concentrated work of genius translated as *Notes
from Underground*.[52]

We shall analyse it in detail later: here we are merely concerned to determine its sense of direction. The narrator and anti-
hero is a sensitive spiteful intelligent exasperated retired civil
servant, living on a pittance and spitting defiance at things in
general. The question is: how much of him is Dostoevsky? How
much is clinical observation and how much personal confession?
The narrator sets out, clinically enough, to 'explain the causes
which have created his personality', 'a personality due to the
milieu which all of us share in Russia',[53] but he ends, with a
triumphal flourish, 'I have only carried to a finish in my life what
you have not dared to carry half way . . . I have been more *alive*
than you. That is all.'

One thing is certain: no theory will suffice which holds either
that Underground Man is being merely exposed or that he is
being wholly commended. On the one hand, he shouts from his
cellar one of Dostoevsky's permanent convictions: that no
amount of organized mechanical perfection either should or in
the long run can deprive man of his freedom. Better the surly
rumbling from underground than the flat finality of the Crystal
Palace. Christ might emerge from these blasphemous catacombs;
there is no place for him among perfected robots. On the other
hand the *Notes from Underground* are definitely distanced. A
historical distancing is suggested in the author's preface: the

---

[52] Literally 'cellar': the sort of underground that disturbs the people above and
where mice run about.

[53] From the author's preface to the narrator's story: i.e. Dostoevsky speaking
in propria persona.

narrator is referred to as 'a representative type of the generation which has not yet passed away'. A distancing of valuations is disclosed in the harrowing illustrative sequel, 'Damp Snow', in which the editorial sympathies of the author (Dostoevsky) are wholly with the narrator's victim and not with the narrator himself.[54] Moreover, we now have the recently discovered text of the meditation written by Dostoevsky on the death of his first wife,[55] in which he says, among other things, that the main business of the 'I' is to annihilate the 'I' – and this in a definitely Christian setting. As the meditation is exactly contemporary with *Notes from Underground*, it is clear that its querulous antihero is being placed in a perspective not his own.[56]

All the same, Dostoevsky goes with him in his denials. He endorses and enjoys the onslaught on rational self-interest, mathematics, Utopia, determinism and other evils which he puts in the Undergrounder's mouth. He shows up the contradiction in liberal ideology by using the volitional anarchist to defeat the Utilitarian. He is weighing up his aversions to discover which is the more formidable; and he is able to eliminate the Utilitarian determinist as failing to account for the self-destructiveness of which, thanks to his experience among the 'insulted and injured', he was more than usually aware. Having, as he thought, disposed of the determinist anthropology by citing facts, he can then face up to his conflict of values with the volitional anarchist. He does not say so: he always had the merit of letting the devil speak for himself, and so far from selecting a long spoon before supping with him, identified with him to the point of perplexing his readers. He is content to indicate his attitude by orchestrating the Undergrounder's manner of narration. He has to, because he accepts his factual theses. His next problem is to consecrate them. There will be no peace for him till the desperate Underground plea for human freedom has found its place in the sight of God. Even in the *Notes* he foresees that 'if we were given complete

[54] See pp. 172ff. below.
[55] Part of it is translated into English by David Magarshack in *Dostoevsky's Occasional Writings*, pp. 305–6, and the whole of it appears in French in Pierre Pascal, *Dostoïevski*, as Text V, pp. 114–18.
[56] The connection might be clearer but for the Imperial Censor. See pp. 86ff. below.

independence . . . we should very soon ask to be taken in hand again'. We seem to be listening to Shigalev in *The Possessed*: 'Starting with unlimited freedom, I arrive at unlimited despotism.'[57] Nevertheless, we do start with freedom: all we can do is use it so that each enhances all by transcending himself. The only solution lies in Christian humility – and that consists not in lying down, but in standing up, one by one, in the other's shoes. That, however, is still to come: what we learn from the *Notes* is that freedom is both the fundament of human nature, and its fatality.

Nevertheless, we can now foresee the direction which Dostoevsky's religion was to take. If freedom and togetherness can come together only in the transcendence of 'I' in voluntary community, the experience of the Russian people supplies the clue. They had never been Western individualists and had nothing to unlearn. And their togetherness was supremely expressed in their religion. The great obstacles to togetherness in general are moralism, which leads some people to set themselves above others, is consequently denounced in the Gospels and is the mainspring of Western religion; self-sufficiency, which protects even men of goodwill from having to share the experiences of the less fortunate; and, underlying these and all others, pride, for it excludes in advance the humility which is the true antithesis of self-will. From these vices the Russian people and their religion were still happily free. On the other hand, the Western-inspired revolutionaries were living examples of them; Dostoevsky, at least, found them unkind, arrogant, and, in their topsy-turvy way, unpleasantly self-righteous – 'Be my brother or off with your head.'[58] But even in his latest years he wrote about 'our Russian socialism', and the one thing that cannot be urged against him is that he was any sort of an individualist.[59] Any religion to which he could adhere would have to be based, not on

---

[57] *The Possessed*, p. 376.

[58] The type, apparently, does not change.

[59] 'Our Russian socialism, the ultimate aim of which is to establish an ecumenical church on earth.' *Diary of a Writer*, II, p. 1029. He distrusted secular socialism as a conspiracy of intellectuals without grass roots. But he disliked every bit as much as its exponents the irresponsibilities of economic individualism.

authority or on independence but on the mutual interplay of disparate but converging elements within a circumambient consensus.

We have now taken the story to the point at which *Crime and Punishment* comes into view. In fact it is the next landmark; for those looking for evidence of Dostoevsky's religious development from 1864 to 1867, his correspondence is only peripheral. He had lost, in 1864, his wife, his favourite brother, and one of his best friends; the journals by which he had set such store had been suppressed; he had been driven abroad to escape his creditors; he had developed a passion for gambling; he was busy both with mistresses and a proposal of marriage; and his correspondence is understandably but tiresomely concerned with money. Once again, it was Christian believers who helped him out; an Orthodox priest named Yanyshev at Wiesbaden, and his old friend Vrangel, now a diplomat in Copenhagen. But he was too preoccupied to meditate about religion, and he did not practise it. The evident religious concern in *Crime and Punishment* exceeds anything one might have expected from his reported activities in the years immediately preceding it. Even so, the spotlight in that novel is not on Christianity, but on the ethics of utility and/or unlimited freedom, and in finding them wanting Dostoevsky called in the worldly wisdom of Porfiry Petrovich as well as the specifically Christian wisdom of Sonya. It is easier, when one is unsure, to use Christianity as a control than to submit it to scrutiny. In any case, as we shall see, as a crucial instance Raskolnikov is not good enough; he is too weak a vessel. That is probably why the more formidable figure of Svidrigaylov looms up behind him, generated almost out of nothing, and, as the notebooks show, at the last minute. Sonya finally wins Raskolnikov round; could she have wheedled Svidrigaylov? The most that can be said is that an average well-brought-up young man who is not quite as important as he would like to think he is can pass through a criminal act to a problematical Christian recovery. *The Idiot* is another thing altogether: but here we must sit back and watch Dostoevsky's private development.

From the period up to 1869, when *The Idiot* was published,

three factors may be singled out as helping to determine the style and accelerate the growth of Dostoevsky's religion. In the first place there was the Polish insurrection of 1863. It is surprising how vehemently Russian even the radicals showed themselves in this crisis: Herzen, the best and ablest of them, living abroad, took up the Polish cause, and lost his following and circulation overnight. It is less surprising that Dostoevsky, already inflammably nationalist, should have gone with the pack. The episode forced on his attention the difference between Polish Catholicism and Russian Orthodoxy. He now knew at least what he had to reject. Poles are henceforward lampooned, immediately and ferociously in *The Gambler*, and after long reflection and no less unfairly in *The Brothers Karamazov*, and the bias against Catholicism is revealed in Myshkin's ill-timed speech in *The Idiot*, as well as figuring as the ostensible issue in the legend of the Grand Inquisitor.[60]

In the seond place, living abroad for long periods (1864–65 and 1867–71) he felt himself more Russian than ever: and not only did the experience incline him further towards Orthodoxy, but it endeared to him what he thought to be a typically Russian trait – the unlimited spiritual capaciousness which transcends contradictions, so sharply in contrast with the compartmentalism, the fixed moral and social barriers, which so exasperated him in Europe. He developed almost a fixation on the *Vsechelovek*, the 'all-man', who can encompass the whole of human experience, discrepancies included. 'I have exceeded the limit all my life', he wrote to Maykov;[61] one might add, in all directions at once. The *Vsechelovek* was both irresistibly attractive to him, and a grave temptation. It took, to exorcise him, the agonized confrontation, in *The Possessed* and *The Brothers Karamazov*, between the man-God and the God-man. In the meantime, providentially, the appeal of the Russian way of life took him through the Russian God to everybody's God.

[60] Protestantism was not even a starter in this race. Dostoevsky particularly hated Geneva which (like London) he found to be both gloomy and drunken. He thought the reformed religion fundamentally unconstructive and lapsing into atheism anyway.

[61] 18 August 1867 (*Pisma* II, p. 24).

In the third place, and principally, there was his second marriage. The first, with a widow in Siberia, had not been wholly a success. She wanted someone who would bring order into her life, and found to her cost that anyone who was to live with Dostoevsky would have to bring order into his. She needed soothing and regularizing, and Dostoevsky, who was capable of utter devotion but could also be irritable and inconsiderate, could not rise to the situation. Her personal characteristics and something of her temperament are recognizable, in adolescent form, in the Lise Khokhlakova of *The Brothers Karamazov*, and the picture of Alyosha firmly humouring Lise may be read as a piece of rueful self-criticism. Yet he was devotedly at her bedside in Moscow in 1864 when she was dying and took over, with more loyalty than judgment, the care of her insufferable son by her first marriage. It is not our purpose to follow him as a lover or a suppliant over the next few years: the women concerned figure in his novels as models, especially the most brilliant and perverse of them, Apollinaria Suslova, who is the Polina of *The Gambler* (even down to the name), and enters into the making of Lizaveta Nikolayevna in *The Possessed* and of Katerina Ivanovna in *The Brothers Karamazov*.[62] We take up the story again with the arrival of Anna Grigoryevna Snitkina straight from a secretarial college to cope with an almost impossible publisher's dateline for the delivery of *The Gambler*. Between them they made it, with not a day to spare, and three months later they were married. Anna was twenty; he was forty-four. She had a profound respect for a literary genius which she did not fully understand; she was precise and orderly (half-Swedish, which some Russian writers seem to think accounts for it); she was strong-minded and decisive, as she showed in her breaking up of the Dostoevsky family communism; she was practical, possessive, bourgeoise to her finger tips, and unswervingly devoted, despite poverty and her husband's gambling habits (it took her four years to cure them, but she did it); she was an admirable secretary, a self-taught nurse, sexually compatible (his recollections in his letters to her

---

[62] Those interested may consult Marc Slonim, *Three Loves of Dostoevsky*, Alvin Redman, London 1957.

were so glowingly circumstantial that she red-pencilled them before handing the correspondence to its editors); she was the mother of four children, household organizer, business manager, and on one famous occasion the promoter of a publishing company for her husband's benefit; she gave him a quiet domestic background and a deeper personal happiness than he had ever known; and, finally, she was an honest-to-goodness not-very-reflective Christian.[63]

Her Christianity enveloped him, so to speak, from two sides. In the first place, she tactfully nudged him into resuming relations with the Orthodox Church, from which he had kept aloof, though increasingly drawn to it by a common enemy and a sense of need which he could not justify. It required patience: when she arrived with him at Dresden, little more than a bride, in 1867, she had to search by herself for the Russian church, and though she attended it with his permission, he did not accompany her.[64] The public date of the change was 1871, when he finally returned from abroad; the efiective date was probably 1868 when he first projected an enormous novel to be called *Atheism*, and planned for himself a strenuous course of religious and anti-religious reading. The dates suggest that his deeper commitment was not unconnected with his marriage.

It was not an intellectual commitment: Anna was not an intellectual. But (her second contribution) she gave him the peace of mind and the material contentment which he needed, not so much as a writer – he had shown that he could write under almost impossible conditions – but as a pilgrim. She did not exorcize his doubts and she probably did not understand them. But he could now face in faith, and therefore more ruthlessly, the problem which had always tormented him: the problem of God.

<hr>

[63] The third good Christian and the most influential in his adult life. For Yanovsky and Vrangel see pp. 9, 32 above.

[64] *Dnevnik A. G. Dostoevsky* (Diary of A. G. Dostoevsky), Novaya Moskva, 1923, p. 30 and p. 35. From the same source (p. 135) there is an account of Dostoevsky's extreme rudeness to the Russian consul in Dresden – an ex-convict's reaction to the official type? All these episodes are related in a deadpan schoolgirl recitative which is much more impressive than any possible comment.

IV

In 1869 appeared what many critics regard as Dostoevsky's literary *chef-d'oeuvre*, *The Idiot*. To those interested in his religion it has always been something of a puzzle. We shall attempt to analyse it later: here we simply consider its background, and state the problem.

We now have the shavings from his workshop: the successive drafts for the proposed novel. In his letters to Maykov and to his favourite niece, Sofya Ivanova, in January 1868, he explained that he wanted to portray 'a wholly beautiful human being'.[65] We now know that this was not his original intention. The first sketch of *The Idiot* (always known by that name) reads more like Stavrogin; there is a strong suggestion of the 'all-man'. At a guess, Dostoevsky found it impossible to contain in one human frame the discrepant activities of his original hero. He had not contrived the machinery for the purpose in *The Double*, and he managed it in *The Possessed* only by setting much of the action back into a past history in which the contradictory phases of the 'all-man' are located successively. At any rate, he tells Maykov that only a desperate situation had forced him to take on such an immeasurable task; he was pressed for time and money, and in the original form the story would not go. As Rogozhin also takes shape in the seventh draft, along with the reformulated Idiot, we may surmise that the original double character was split into two. The consequence was a change in direction of the novel. On the original plan the two parties to the action would have been the doubled-up embodiment of passion and purity on the one hand and the sordid commercialism of conventional society on the other. As it is, the duel between passion and purity takes the heat off the social set-up,[66] though traces of the original intention remain in Part One. Both Myshkin and Rogozhin, though now separately and competitively, stand in the way of the Yepanchin-Totsky deal over Nastasya Filippovna.

[65] The word is *prekrasnogo*: good, indeed, but good in a beautiful way: it would include St Francis of Assisi but not St Ignatius (or Calvin). To Maykov, *Pisma* II, p. 61. To his niece, *Pisma* II, p. 71.

[66] Greatly to the chagrin of the Soviet critics, but in conformity with Dostoevsky's world-outlook.

The *vsechelovek* being thus split and postponed, we have the 'wholly beautiful human being'; and Dostoevsky is under no illusions about the difficulty. As he tells his niece, 'the beautiful is an ideal' and the ideal is far from having been elaborated either in Russia, or in 'civilized Europe' (the phrase comes off his pen with a splutter). Words like 'ideal' have subtle over-tones in different languages: it has been observed[67] that Dostoevsky's use of the word 'idea' is Platonic, and 'ideal' could be similarly slanted. In that case it refers to what in the nature of things does not belong to this world at all: and how can that be when what is to be portrayed is flesh and blood?[68] The result, on these terms, must be a failure, and that is just what it is. That discerning Soviet critic, G. M. Fridlender, sees the point and pounces on it: 'the beautiful is in profound contradiction with life'.[69] He promptly blames Dostoevsky for letting his Christianity stand in the way of his discernment. He cites 'the ascetic principle', the 'separation of flesh and spirit', and 'the idealization of humility and suffering'. As a matter of fact, apart from some straining of the word 'ascetic',[70] he is perfectly right. But he debits it against the Christian religion; the alternative view is that it results from an insufficiently Christian view of religion; if you will, of the Christian religion. If 'the beautiful is in profound contradiction with life', there is no question: so much the worse for the 'beautiful'. And it is Dostoevsky who is as fault. Try as I may, I cannot interpret *The Idiot* as a deliberate clinical exercise. Myshkin is put forward as the best thing available, and his failure (as we shall see it is) is a genuine tragedy. It is possible because Dostoevsky, by relentlessly working out his current religion in terms of human psychology, finds his hero turning against him.[71] His chosen and greatly beloved creation is unfit

[67] By J. Steinberg, *Dostoevsky*, p. 85.

[68] In Christ, perhaps, but he was God: he is the one case of perfect identity: and he can never be repeated.

[69] In 'Roman Idiot', *Tvorchestvo Dostoevskogo*, p. 191.

[70] In the sense of 'ascetic' to which we are accustomed, Myshkin was not an 'ascetic' at all. There is no overtone of 'going into training'. Myshkin is just *not* trained, Christianly or otherwise.

[71] This point is taken by Fridlender, op. cit. p. 190, and once again he is quite right. About Dostoevsky he is nearly always right. What he is wrong about is Christianity.

for the task. So, of course, are many Christians; it is usually possible to say why, and in this case the answer is a Christian answer: he is not sufficiently incarnate. He is a living presentation of the insufficiency of the 'ideal' to which Dostoevsky outside his art had been attaching a high importance. It is neither the first nor the last time that his artistic insight makes short work of his prose convictions.[72]

The problem then is (and this is our second point): is there no way between the *vsechelovek* (almost the man-God) and the ideal man, lacking in the all-too-human qualities which make a man? The answer is the God-man and his presence among the faithful; to this concept *The Idiot*[73] is a painful dialectical introduction.

As far as we can fathom from external evidence, in 1869 Dostoevsky was aligned with the popularist anti-enlightenment; he was full of religious sentiment and less suspicious of the church than formerly; but he was still in trouble on the intellectual front.[74] He tried to persuade himself that it did not matter: it was in that spirit that he put Myshkin up to declare that 'the atheist is always talking about something else'. 'The essence of religious feeling does not come under any sort of reasoning or atheism, and has nothing to do with crimes and misdemeanours'.[75] 'Compassion is the chief law of human existence' – irrespective of whether it wins through, whether there is anything in the world to respond to it or not. That is the religion which is tested out with merciless honesty in *The Idiot*; and, as we shall show in detail, it fails; not, as Fridlender thinks, because it is Christian, but because it is not Christian enough.

There are signs of his increasing preoccupation with the sub-

[72] We have here anticipated the detailed account of *The Idiot* on which this conclusion is founded. See Ch. 4 below.

[73] It is beginning to show up that Dostoevsky in his works set out to test his prose convictions, and found them wanting. But on each occasion he came back with new ones, with the same results. This is what is meant by calling his method 'dialectical'. His novels present the 'negative moment', and he proceeds to reconstruction on a higher level. In *The Brothers Karamazov* he is both more ruthlessly dialectical, and nearer to finality, than ever before.

[74] E. H. Carr seems to be right in deferring Dostoevsky's final religious commitment to the last ten years of his life.

[75] *The Idiot*, p. 219.

ject. The first is in his letter to Maykov of 23 (11) December
1868, in which he announces a big novel to be called 'Atheism',
in which the principal character is to lose his faith at forty-five,
and to seek among 'the atheists, Slavs and Europeans, Russian fanatics and hermits, a Polish Jesuit proselytizer and Russian
flagellants, and finally to discover on Russian soil the Russian
Christ and the Russian God'. At this stage he was clearly
anxious to survey the varieties of contemporary religious (and
irreligious) experience, and to conclude with the *Russian* God.
'I shall [then] have expressed the whole of myself.'[76] This
ominous conflation of Christ and culture re-echoes throughout
the *Diary*, and leads to militant talk about the Third Rome and
the recapture of Constantinople, all in the name of Christian
humility. It is perhaps only fair to distinguish on his behalf between 'The Russian God' and 'The Christian God whom Russians, because of their humility, are best qualified to discern'.

It remains to be noted that this novel was never written. We
do not find anywhere in Dostoevsky a complete review of contemporary trends in religion; the proposed plot obviously failed
to inspire him. That was to be expected: Dostoevsky's religious
passion expressed itself concretely in his anthropology. It is a
serious but common mistake to suppose that Dostoevsky was
writing about 'ideas'. He was not; he was writing about people
who were bitten by ideas. The proposed 'Atheism' would have
meant placing ideas in the centre and making his hero work his
way through them. It was fortunate for his readers, and a tribute
to his (often underestimated) literary judgment, that he did not
make the attempt, but split the inspiration between the great
works to follow – *The Possessed* and *The Brothers Karamazov*.

The next reference to a major project is in another letter to
Maykov, on 6 April 1870.[77] Here Dostoevsky proposes a novel
comprising 'five long stories', to be entitled as a whole *The Life
of a Great Sinner*. One item from 'Atheism' is carried over with
this project; 'the hero in the course of his life is now an atheist,

[76] See for the whole letter in English, J. Coulson: *Dostoevsky: a Self-portrait*;
pp. 179f. (*Pisma* II. p. 179). There is a less explicit letter to the same effect to
Sonya Ivanova, 20 March 1869 (*Pisma* II, p. 175).
[77] *Pisma* II, p. 264.

now a believer, then is a fanatic or sectarian, and then an atheist again'. The reference here is to the first of the constituent stories, which eventually took form as *The Possessed*. It contains, in fact, a valuable clue to it. We do not observe these changes in Stavrogin because the action of the novel takes place many years later; but he has been through a Russian-Christian phase in which, spiritually speaking, he begat Shatov, a 'fanatic' phase in which he begat Kirillov, and a social-atheist phase, in which he begat Pyotr Verkhovensky. All these disciples owe their inspiration to him and revere him as their leader. But he was an atheist from the start and all through, merely willing the various phases to escape the horror of a life without an object and incapacitated by a sense of guilt.

But the letter to Maykov goes further. 'The second story will take place in a monastery'; and 'I have concentrated all my hopes on it'. As outlined to Maykov, it does not correspond with *The Brothers Karamazov*, and the discrepancy is extremely interesting as an instance of how the planning of it was transformed by the necessities of plot and character. He proposed to study a thirteen-year-old boy who had taken part in the committing of a crime and had been placed under restraint in a monastery by his parents. This character is to be 'the future hero of the whole novel'. In the monastery he is to meet an elder who shall be the historical Tikhon Zadonsky under another name – the elder appears almost unaltered as Father Zosima. But the Alyosha of the novel is not an ex-criminal; he is on the edge of a crime, but in no sense implicated, and his early career is covered sufficiently to show that he could never have been the 'young wolf and child-nihilist' outlined to Maykov. Dostoevsky did produce what he meant to produce, 'an imposing, *positive*, saintly figure', but the child-nihilist has evaporated and his place taken by the next-generation saint on trial. Yet the nihilism is there, in Ivan and Smerdyakov, and so is the interest in children, which, however, is almost shunted off into a special siding. Alyosha is certainly to be tempted, and he will reel, as a Karamazov must; but he will not collapse, as Myshkin did, for lack of a proper physical backing; he is not ideal, but incarnate. It is the 'rooted' religion of the Russian tradition rather than the 'ideal' religion springing from Western philosophy which must be brought in to confront the nihilist, and not at the political and derivative but at the primary psychological level.

V

We have now reached the period of Dostoevsky's religious conformity; and we are required to ask what it amounted to. Publicly, it was orthodox enough. The *Diary* is full of sententious proclamations.[78] This is not merely nationalism; in particular, there is an increasing insistence on immortality, without belief in which he declares love for mankind to be impossible.[79] Nor is it 'ethical Christianity': for the ethics of Christianity were always for him conditional: that was precisely his agony; he had pinned all his being to them for years, and dreaded that the foundations might be dragged from under them. Moreover, he had put to himself the disturbing suggestion advanced to explain Versilov by Vasin in *A Raw Youth*, that some very proud people respect God because it absolves them from respecting men. Nor was it just mysticism: Dostoevsky's personal experience of mysticism was restricted to the moment before an epileptic fit, and his temperament remained to the end restless and unsettled. Still less was it old-fashioned ascetic-monastic discipline: that is portrayed in Father Ferapont in *The Brothers Karamazov*, who is unfavourably contrasted with the world-oriented Father Zosima. What became central for Dostoevsky in his later years was the Orthodox concept of *sobornost'*, 'togetherness', expressed in Zosima's formula by 'the responsibility of each for all'.

Sobornost' was a vital part of the Orthodox tradition, and even persists, unfrocked, in the Russian type of Communism. It begins with the presence of the Holy Spirit with the assembled congregation. Right from the time of Constantine what distinguished the procedure of the Senate from that of an Episcopal

---

[78] The Turkish war is 'in defence of Christianity' (*Diary of a Writer*, p. 858). In another vein: 'Christ is the only love of the Russian People' (ibid. p. 39).

[79] He also remarks that 'the promise of eternal life binds man all the more closely to the world' (ibid. p. 540).

Council was that in the Senate resolutions were carried by a majority vote, whereas the bishops' verdict had to be unanimous – unanimity being the sign of inspiration by the Holy Spirit. It has been the view of the Orthodox Church that under Catholicism the Holy Spirit is confined to absolutist papal decisions, and under Protestantism identified with the secular formula of majority rule. It is easy to object that unanimity is a difficult requirement. Constantine found that out when two bishops stood out against the Athanasian formula at the Council of Nicaea. He promptly had them dismissed, and there was unanimity. The requirement of unanimity led directly to the intervention of the secular power. It is none the less true that majority rule in spiritual affairs seems to limit the personal religious response, as Quakers testify when they try to avoid voting and to ascertain instead, through the Chair, 'the feeling of the meeting'. The tradition of dissentience, as the Orthodox sees it, starts from an unworkable absolutism and proceeds to an unworkable fragmentation. So they have concentrated on what congregations can do in common, and have played down the issues on which they might divide. Hence their emphasis on splendour of worship and, down to Solovyov, their weakness in theology. The Russian word for orthodoxy is *Pravoslaviye*; the Greek word *doxa*, which may mean either 'opinion' or 'glory', has been taken by the West, Catholics, Protestants and atheists alike, in the former sense, by the Russian Church in the latter. Worship is the focus; but ideally at least it extends to the pieties of everyday life (*bytovoye blagochestiye*), covering all aspects of personal and social morality. These are preserved, not by obedience nor by discussion, but by a kind of prior unanimity. This was what was distinctive in pre-Tatar Russia, and it was the glory of Orthodox Eastern worship which moved Prince Vladimir to accede to the Eastern rather than the Western Communion. It was made possible by the use of Scripture in Slavonic: Scripture, worship and daily experience were linguistically united.

The situation in Dostoevsky's youth was vastly different. The Russian Church was tied at least as closely to the secular Tsarist absolutism as it ever was to the religious absolutism of the popes. Peter the Great created the Holy Governing Synod, nominating every bishop himself, and for good measure installed a procurator as a secular political watchdog. The model was said to be Lutheran; it was a misfortune that Peter, who turned to the Dutch for ship-building, turned away from their freewheeling ecclesiastical politics. The result was that Catherine II appointed open atheists and free-thinkers as procurators, and that the reading of the New Testament in Russian was forbidden under Nicholas I and his procurator Protasov (a general!) from 1825 to 1863. Much has been written about the procurator K. V. Pobyedonostsev, a friend of Dostoevsky's, who encouraged and is said, absurdly, by some recent critics to have commanded *The Brothers Karamazov*. As a matter of fact, unlike his predecessors, he was a man of learning and piety, and secured for the church some measure of freedom; he became an overt reactionary only after the death of Dostoevsky (and of Alexander II) in 1881. The situation which Dostoevsky left behind in 1849 had in fact improved during his absence. The abolition of serfdom, one of the objects of the society for belonging to which he was condemned, took place in 1861, and the manifesto which proclaimed it was actually drafted by the Metropolitan of Moscow. But, even more significantly, the Slavophiles had come into prominence.

The Slavophiles were in the first instance amateur anthropologists, concerned with the distinctive character and essential unity of those speaking Slavonic languages.[80] But their abiding passion was what they believed to be the distinctive content of Slavonic civilization. This was a village-based conception of community as both integral and consentient: as far as possible from the 'proud pagan individualism' of Rome.[81] Their culminat-

---

[80] Nicholas I did not like them because they threatened his concord with the Hapsburg and Hohenzollern empires. They themselves had doubts about the Catholic Poles and the Catholic-Protestant Czechs. They were most in earnest about the liberation of the Orthodox Serbs and Bulgarians, and hailed the Turkish War of the 1870's as 'holy'. Disraeli, using his diplomatic initiative against them, with uncanny foresight, described the Russian intervention as 'Socialist'.

[81] The rejection of Rome, both pagan and Christian, was a main feature of their programme; and it is subtly evident both in Dostoevsky and in the whole structure of Russian society, before and after the Revolution.

ing concern was religious. The most interesting and best-known of them, Alexei Khomyakov (1809–60), had travelled widely in Europe and, like Dostoevsky, hated it; unlike Dostoevsky, he made an exception of England, and especially the University of Oxford which delighted him. He was convinced, from what he saw of religion in Franco-Germany, that that complex was set on the road to atheism. His basic conviction was that both Catholics and Protestants were basically wrong about religious authority. The pope was too distant in space; the Bible was too distant in time. Under the earlier and better Christian tradition the entire community of believers was inspired and guided by the Holy Spirit. He proclaimed the freedom of that community (against the political establishment) and the total communion of its members (against liberals and individualists). Those who think that religion and the establishment in Russia in Dostoevsky's day were synonymous will be surprised to learn that he was not allowed to publish during his lifetime; the political controllers of the church held up his works on various pretexts till 1867.[82]

There is no doubt that Khomyakov correctly interpreted the pre-Petrine tradition of the Orthodox Church. An Orthodox is one who praises God in the right spirit as a member of the religious community. So for the Slavophiles, dogma took second place. 'Nothing that has not some direct bearing upon divine worship need be dogmatically defined.' 'The confession of faith is part of doxology.'[83] The doctrine of incarnation is central to the form of worship and is governed by dogma. 'Minor issues' (many of them important to Western theologians) are settled by 'theologumena' on which doctors disagree. That is the background for the Orthodox reply to the papal encyclical of 1848: 'The Pope is greatly mistaken in supposing that we consider the ecclesiastical hierarchy to be the guardian of dogma

[82] Concerning *sobornost'* (a word he constantly uses): Khomyakov defined the church not as a centre of teaching or authority, but as a congregation of lovers in Christ' (*Russian Philosophy*, ed. James M. Edie and others, II, p. 161), and its members are united 'organically' and not 'organizationally' (ibid. p. 162).

[83] The summary is quoted from N. Zernov, *Eastern Christendom*, p. 230; much of the above information is taken from the same source. My excuse for this theft is that it is not taken into account by literary critics of Dostoevsky.

. . . The unwavering constancy and unerring truth of Christian dogma does not depend on any of the hierarchical orders; it is created by the totality of the people of God, which is the body of Christ.'[84]

Dostoevsky was in sympathy with the nationalist emphasis of the Slavophiles; he wrote in 1877 that he shared most of their opinions;[85] but his whole background was utterly different. Khomyakov, for example, was a landowner with the soil in his blood; so were the distinguished brothers Konstantin and Ivan Aksakov. Dostoevsky till late in life moved among the alienated urbanized new poor: unsuccessful clerks and government servants, and of course students; he preferred Petersburg, with its window on Europe, to Slavophile Moscow; and his conception of religion was almost indelibly stamped with the Western brand before his experience of the 'people' in Siberia. He shared with Khomyakov the conviction that religious consentience has political repercussions. Khomyakov appealed to the ancient Slavonic institution of the *obshchina*, or village commune, and rejoiced that Russian Christianity had such a congenial pagan soil to sink its roots in. Dostoevsky knew about peasant life from those who had been violently detached from it by the penal system. He could not in the nature of things be a continuing conservative: to the extent that he followed the tradition, it was by a deliberate act of adherence, based on an equally deliberate renunciation of his own past. As happens in such cases, the process was incomplete – a fact which did not escape the notice of the more instinctive conservatives whom he so carefully cultivated. He remarked, as late as 1876, 'the Russian people are not conservative, because they have nothing to conserve'.[86] No Slavophile could have said that, even by accident. He was taken up by genuine conservatives as a formidable reputation, but they never quite trusted him: and when he turned to his old radical crony, the poet Nekrasov, for the publication of *A Raw Youth*, his political friends, Maykov and Strakhov, turned cool,

[84] Quoted by Zernov, op. cit. p. 231, cf. his comment p. 232: 'So long as Christians remain within the Eucharistic fellowship they will be able to disentangle truth from error.'

[85] *Diary of a Writer*, II, p. 779.   [86] Quoted by Lossky, op. cit. p. 119.

and Strakhov positively spiteful. As Lossky observed, 'he was not really a party man'. And then there was his hesitation about accepting a role on the platform at the Pushkin celebrations in 1880. Rightly convinced that no political party could put Pushkin in its pocket (he was the universal Russian if ever there was one) he decided to go, partly because he was not going to let the Westerners take possession, and partly because he feared a lack of popular appeal in the Slavophile Ivan Aksakov; he thought him too old (he was in fact two years younger than Dostoevsky) and too remotely sectarian. He judged rightly: he was an enormous success, from a point in the middle of the road. For once, his capacity for entertaining contradictories had resolved itself into a working synthesis.

It is, then, a mistake to underestimate the pull of his Westernizing past on Dostoevsky's *religion* – a mistake enshrined in jargon such as 'his reactionary religio-idealist idea'. The conflict in Dostoevsky is not between a forward-looking humanism and a backward-looking religion,[87] it is a conflict within his religious consciousness between the Western priority of intellect and the Orthodox priority of *sobornost'*. It is resolved far more adequately in *The Brothers Karamazov* than it is in the *Diary*, where he plays his doubleness down instead of facing up to it. What turns the scale is the Orthodox conception of worship as a centre of action. If a man is properly disposed, he will see and act accordingly: if he is not, the best he can do is to be incredibly ingenious. Dostoevsky ends his intellectual difficulties by subordinating the intellectual approach.[88]

1. We may recall that from the beginning Dostoevsky had laid supreme emphasis on freedom. We may also recall that freedom for Dostoevsky was never, as for Kant, for example,

---

[87] Belkin's analysis in N. L. Stepanov (ed), *Tvorchestvo Dostoevskogo*, p. 266.

[88] Khomyakov wrote: 'In adopting the concept as the sole basis of thought one destroys the world, for the concept turns every activity belonging to it into an abstract possibility' (apropos of Hegel: and remarkably similar to Kierkegaard on the same subject. Letter to Y. F. Samarin, cited in James M. Edie(ed.), *Russian Philosophy*, II, p. 282, cf. editorial comment, ibid. p. 162, on 'organic togetherness in cognition' – 'rational cognition is a secondary and derivative form of knowledge'. Dostoevsky had certainly heard this kind of discussion, and approved it – it was one of the 'many respects' in which he went with the Slavophiles.

'rational freedom'. It is illustrated in the supremacy of will over the eternal verities, e.g. $2 \times 2 = 4$. The Russian *volya* is etymologically connected with 'will', and that is in fact one of its dictionary equivalents; but it also means 'freedom', with an overtone of 'not forced'. It is eroded not only by absolute subjection but also by binding constitutional understandings.[89] How far this reaction is typically Russian it is not for a foreigner to say. Dostoevsky thought it was, and he found the dutifulness of German behaviour, and above all the unfailing German punctuality, intolerably restrictive. The result is a certain 'natural anarchism' of which Dostoevsky had at least as much as his fair share. How can freedom, so interpreted, be reconciled with any kind of organization whatever? There is only one possible answer: only if everyone spontaneously wants the same thing. That, in the crowning moment of worship, is exactly what happens.

2. Read back into the multifarious activities of people out of church, *sobornost'* would seem to be, at the best, a counsel of perfection. Unanimity of feeling in all contexts is much too good (or too bad) to be true: particularly for a man like the author of *Notes from Underground* with his highly developed irritable insistence on the punctilio of irresponsibility. Unless unanimity can be restructured so as to arise spontaneously in all contexts, the quest is in vain. The principal and apparently invincible obstacle is self-will, which is also, in Dostoevsky's world, the strongest motive (far stronger than self-interest, to which it is normally opposed). We shall study in the novels the vicious circle of hurt-and-be-hurt, a subject to which Dostoevsky returned incessantly: for the moment, we just note that at every turn it jeopardizes the unforced unanimity of the Christian order. The contrast is so clear that it is tempting to say: Dostoevsky is consoling himself with an imaginary harmony and sees it as an 'ideal' not as a solution. The critic V. V. Rozanov, who married Dostoevsky's ex-mistress, Suslova, and could have had inside information,[90] said of him: 'In our literature there has

[89] Cf. his contempt for a 'written sheet of paper', *Diary of a Writer*, II, p. 1033.
[90] True or false.

never been a writer whose ideals were so completely separate from contemporary actualities.'[91] The same charge comes from within the Soviet Union; naturally from the opposite angle: his sense of actualities did a good deal to counter the remoteness of his Christian 'ideals'. Both ways, I believe this interpretation to be wrong. At the very least, Dostoevsky *thought* of *sobornost'* as a meeting ground for his religion and his passion for freedom, and we must follow him as well as we can.

In the discourse of Father Zosima in *The Brothers Karamazov* which was intended as the reply to Ivan's agonized unbelief, there appears the intimation, 'Each is responsible for all.' 'There is only one means of Salvation . . . make yourself responsible for all men's sins . . . as soon as you sincerely make yourself responsible for everything and for all men, you will see at once that it is really so, and that you are to blame for everyone and for all things. But throwing your own indolence and impotence on others you will end by sharing the pride of Satan and murmuring against God' (pp. 340–41). The importance of this passage is that it shows how *sobornost'* works out in practice. You can be together with people as at the moment of worship if you pull down your walls and so humble yourself that your help and availability will humiliate nobody. In Dostoevsky the question was not *merely* self-interest. Even at the height of his crusade against bourgeois individualism, in *Crime and Punishment*, and the first part of *The Idiot*, he realized that it was not enough to give oneself to another or for another: the real problem was to do it without humiliating. For pride is perhaps all that the other has left to him, and in the name of all that he is he will stand out against the kindness which threatens to deprive him of it. As has often been pointed out, Raskolnikov does not commit his murder for gain, but to show that he is somebody; and Nastasya Filippovna rejects Myshkin because she will not accept her restoration at the hands of a redeemer, particularly one as selfless as he. The difference between the two cases is not simply that Nastasya is a stronger character than Raskolnikov; that is certainly so, but it is not decisive. The main difference is that Sonya

[91] *Legenda o Velikom Inkvizitore*, Berlin Izdatelstvo Razum, 1924.

really loved Raskolnikov, and Myshkin did not whole-heartedly love Nastasya: he was mesmerized by her suffering. The point of Zosima's utterance is that people can only remain in spiritual togetherness if there is absolutely no assumption of superiority (especially moral superiority) and if all set to work with each other on the assumption that all crimes and merits are shared out. Thus togetherness is combined with an acute sense of individual responsibility. Freedom is delivered from self-will, collectivism is delivered from tyranny, under a formula which the Church in Russia had recovered from its own past and which would enable it to ride triumphantly the storm which Western Christendom was due to be drowned in.

This is Dostoevsky's final conclusion. It marks the triumph of the religious over the Satanic strain in him. It is not simply a public stance; after many vicissitudes it appears decisively in the fiction itself. It is not above criticism, especially when it is given a political twist; to suggest that the State can be absorbed in the Church, or even be conducted on the same assumptions, is to miss the role of the State entirely; and to claim that the Tsar presides over unanimity as the Holy Spirit was supposed to do is surely blasphemous. E. H. Carr pointed out at the beginning of his percipient work that Dostoevsky grew up in the close society of a large family and never learnt to rub along with acquaintances; it was either intimacy or nothing. Such a training is a good preparation for religious fellowship, and a bad preparation for politics. But our object at this stage is not to cavil but to understand, and it is in the traditional Orthodox concept of *sobornost'* that Dostoevsky's long religious anguish comes to an end.

But with a difference. The expression of *sobornost'* in personal relations is *active* love. Despite his late interest in monasteries, Dostoevsky does not end by preaching contemplative mysticism, let alone passive resignation. Aloysha is ordered out of his monastery into the world; it is in the world that the struggle for faith has to be decided. Fyodor Karamazov is not a sympathetic character, but some of his jeers carry conviction. 'Here in this hermitage there are twenty-five saints being saved. They look at each other and eat cabbages' (p. 33). Lise is not an easy character either, but she, too, sending Alyosha on an errand of mercy, says to him: 'I told Mamma you'd be sure not to go. I said you were saving your soul' (p. 51). Both these impertinences are allowed to pass. Dostoevsky evidently sympathizes with them. The religion to which he finally adhered was not only a corporate religion but a religion of action. Its final expression is found in Zosima's reply to that effusive 'lady of little faith', Mrs Khokhlakova: 'Strive to love your neighbour actively and indefatigably . . . In so far as you advance in love you will grow surer of the reality of God and of the immortality of your soul. If you attain to perfect self-forgetfulness in the love of your neighbour, then you will believe without doubt, and no doubt can possibly enter your soul. This has been tried. This is certain' (p. 53).

We have now traced the main stages of Dostoevsky's religion. After breaking away from his family pieties, he passed through a Social-Utopian phase, all but, if not quite, atheist, but as it were dedicated to Christ. As the result of his Siberian misadventures, he came to see how powerful and how personal evil is, its principle, self-will, being at the same time the basic drive of human action. It cannot be extinguished, for humanity would perish with it; it can only be stood on its head and become humility. But humility is so often inefficacious; it disarms the ordinary natural man, but not one who is 'possessed' like Nastasya Filippovna or Stavrogin. It needs roots in the soil (hence the Russianness of Shatov and the *Diary*), and it needs the concurrence of a body to match; it has to be tried out in the flesh and in the world (herein is the superiority of Alyosha). But all through the question keeps arising: how are these various models for practice related to philosophical assumptions about God? Towards the end, Dostoevsky took notice of it, and deliberately declared theory to be a constituent of practice.[92] He thus provides for the Undergrounder who thought intellect to

[92] Cf. John 7.17, 'If any man will do his will, he shall know of the doctrine', and Karl Marx, Eleventh thesis on Feuerbach: 'Philosophers have tried to understand the world: the task, however, is to change it.'

be a part and will the whole, but only on condition that the will itself is integrated in the whole consentience of humanity. He provides for the proud, who do not have to take their forgiveness from others, because the others are equally culpable.[93] But, in providing, he overturns. The possessed pass out into freedom undiminished. That is what happened when Jesus said to his patients 'thy faith hath made thee whole'.

God is then to be understood, but he cannot be understood from the theorist's angle. Dostoevsky had in fact been convinced of this from 1846 onwards; the trouble then and for long afterwards was that he thought it a fatal flaw. He was reconciled when he saw how from the heart of Christian endeavour could arise a different kind of understanding: God being present only in the endeavour, there could be no way to him except *through* the endeavour. There is here some justification for otherwise implausible attempts to relate him to Kant – *prima facie*, two characters could hardly be more dissimilar. But, on the whole and perhaps because he is not rigorous enough, Dostoevsky avoids treating a presupposition as problematical. God *is*, even if it is only in serving him that we know it.[94]

[93] This is subtly different from Tikhon in *Stavrogin's Confession*: if you can forgive yourself, you are forgiven; but it shows the same delicacy in the preservation of self-respect.

[94] It is tempting to speculate on the possible influence on Dostoevsky of N. F. Fyodorov (1824–1903) who attacked the notion of pure scholarship and demanded from thinkers that they enter the service of action. In a letter to N. P. Peterson, 24 March 1878 (*Pisma* IV, pp. 9–10) Dostoevsky expressed great interest in the 'thinker' (actually Fyodorov) whose views his correspondent had reported to him, and says he is 'in entire agreement'. But he goes on to discuss, not Fyodorov's general thesis, but his particular and picturesque interpretation of the 'resurrection of the body': namely, that it is happening in this world here and now, and if only we get to work scientifically we may re-establish contact with our ancestors. To our surprise, Dostoevsky reports his sympathy with the suggestion, and that he talked it over with Solovyov who sympathized also. There is no hint whether he was also referring to the broad, and for us, far more relevant issue, or whether he followed it up. At the very least he exhibits, in a mild form, the persistent anti-rationalism of his conservative contemporaries and he seems to have shed the rationalist scruples which had kept him so long in such great anxiety. They went out in a blaze of glory when he wrote up Ivan Karamazov.

✖ TWO ✖

Dostoevsky as a Christian Novelist

I

The first business of a Christian, said Kierkegaard, is to become one. It follows that no Christian is just a Christian, or wholly a Christian: if he were just a Christian, he would be less of a Christian; to be effective in his witness, he is called to excel at some point in the secular world, and in any case to surpass what he is now. And no man is wholly a Christian; every Christian carries the weight of imperfectly Christianized impulses which are liable under stress to take an anti-Christian direction. Of some of them he is aware, and he takes measures accordingly; of some he is not, and they are apt to erupt all over him when he least expects it.

All this is platitudinous, but it bears on the predicament of the Christian novelist. If the Christian agent sometimes betrays an un-Christian ferment inside him, it is likely that the Christian who is also an artist will bring the matter into the open. But his is a special case. All Christians are agents; only some Christians are also artists.

Christian action is a response to the love of God, expressed in an unforced and unlimited concern for a person. *All* persons: being God-centred, it is above all things not selective. It collides at an early stage with the motives of self-aggrandizement and self-importance; it collides at a higher level with the exclusiveness which reserves concern for particular kinds of people – fellow-nationals, for example – or, what is more important for our purpose, *good* people. That a Christian should be wholly pervaded by this concern is not possible: it is always a matter of more or less. The agencies of interference (more simply described by our ancestors as devils) are infinitely various ('our name is legion'), and in eluding one he can easily become the prisoner of another. There are intellectual dubieties and deviations: it is unreal, as well as an insult to intelligence, to claim that they have no effect on action. There is the temptation to play for a draw by observing the formalities and looking no further. There is the tragic involvement in a civil war between those natural partners, flesh and spirit. Above all, there is the experience of humiliation; if one's sense of significance has been mauled or stunted or deformed it is bound to appear in an exaggerated form, and to be particularly intractable. The sequence can be worked out in the public arena, but it is in private dealings that the crucial cases occur: a thwarted citizen will act reasonably unless he is also a thwarted person. This experience is Dostoevsky's special subject; and in thinking that pride is the first problem of a Christian, both in himself and in others, he has the weight of Christian precedent on his side. All these interlopers, and combinations and permutations of them, have been canvassed by Christian novelists. What is common to them is that they are all deeply impressed by the power and malignity of evil. The accusation of taking evil too lightly, constantly levelled against Christians but applicable only to deists, is particularly misplaced when directed to those Christians who are engaged in exploring the human condition.

So far, we have considered, with inevitable previews on literature, the general predicament of the Christian. Suspended between the challenge of perfection and his own defects (why not 'sins'?), he will make what he can of an imperfect world, and he will ascribe such success as he achieves to 'the practice of the presence of God'. He will not presume on his achievement; he knows he has to 'work out his salvation with fear and trembling'; and if his account anywhere near balances, he will be grateful and happy and take none of the credit for himself. This will hold no matter what his particular devils may be; though if he does not

reckon with those evoked by Dostoevsky, he is asking for
trouble. But the ordinary Christian is concerned with the management of his corner of the world, and of himself. If he resorts to
introspection and analysis, it is with this strictly practical end in
view. The case of the Christian artist is more complicated. Like
the Christian thinker, he has not merely to deal with situations
but to dwell on them; and because the situations are not assured
or stabilized, what he reveals will be a checkerwork of light and
shade, the shade being thrown into relief by the light. Unlike the
Christian thinker, he cannot, as he explores situations, focus on
what lies beyond them. He does not, for example, write novels
about God; he writes them about people in their perplexities
about God. He may, indeed he cannot but, reveal his personal
convictions, but it will be dissolved in the structure of the novel;
it is the people, with their unfulfilments, their stresses, their
defiances, and also their complacencies and compromises, and
their exposure to the light which they may accept or decline,
which absorb his attention. It is not his business to explore the
universe but, if he has the power, rather to convey it; what he
explores is character. And this, too, holds no matter what
particular devils he is concerned to evoke.

Some Christian novelists have been concerned mainly with
false doctrine; implicitly about God, but explicitly about men.
For example, Paul Bourget in *Le Disciple* puts the blame for his
student's crime squarely on the shoulders of a personally blame-
less rationalist teacher who suggested, academically and with no
intention to act on it, that controlled experiments on human
beings should be allowed in which, for pure purposes of observation, vices should be practised as well as virtues. The case is
particularly instructive for us because Bourget's 'disciple', like a
Dostoevskian *vsechelovek*, sets out as a programme of study
'multiplier le plus possible les expériences psychologiques',[1] and because Bourget himself shares with Dostoevsky a detestation of
the scientific reductionism which threatens the belief in responsibility. Indeed, on the intellectual plane they are remarkably akin.
Where they differ is that in Dostoevsky intellectual assertive-

[1] Reprint in *Bibliothèque Plon*, p. 42; Eng. trans., London 1901, p. 58.

 the danger of clumsiness and insensitivity in those who for-
. Dostoevsky, who explored these regions in depth, could
ighten them.

We are thus brought back to the Christian concern about evil.
 world, as the Christian understands it, is full of evil: not
t, the high-minded sort of evil which ended in the crucifixion.
 Christian novelist, having to compress it within the covers
book, will see it, if anything, a little larger than life. From
yan downwards, he knows that there are people who exude
. They are not all of them 'bad' people by conventional
dards; they may be upright in their way but empty at the
; or they may have a high potential for good but are
nded and desperate. The distinction between good and evil
 t the comfortable distinction between right and wrong. Evil
fferent because it has a religious dimension. That consider-
Christian novelist, Graham Greene, is a specialist in this
 nowhere more clearly than in his early work, *Brighton*
 The younger gangster, 'Pinkie', a Catholic gone wrong but
aunted by his early training, especially hell ('hell lay about
in his infancy'), moves in and in his uneducated way
nds to the religious dimension; and, knowing himself to be
does not begin to take his wrongness seriously, even when
bs to the point of murder. ('The word "murder" conveyed
re to him than the word "box", "collar", "giraffe"'). So
Rose, the little Catholic waitress whom he marries, so that
nnot give evidence against him; she too moves in the
us dimension, acutely aware of evil, and loving him enough
 his evil in her stride, and his injustice with it. There is a
ss of contrivance in Greene which Dostoevsky never com-
, and a touch of cynicism which Dostoevsky might not
nvied; but they both inhabit the same frozen regions
the home comforts of the just and the unjust. Awareness
dimension is to be expected of the Christian novelist; he is
 and uneasy about it and not at all comfortable to live
o be wholly out of the range of evil is not the privilege of
t; it is a fictitious alibi for the self-deceiving.[7]

lurring of 'wrong' in the context of 'evil' may seem to be morally repre

ness is only one illustration of the more generalized spiritual sin
of pride, for Bourget it is the heart and centre of it.[2] It cannot be
said that as a Christian Bourget was wrong to concern himself
with ideas as a source of moral corruption; they are a fact of
human experience, and deserve the implacable study which he
devotes to them. But they are a symptom rather than the cause
of the malady. For Dostoevsky, at least, they are a disease of the
will. And it cannot be said that his approach is not authentically
Christian. It is the pathological inversion of that outstanding
text (John 7.17): 'If any man will do his will, he shall know of
the doctrine.'

Again, some Christian novelists have found their main theme
in the conflict between flesh and spirit. This heretical preoccupation of the Albigenses has re-echoed in French Catholic
orthodoxy, from the *Phèdre* of Racine to the fiction of François
Mauriac (*Le Fleuve de Feu* is the extreme case). Again, these
things happen: diabolical possession may take the form of
sexual abandon, though it is the abandon, and not the sexuality,
which is at odds with the Christian dispensation. But the role of
pride in this conflict is ambiguous; in *Phèdre*, though inefficacious, it is on the side of the angels, while the victims depicted by
Mauriac have lost it and are simply powerless.[3] For Dostoevsky
it is both intensely operative, and diabolical: and it is central.
As has often been pointed out, there is not much in the Gospels
about sexuality (we have to work it out for ourselves in accordance with the over-all Christian pattern); but there is a great deal
about pride, and especially about the moral self-congratulation
of the righteous. On that showing, it is Dostoevsky rather than
Mauriac who is at the centre of the picture. He is not unobservant of sexual passion, but what particularly interests him is the
way it is disoriented when it enters the vicious circle of hurt-
and-be-hurt. The outstanding cases are the tragic doubleness of

[2] In fact, Bourget admires pride in a military context as much as he dislikes it in
an intellectual. The intervention of Count André, which gives the book its unexpected and utterly proper conclusion, is motivated by pride from start to finish.

[3] Jean-Paul Sartre complains that Mauriac treats his characters as puppets,
adding characteristically: '*Dieu n'est pas romancier, M. Mauriac non plus.*' The truth
behind this crack is that he sometimes *displays* them as puppets, being sorrowfully
convinced that they are.

Nastasya Filippovna in *The Idiot*, and the self-immolating convolutions of Katerina Ivanovna in *The Brothers Karamazov*. Incidentally, but still to the point, in the latter novel Dmitri's points of honour are heavier with disaster than is his infatuation.

Many Christians, especially if Anglo-Saxon, have found the centre of their religion in the moral law. It is interesting to reflect that they include no novelists of quality: even *Eric, or Little by Little*, rises beyond this restriction at its better moments. There is something about the quasi-legal approach which seems to antagonize them. The fact is that, not having to act, they are spared the temptation to standardize and abbreviate and, having to imagine, are impelled to place themselves on the inside of their characters and to love them as themselves. Even Bunyan, who dealt allegorically with types and generalities, used them to discredit typical and generalized morality in favour of the pilgrim; even T. S. Eliot, concerned to celebrate Christian orthodoxy as the answer to chaos and despair, distilled it from the unheralded and unpredictable instant, for which there is no recipe and certainly no legislation. More wayward than either of them, Dostoevsky viewed the whole concept of law, civil or natural, with unconcealed suspicion. He knew that the devil (whom he seems to have taken more than half literally) could disguise himself in the most unimpeachable moral dinner-jacket, and that the hard line between sheep and goats is more than anything else fatal to human brotherhood. It was his deepest conviction that if you cannot love men in their sin, you are (the language of the Gospels) a whitewashed tombstone; you may sparkle in the appropriate moral sunlight, but you are prematurely dead inside. With Christianity understood as obedience to law (or, for that matter, as the apprehension of propositions or, in general, as any sort of rationalizing device for streamlining humanity out of its freedom), Dostoevsky had nothing to do. He interests some of us just on that account: he seems to be so much closer to the original Christian emphasis. But, right or wrong, we shall not understand Dostoevsky as a Christian moralist unless we accept, or at least are prepared to explore, his conviction that the central issue is the wholly personal issue of

pride. It will be remembered that Lucifer fell th devil is not a mudlarker, but a fallen angel.

That being so, we are none of us 'in the clea pull of self-assertion, and if we are sensitively easily become 'frustrated' and experience 'ali we are practised in our religion and can pul tanglements, that is not the end of the matter only enjoins humility on each of us individua us to devote our humility to the service especially if he is running into trouble. But without love may be just a complicated form other end, being helped may be felt as an their alienation will cling to it as the last r respect. Above all they will not consent to *facie*, forgiveness is an unequal relation; eve the need of it, he is humiliated in his own This leads immediately to one of Dostoevsk most difficult paradoxes: that it is harder forgive. The only people in fact who can be ness are those who at the same time ackno in sin with the forgiven. Otherwise, forg an instrument of oppression. In these re easily misled by his own finer feelings. excellence which the devil cannot simulat percipiently remarks,[5] he 'finds his m Dostoevsky's world as in traditional C sublime virtues'. 'The moment of choice to its own use.'[6] Christians will admit th case of courage in a burglar or attention of forgiveness, as of other canonical vir say: here, at least, there is no foothold they underestimate the obduracy of inju

[4] The parallel between Dostoevsky's Russia a ominous and remarkable.

[5] *Dostoevsky: the Major Fiction*, p. 57.

[6] Cf. Prince Valkosvky in *The Insulted and Inj* in the best actions, and the better the actions the character, but his author is prompting him.

II

It will be said: this is all very well, but not all Christian novelists conform to the description. Some do: Bunyan, to start with, and Greene, certainly; also a whole cohort of French Catholics, including Bourget, Mauriac, and most eminently Georges Bernanos; and they are accompanied in their respective countries by affiliates in poetry and the drama – Eliot in England, and Péguy and Claudel in France. But there are others who show little sign of contrition or self-examination: Charles Kingsley's studies in religion are mainly social-humanitarian or Protestant-controversial, and those of Maurice Barrès French-nationalist or Catholic-political. Others, described by Dostoevsky as 'Christian' – Dickens, Victor Hugo and George Sand – did not devote themselves to an analysis of the religious consciousness and can be included only if 'Christian' = 'humanitarian', pure and simple. Others, again, are Christians *and* novelists, the two characters rarely interesecting. Both Jane Austen and Sir Walter Scott were good parishioners, but neither of them examined their beliefs in their fiction.[8] They were an assumption, not a passion or a problem. Moreover, the exploring of the Christian consciousness has been movingly practised by ex-believers, such as George Eliot in her earlier phases, and by the much underestimated Mark Rutherford, and by positive unbelievers like Anatole France in *Thaïs* – in this case, with discomforting illumination. The threads are properly tangled; and, looking at the dates of these writings, if we set Bunyan aside as a special case we note that the earliest of them is contemporary with Dostoevsky, and the most significant, those of Bernanos, quite

---

hensible. The Soviet critics find it so in Dostoevsky; and the good old-fashioned proponent of the Puritan ethic will agree with them. For the critics it may be said that the human cash value of 'evil' is 'wrong', and that 'wrong' is none the less 'wrong' when it enters the orbit of 'evil'. But to those who move in the religious dimension it does show up as derivative; and that is what Greene (and Dostoevsky with him) is trying to put on record.

[8] Scott did provide, in *Old Mortality*, a masterly study of a seventeenth-century Covenanter as ruthless, splendid and impossible. But in this and similar ventures he uses history as an alibi; he does not probe the contemporary condition.

obviously indebted to him.[9] It begins to look as if something happened to the novel in respect of religion in the latter half of the nineteenth century, and that Dostoevsky was both a symptom and a cause of it. At the same time, the turn then taken was one which had to be taken if religion were to be properly focussed in the novel. If not an average sample, Dostoevsky is at least a paradigm case.

Now the novel, as an art-form, is in some sense a secularist discovery. It grew up as a humane diversion for a new public made available by leisure and the printing press; it was directed to a mixed *clientèle* of varied allegiances; it had to assume that it would be read aloud in the family circle; so that it could best promote itself by avoiding controversy and concentrating on the human predicaments common to all types and conditions. Neither in its realist or in its romanticist expressions, neither by concentrating on the matter-of-fact features of the world nor by contracting out into history or fantasy, was it called upon to invoke religion or, for that matter, anti-religion. Its field was the tragedy of human conflict and the comedy of human manners. Thus in undertaking to explore the religious consciousness, the novel exceeded its original social specifications. And, before it could so so, two conditions had to be fulfilled. In the first place, there would have to be a cultural *milieu* in which religion was no longer taken for granted, and could be probed in the presence of readers (including readers-aloud) like any other phenomenon. Secondly, some author of genius would have to arise, Christian enough to know what he was talking about, but fully aware, in himself and in others, of the conflict between faith and denial, and eager to make it available to a general public now ready to receive it. Both conditions had been fulfilled by 1860; and the innovating genius was Dostoevsky.[10]

[9] The Mouchette of *Sous le soleil de Satan,* who cannot endure the pity which threatens her defences, is an eminently Dostoevskian character; and the devil's interception of the priest on the plains of Picardy contains even verbal reminders of his earlier encounter with Ivan Karamazov. So with the coruscating author's allocution on the turning of good to evil, ending *'sa haine s'est reservé les saints'* (*Oeuvres* I, Paris 1947, p. 109).

[10] There remains Bunyan. But he too belonged to a period of religious disturbance, in which religious problems were both central and disputed; and he too was

III

He was aware from the beginning that he did not quite conform to type; but, being a novelist, he naturally saw his unorthodoxy as technically artistic. In fact, it was his technical revolution which enabled him to encompass without omission the dichotomy of the religious consciousness; but that was incidental to his main objective which was to show up the third dimension of character by studying its divisions and duplicities in general. The novelist was traditionally expected to consolidate his characters by 'multiplying their similarities' – the phrase comes from Dostoevsky's compatriot and contemporary, Goncharov, and is admirably illustrated in his great creation Oblomov. Each character is thus a strongly marked type; the disturbing waywardnesses are excluded. That does not mean that the characters do not develop; indeed, their central unifying traits are deployed on many fronts, and the reader is able to assess their habitual deportment through the variety of their contacts. Even so, this kind of fiction seemed to Dostoevsky unreal, and his so-called 'realism' is in the main a revolt against it. His method was the multiplication of *dis*similarities. To variations on a main theme he preferred counterpoint: within the limits of the work of art, the bass which equally with the melody constitutes character rumbles along in its own way.[11]

There are several stages of the revolt, and Dostoevsky is almost unique in refusing to stop at any one of them. In the first place, unity of character may be fixed by some social norm. Figaro is a valet carried to the point of genius, but everything he does is tied to his being a valet. Dostoevsky is singularly unconcerned with social placement; it is a fair complaint against

---

a man of faith who knew better than most where the pitfalls lay. But he was a forerunner; by the time the novel as an art-form got into its stride, the lucid eighteenth-century interregnum was upon it, and it was not called upon to discuss what almost everyone assumed and almost no one was disturbed by. In England the only significant religious movement, Methodism, was lamentably only a joke for the novel-reading class; and it never produced a Bunyan. So the forerunner's work had to be done all over again; in a new idiom, to encompass the new perplexities.

[11] The analogy is used by Bakhtin, *Problemy poetiki Dostoevskogo*, p. 60.

him (carried to an extreme by virtuous Soviet critics concerned about the weakening of the work-force) that his characters have nothing to do but interact. They either have money or they have not, but in neither case do they work for it. His persistent avoidance of this central compartment of life can hardly not be deliberate. He is determined to explore the recesses of character which are smoothed over in the professional stereotype.

Secondly, unity of character may be fixed by psychological coherence. Here, again, Dostoevsky dissents. He does not identify his personages by single traits, or pin them down with a *Leitmotiv*. There are, it is true, one-piece characters in his gallery; but they are either comic (as in *Uncle's Dream*), or early (like Makar Devushkin and Varvara Dobroselova in *Poor Folk*), or subsidiary (like the wonderfully drawn Darya Pavlovna in *The Possessed*). They do not include Alyosha (he is only just starting) or Myshkin, whose type-qualities break down under him as the story proceeds. There remains Sonya who will have to have a section to herself. In general, unity of character is fixed in his novels by psychological *in*coherence.

Finally, unity of character may be fixed by individualizing abstractions. This is the technique of Bunyan, and particularly to our point, for his fiction not merely depicts the religious consciousness, but is saturated with it. Bunyan has an eye for character, but his vocation is typing and classifying: Mr Worldly Wiseman is truly embodied, but only as worldly wisdom. In displaying the great difficulties of the Christian pilgrimage, Bunyan anticipates Dostoevsky; he knows that key points on the highway are controlled by the devil's junior executives. He knows, too, that smugness and respectability are the air they breathe. But they are nothing but what they are; we are rarely moved to pity their humanity:[12] they are lifelike exhibitions of their dominant qualities. It is the same with the pilgrims; they are subject to temptation but they are not divided; the evil they encounter finds a response in them, but they have absolutely no doubt of their vocation. Brilliantly inventive as the details

---

[12] It is perhaps permissible to pity Giant Despair when it transpires that his wife is Diffidence, and vice versa.

frequently are, they are not for contemplation, but for use; they are part of a guide-book for travellers to heaven. Now Dostoevsky did not embody abstractions: he created characters, and the characters evolved the ideas, often to his own discomfort. Ideological stereotypes were as alien to him as social and psychological. His main claim as a student of character was to have discerned the 'double' which breaks up stereotypes of every sort.[13] It was his genius, within the same character, to reveal incongruity and so to penetrate by way of the apparently fantastical to a layer of reality untapped by rationalizing psychologists or well-bred observers of the social surface.

With this reinterpretation of 'realism', Dostoevsky resorts to the methods of the adventure story, rather than to those of the traditional novel of character. Speed, intensity, incident piled on incident, action and dialogue rather than description, a leaning to the unities, especially of time, an almost Aristotelian preference for the plausible impossibility over the unpersuasive possible – these are the technical hallmarks of Dostoevsky in full spate. For the most part, the torrent is sufficiently impetuous to carry with it boulders which would block the progress of any normal novel. Since the publication of the *Notebooks*, it has become clear that his first prerequisite was plot; the second, characters; the third, consequentially, and sometimes inconsequentially, ideas. Plot being conceived in terms of events, his models are not only the great writers, but also the good story-tellers. He is in many respects indebted to the 'Gothic' novel – not only to Hoffmann[14] but also to the English spine-chiller, Mrs Radcliffe (1764–1823), whom he claims to have read at the age of eight.[15] He lived

[13] It may be that the 'double' was a Western romantic discovery:

Cet étranger vêtu de noir
Qui me ressemblait comme un frère:

and it is said by E. H. Carr to have been cleverly utilized by the then fashionable E. T. A. Hoffmann (1776–1822), author of *Die Elixire des Teufels* and *Nachtstücke*; but Dostoevsky used it not merely horrifically, but for revelation. He refers to Hoffmann in an early letter to his brother Mikhail, 9 October 1838 (*Pisma* I, p. 47).

[14] See note 13 above.

[15] Letter to Y. P. Polonsky, 31 July 1861. She is best known for *The Mysteries of Udolpho* (1794) and is commended by a writer in the ninth edition of the *Encyclopaedia Britannica* (1883) for 'ingenuity of plot, fertility of incident, and skill in

before the days of the detective story, but being fascinated by the study of crime and incurably addicted to surprises, he found himself writing one – trial scenes and all – and it grew into his most ideological creation, *The Brothers Karamazov*. In all this he claims to be the true realist: the turbulent and distracting course of events throws the characters off balance, and they are revealed for what they are.

This reinterpretation of character as a unity of contradictories may fruitfully be extended to the novel as a whole. In his important work, *Problemy poetiki Dostoevskogo*, M. M. Bakhtin attributed to Dostoevsky 'a completely new type of artistic conception, which we have provisionally called the polyphonic'.[16] It is distinguished by the presence of independent consciousnesses, 'a polyphony of voices, each given its full value'. In the normal 'monological' novel everyone and everything is limited to the author's horizon. Dostoevsky's characters are created not as objects, but as subjects, as independent voices, not completed by the author in advance, but set up by him with the law of their own development inside them. 'What is important is not how the hero appears in the world, but how the world appears to the hero.'[17] 'Not for a moment does a Dostoevsky hero coincide with himself.' He is 'not a finite substance, but an infinite function'.[18] In language reminiscent of J.-P. Sartre, we are told that 'it is impossible to apply to man the formula of identity, A is A'.[19] He is not a 'thing-like being',[20] 'which can be surveyed,

---

devising apparently supernatural occurrences capable of explanation by human agency and natural coincidence'. The first two of these virtues are pre-eminently Dostoevsky's; as for the third, it is exhibited in some of his more horrible dreams (e.g. Raskolnikov's and Svidrigailov's in *Crime and Punishment*) and raised to the highest possible imaginative power in Ivan Karamazov's hallucinatory encounter with his diabolic 'double'.

[16] *Dostoevsky's Problems of Composition*. In the series *Sovyetsky Pisatel'*, Moscow 1963. The main thesis was stated earlier in *Problemy tvorchestvo Dostoevskogo*, 1929; the later book is in effect a 'second edition' (p. 4), 'revised and significantly augmented'.

[17] Op. cit. p. 63.

[18] Ibid. p. 68.

[19] Ibid. p. 79. The following shorter references are scattered about in the same chapter.

[20] *Veshchnoye bytiye*: cf. *chosiste* in Sartre.

defined and predicted, irrespective of his will and behind his
back'. 'The genuine personal life is accessible only to those who
enter into it dialectically.' The author does not push his characters about; he mingles with them on equal terms: 'the conversation is not *about* the character, but *with* him'. They are
'undefined' and 'incomplete'; they may add to themselves, inopportunely, at any moment. The 'word' they carry lies
'alongside' the author's 'word'. They are subject to no objective
constraint except the pressure of other characters similarly independent. Even the material world is refracted wholly through
their consciousness; for example, Petersburg figures as a vivid
presence in *Crime and Punishment,* but it is presented entirely
through the lived experience of Raskolnikov and Svidrigaylov.
Similarly, the author does not explain his characters; he makes
them throw light on each other. The objective world of the novel
is at the point of intersection of consciousnesses.

What Bakhtin says about characters he proceeds, in the next
chapter, to say about ideas. Dostoevsky, he observes, never
attempted disembodied discussion, which is anyway the business
of philosophers rather than of novelists. He thought the truth
about the world to be 'inseparable from the truth of personality'.[21] He tells Pobedonostsev that he will not answer Ivan's
indictment 'point by point' but 'as it were in an artistic picture'.[22]
All his ideas are tested dialectically through their embodiments.
There is therefore no conclusion, only confrontation. The author
does not dictate affirmation or denial; if he did, he would exclude
the imaginative presentation of the idea: in fact, monological art
renders impossible both the 'reciprocity of consciousnesses' and
'real dialogue'.[23] Dostoevsky, on the other hand, polyphonically
elaborates ideas foreign to him as if they were his own, as,
indeed, artistically speaking, they are. He makes no exception of
ideas which as a publicist he vehemently maintained. Sonya,
Myshkin, Zosima are 'liberated from the monological exclusiveness' which Dostoevsky displayed in the *Diary.*[24] All ideas
enter into the dialogue with 'completely equal rights'.[25] As all

[21] Op. cit. p. 103.   [22] Letter, 24 April 1879 (*Pisma* IV, p. 109).
[23] Bakhtin, op.cit. p. 107.   [24] Ibid. p. 124.   [25] Ibid. p. 122.

characters have equal rights, and ideas are presented only through characters, the conclusion necessarily follows.

As a literary introduction to Dostoevsky's way of thinking, Bakhtin's book is brilliantly illuminating. It explains why we should be more than usually cautious about attributing the 'word' of his characters to Dostoevsky, and why his own 'word' is so difficult to discern. He is in fact so polyphonous that one is tempted to go further, and to say that his 'word' exists only as incapsulated in the various 'words' of his character; that, for example, in *The Brothers Karamazov* it is not Dmitri or Ivan or even Alyosha, but the interaction of these and the other principal characters; it consists of getting the whole bagful right for the record. This is more than what Bakhtin asserts: his view is that the 'word' of the character lies 'alongside' that of the author. His caution is justified: sometimes the narrator offers an opinion in his own name, as in the deliberate accrediting of Radomsky at the end of *The Idiot*; though it may transpire that in making this necessary admission Bakhtin allows for a possible priority on occasions for the 'word' of the author. But in general Dostoevsky does not restrict his own 'word' to those who reflect his own everyday opinions. It is expressed in Ivan, whom he wished to refute, no less than in Alyosha, with whom he agreed. The refutation of Ivan, if it is one, is in the implacable course of events. Dostoevsky never silences a character with an ideological hammer.

His permissiveness in the matter has a direct bearing on our thesis. It could mean that his (generally Christian) 'word' has no special standing inside the novel, and that an essay on 'the religion of Dostoevsky' could have only a biographical significance. To this point we shall return: in the meantime, the objection may be offered that his artistic polyphony is somehow not quite Christian :[26] as if it were the business of a Christian novelist to force his creatures to embody a Christian conclusion. But if force is used, that can only be because Christianity is felt to be

[26] Bakhtin seems to think so; which is fortunate, for it enables him to enter into the feelings of Christian characters without what for him would be the embarrassment of personal commitment.

unequal to the course of events: here, as elsewhere, violence springs from insecurity. So the Christian artist, like Christians everywhere, has to take risks: from within his Christian frame of reference, with agony in his heart, he has to watch his characters 'doing their own thing'. Dostoevsky cannot coerce Ivan Karamazov; he can indicate his conviction only by telling the story of his struggle and final collapse.

To show that his case, though highly individual, is not wholly idiosyncratic, consider, for similarities and divergences, the imaginary dialogue in Dorothy Sayers' important work on the boundary of theology and literary criticism, *The Mind of the Maker*. She was a convinced Christian, but her eminent creation, Lord Peter Wimsey, does not figure in that category, either as a model or, for that matter, as a warning. She pictures herself being confronted with an interfering interlocutrix, and the dialogue proceeds:

> 'I am sure Lord Peter will end up as a convinced Christian.'
> 'From what I know of him, nothing is more unlikely.'
> 'But as a Christian yourself, you must *want* him to be one.'
> 'He would be horribly embarrassed at any such suggestion.'
> 'But he's *far* too intelligent and far too nice, not to be a Christian.'
> 'My dear lady, Peter is not the Ideal Man; he is an eighteenth-century Whig gentleman, born a little out of his time, and doubtful whether any claim to possess a soul is not a rather vulgar piece of presumption.'
> 'I am disappointed.'
> 'I'm afraid I can't help that.'

Footnote: in brackets and italics. 'No, you shall not impose either your will or mine upon my creature. He is what he is, I will work no irrelevant miracles upon him, either for propaganda, or to curry favour, or to establish the consistency of my own principles. He exists in his own right and not to please you. Hands off.!'[27]

It would seem that Dorothy Sayers was not troubled by the difference of religion between herself and her creature, partly because Lord Peter is so well-mannered, partly because he does not raise religious issues (Bunyan might have called him My Lord Sagacity from the Mansions of Incredulity), and probably (though this is surmise) because Dorothy Sayers was the kind of

[27] *The Mind of the Maker*, p. 105.

Christian who could compound with eighteenth-century Whigs – just as Dostoevsky was the kind of Christian who could compound with nineteenth-century Russian populist nationalists. Where she made it easy for herself was in avoiding situations in which Whig values and Christian values would be incompatible. She was well within her rights: no writer has to raise religious issues unless he wants to, or his characters call for it. But, Dostoevsky did raise the religious issue; he did, as an artist, accord equal rights to his atheists; he did insist that the story should go its own way, without interference, and it is only at the end of it that the gains and losses can be counted. He neither kept religion out of his novels, nor indifferently expounded his pros and contras. While allowing them no privileges, he was right behind his Christian heroes, in their failures as well as their successes, in the faith that in God's world there is no need to fake results to justify his ways to man. Also, as a Christian should be, he was right behind his atheists, as they struggled in their own way towards the light as they saw it, cheering them on while he showed in human terms how they were bravely attempting the impossible. He went on experimenting till in *The Brothers Karamazov* the record looked like coming straight of its own accord. That, and not pushing doubts under the carpet, is what is meant by faith.

The fact is that the artist's polyphonic disengagement, as Bakhtin presents it, is more Christian than he appears to realize. It is the business of Christians to put themselves in all manner of people's places; and the Christian novelist, with the imaginative perceptiveness of his art, is a better guide than 'forms and categories'.[28] It is possible to know *about* people in general, and this knowledge is helpful to those whose interest in them is particular; but in the end they can be *known* only one by one. To insinuate himself into the unique predicament of a character is

[28] Bakhtin (op. cit. p. 130) quotes from Dostoevsky's reply to his critic, Kavelin, included in the collection *Biography, letters and notes from minor writings*, 1883: 'better remain with a mistake, with Christ, than with you; you have nothing left but forms and categories, and it looks as if you were glad of it': and Bakhtin observes: 'Forms and categories were foreign to his nature.' What he is seeking is a personal assurance which concept chopping cannot provide. See below.

the polyphonic novelist's special accomplishment. The case cited by Dorothy Sayers is relatively simple; this Christian writer does no more than *suspend* her religion while delineating her hero; she identifies with him, but because the difference between them is not brought out in her novels there is no polyphonic effect. Dostoevsky is through and through polyphonic; he stakes his fondest hopes on one set of characters, goes violently into reverse to identify with another and maintains his own equilibrium, all at once.[29] What they present in common is what the theologians call *kenosis* – the emptying of their Christian consciousness to achieve identification with their creatures, and not only their Christian creatures: and that is the point of our comparison. Dostoevsky, however, goes further, using this authentically Christian procedure to set up conflict-situations among his creatures, and between his creatures and himself. He has to, for his eye is not merely on objectivity, but on redemption.[30]

We are thus brought indirectly to consider the style of Dostoevsky's personal religion. Bakhtin makes and cites a number of illuminating comments. He observes that Dostoevsky 'thought not with concepts, but with points of view'[31]; that is, he took into account not so much the truth of concepts as such, but also the viability of the total affective structure to which they belong. In the same strain he writes of Dostoevsky's world as 'not a world of objects, but a world of reciprocally enlightening consciousnesses';[32] the truth about it is a truth about (or of) people, and the ordinary categories for the subsuming of objects are inadequate. It is natural that Dostoevsky should have carried this way of thinking into his religion – a man's religion is his character, blinking in a vast inflow of light. His option for Christ is not ideological but experiential, 'there is only one verification:

---

[29] How far the despair of the alienated was also his own and how far the product of imaginative sympathy, makes no difference. From what we know of Dostoevsky, in and outside the novels, it was a little of both.

[30] In *A Man Born to be King*, Dorothy Sayers created a Judas in the manner of Dostoevsky, full-voiced and independent: a high-minded man who understood his Master's purpose better than any other disciple, but was too clever to trust him.

[31] Bakhtin, op.cit. p.124.

[32] Ibid. p.130.

Christ'.[33] A verification: not an object to be contemplated but a guide for people in action. As he grew older, Dostoevsky tried to keep up with the theologians, but it was not his *forte*. As Bakhtin says, in words it would be hard to improve upon, 'he is looking for a higher authoritative order, and receives it, not as his own true thought, but as another true person and his word'.[34] Dostoevsky, who generated 'persons' and 'words', polyphonically, knew when they spoke 'with authority and not as the scribes'.

IV

There is thus no Christian reason for resisting Bakhtin's conclusions, and they are carefully documented and stated with great moderation. They call, however, for the following comments, which are not necessarily to be taken as criticisms.

1. While what he says about 'polyphony' in Dostoevsky may well be true, 'polyphony' in itself is not quite the discovery it is represented as being. Any novelist of any quality allows his creatures room to grow in, if only because a destiny determined by fiat 'behind their backs' destroys the reader's interest. It is true, however, that some writers build their stories round their own concepts,[35] and that Dostoevsky went to almost any lengths to keep the options open. Both ways, it is a matter of degree: Dostoevsky is unusual in pressing the independence of his characters quite so far.

2. Even so, however, he imposes certain controls – not those of an authorized ideology, but those of a disinterested observer. Bakhtin insists that his central thesis does not depend on, or entail, any particular manner of narration; but even the most polyphonic story must be told by somebody. The usual choice is between the first-personal narrator and the omniscient novelist

[33] Quoted from Dostoevsky's reply to Kavelin, ibid.
[34] Ibid. The concept of a 'true person' leads to a philosophy of practice. See Ch. 8.
[35] Several times Bakhtin cites by way of contrast the intrusiveness of Tolstoy. An extreme case is the short story, *Tri Smerti, Three Deaths*, in which the rich lady, the coachman, and the tree are all shown in the act of dying, and there is nothing but Tolstoy's overriding concept of death to hold the episodes together. Oddly enough, it works: absolute government occasionally does.

in his own capacity; and both of them slant the story their own way. Dostoevsky managed to be polyphonic in the all-disposing third person in *Crime and Punishment*[36] and *The Idiot*, and even the first-personal loquacity of the 'raw youth' reveals incidentally a discordance of 'voices': but to obtain the full polyphonic effect something less obtrusive is required. Dostoevsky discovered how to do it in *The Possessed*, and repeated the experiment in *The Brothers Karamazov*. He tells the story through an inconspicuous narrator on the edge of the action, but speaking nevertheless in the first person. In *The Possessed* he is called G——v; in *The Brothers Karamazov* he has no name at all. In both cases he provides the objectivity needed to balance the pressurizing presences of the principal 'voices'.[37] This is not to say that Dostoevsky fails to achieve polyphony within the traditional methods; on the contrary, to assure freedom of movement to his characters he stretches those methods to breaking point. But it is permissible to draw attention to a device whereby the novelist is saved from brooding too heavily upon his creatures, and the first-personal narrator is prevented from presenting too egocentric a picture of the situation.

3. The 'word' of Dostoevsky can sometimes be gathered from his 'normal' characters. His interest is in the exceptional, and particularly in those who resist the standard Christian procedures they are the hard test cases for a Christian anthropology. Yet he frequently stations sensible people in the margin and sets his sights by them – a device which has received less attention than it deserves. To start with, Razumikhin in *Crime and Punishment* (*razum* = reason, good sense); then, in *The Idiot*, the wordly but perceptive Radomsky; then, in *The Possessed*, Q——v himself, whose interjections subtly highlight the passionate perversities of the protagonists, and the silent patient Darya Pavlovna, always available when needed, and never sufficiently

[36] Originally told by Raskolnikov in the first person. That Dostoevsky changed his mind only at the last minute shows a certain dissatisfaction with both methods.

[37] Even this device has its difficulties. G——v in *The Possessed* has to be anywhere and everywhere, with an improbable confidential access to some singularly unconfiding characters; and in *The Brothers Karamazov* it gives out altogether when Ivan and Alyosha discuss the universe in the pub, and when Ivan is confronted by his diabolic double.

called upon. An interesting feature of *The Brothers Karamazov* is the absence of any such character; the sensible people, Rakitin and Perkhotin, are pure egoists, and the role of dispassionate observer is doubled with that of an active participant, Alyosha.[38] In general, the device is all the more remarkable because Dostoevsky did not sympathize with sensible people; he detested the 'golden mean', and still more the prudent quest for advancement. Still, to keep his more wayward and overwhelming characters in perspective, for the sake of order in the novel if not in life, he had to measure them by a more ordinary norm; and, through that norm explicitly (Radomsky) or implicitly (Razumikhin), he speaks with a more sensible 'voice' than his more dominating heroes and heroines. To use Bakhtin's language, in such cases his 'word' is not merely 'alongside' that of his characters; it is also a sort of corrective. That is not to deny Bakhtin's main point, that a Dostoevsky character has his own way of being, and is not an extension of the author's; otherwise, an author's corrective would be unnecessary.

4. Moving further in the same direction, and further away from Bakhtin, we note that Dostoevsky is not primarily lyrical or confessional, but clinical. The medical heritage was not wholly lost in him. The ordinary clinician does not project himself, he observes. The artist-clinician does project himself, but only to the extent that it aids his observation. The unpleasing writer of *Notes from Underground* borrows, no doubt, from the unpleasing recesses of Dostoevsky's consciousness, but Dostoevsky's part in the matter is to effect a diagnosis.[39] He shows by speaking from inside him that he is a likely product of a competitive society working on excessive sensibility, and he allows him to challenge the world to face realities. But in the very challenge there is an appeal to a normality which is absent both in the protester and in what he protests against. In particular, the editorial sympathy,

[38] Alyosha is deliberately created more normal than an average front-liner in Dostoevsky; in fact, only a firm basis in normality can enable him to face what lies before him. Even so, the doubling of the roles has the effect of making the author take sides just that little bit more than usual.

[39] As we shall see (Ch. 3 below) this does not prevent him from giving his patient some home truths to declaim to his day and generation.

so to speak, of Dostoevsky is with Lise, and against her tor-
mentor, in the harrowing episode of 'Damp Snow'. To that
extent Underground Man is a case, and there is no pathology
without a norm. Similarly Raskolnikov is marked out as a case,
flanked as he is by Razumikhin on the one hand, and Sonya on
the other, and is probed as such by that remarkably acute
magistrate, Porfiry Petrovich. So with Nastasya Filippovna,
Stavrogin, and Ivan Karamazov, in ascending order of complexity. They obtain their power and their terror from the
inexorable framework within which they operate – not the framework of divine justice, in so many words, but the framework of
human sanity. They may well embody the fears, the adumbra-
tions, and even the expectancies imaginatively entertained by
Dostoevsky, but they are exposed all the time to his clinical eye,
even when remedial agencies are powerless to avert the catastrophe. Even the redeemers are caught in the same implacable
searchlight. Myshkin is measured by the good sense of Radomsky, Stavrogin and all his spiritual dependents by the selflessness
of Darya Pavlovna, and Ivan, too sophisticated to be saved by
Alyosha, runs onto the reef which awaits all deviants, mental
breakdown. Dostoevsky knows that these things happen, and the
better to observe them, unrelentingly sets them down.

For these reasons, we must be careful about explaining his
characters as projections of the author. They take their own line
as obstinately as Lord Peter Wimsey. They are not so much
pro-jected as *e*-jected; and as ejects they are reviewed with the
proper clinical detachment. Much has been made of Dostoevsky's
concern with the abnormal: this, for example, from V. Lvov-
Rogachevsky (1922): 'the mournful chart of the gloomy isolated
inmates of this hospital for the poor erected at the expense of
F.M.D. for his doubles'.[40] Hospital, perhaps; but there is a
master diagnostician in charge of it.

[40] Quoted in V. Seduro, *Dostoevsky in Russian Literary Criticism, 1846–1956*,
p. 17. The writer complains, over-earnestly but accurately, that Dostoevsky is not
interested in 'selfless public workers'. Neither do hospital doctors attend the hale
and hearty. The hale and hearty do, however, constitute their frame of reference.
Much earlier, Belinsky had complained that the 'double' was a fit subject for
medicine but not for the novel. He was wrong about the incompatibility but right
about Dostoevsky's medical approach.

It has been noted (pp. 53ff. above) that a Christian novelist can be expected to be preoccupied with evil. Dostoevsky's clinical experiments are a case in point. N. K. Mikhaylovsky in a celebrated phrase wrote of his 'cruel talent'. It is not clear whether the cruelty is supposed to be directed to the reader, the character, or himself; but it is clear that in his diagnosis of the human situation he spared nobody, and himself least of all. He refused to make the best of the world by dwelling on its excellences, or to justify God by percentages. Thomas Hardy wrote in a lyric, 'if a way to the better there be, it exacts a full look at the worst', and the worst so horrified him that he missed the way to the better. Dostoevsky thought along the same lines, though he had the courage and the sheer spiritual vitality to see it through. (No one was ever less of a pessimist than Dostoevsky.) Belinsky had taught him, and he never forgot it, that unless all could be saved, no one had a right to be saved; and he worked this rebellious sentiment into a Christian context.

These are generalities; but they are borne out by his handling of marriage. In a letter written to N. N. Strakhov in 1870,[41] when he had been married to Anna Grigoryevna for four years, he said: 'Marriage makes three-quarters of human happiness, the rest of life a bare quarter.' It is curious that this conviction is nowhere communicated to his fiction. One can understand that he should refrain from using as copy the wife to whom he owed so much; one can even see why he should prefer to draw from his former mistress, Suslova, whose oddities fascinated him, as Nastasya Filippovna's fascinated Myshkin: there is nothing sacrosanct about infatuation. But what does surprise us is that in all the major fiction there is practically nothing about marriages. There is, of course, the unhappy Marmeladov *ménage* in *Crime and Punishment* (hardly a recommendation), and though marriage as a topic is much to the fore in *The Idiot*, the actual married couples presented are the Yepanchins, who have coalesced fairly well but are not the subject of a close study, and the Ptitsyns – a clear case of a woman marrying for money and receiving kindness beyond what she deserves. In *The Possessed*,

41 *Pisma* II, p. 256.

the two marriages on view are those of Stavrogin and Shatov, both to the last degree abnormal; and in the whole of *The Brothers Karamazov* there are no married persons at all. From these casual allusions and remarkable gaps, one would not suspect that Dostoevsky valued marriage as much as he did, and had every reason to do. The fact is that Dostoevsky was concerned as an artist with the misery of the world, tracing it to its source in the pagan virtue of pride and pointing to Christian 'togetherness' as the only remedy. He had to select the dark corners of the world, if only to show that the light which could not penetrate them would not be worthy of worship. In that spirit he was prepared to throw in his own and others' unhappiness and misadventures, but not to put on display the hope which had dawned upon him. Perhaps that is the trait which Mikhaylovsky qualified as 'cruel'.

The first aim of clinical observation is diagnosis; unless we see what is wrong there is nothing we can do. The second phase is therapy: and here Dostoevsky is avowedly experimental. His first attempt to present a hero coping with a major dislocation, in *The Idiot*, conducted with remorseless honesty, ends with his breakdown.[42] But the diagnosis remains, and stands him in good stead when he tries again in *The Brothers Karamazov*. We have been shown how not to set about repairing injured self-esteem, and that it takes a stronger, younger, and more earth-bound therapist than Myshkin to succeed. Alyosha is programmed to be the answer: because he is not a 'perfect knight' or a 'pure fool', but a Karamazov.

v

We can now face the problem raised above (pp.61ff.): if Dostoevsky is to be genuinely polyphonic, what standing can his 'word' have inside the novel? To answer it, we shall have to revert briefly to his 'word' outside the novel. Except for a year or two after the first impact of Belinsky, he would have said,

---

[42] Not counting Raskolnikov who is too much of a light-weight for tragic eminence.

vaguely, that he was a Christian; but almost to the end he was still struggling. It was not so much his early 'dissipation' that clouded the horizon; nor his love affairs of 1863–66; nor his reckless propensity to gambling, which continued till 1871. He held as a matter of Christian conviction that the love of God includes the sinner *as he is*, even, as we shall see, without the precautionary requirement of repentance. He was struggling most particularly on the intellectual front, which was where his line of defence was weakest: the shadow of Belinsky fell across it to the end of his days. Lacking a theology, and spasmodically racked by a kind of anti-theology, he was more than most Christians what all Christians are more or less, a Christian in process. Facing successive difficulties, he set them forth in his novels so purposefully that he has convinced good critics that he found them insuperable. He does not take charge of his characters but he does present through them problems which troubled him: decently distanced, properly subordinated to the demands of the story, and carefully distributed over the characters in accordance with their capacity to sustain it.

It is therefore not only helpful but necessary to consider the novels in order to get to grips with Dostoevsky's religion. He put into the novels the agonizing doubts which he hid beneath the ebullience of the *Diary*, and the caution of his letters to his editors. More precisely, he uses the novel to test out the tentative advances in religion which he had achieved in his personal life: often with the most disconcerting results. He does it *as* a tentative Christian and not as an assured Christian simulating tentativeness for purposes of exposition. Contemplating his incomparable honesty, one is tempted to ask: are assured Christians quite as assured as they look? Not being able to entertain their doubts imaginatively, they overrule them by an act of will where will cannot succeed; or not being able to express them indirectly, as novelists can, harbour them in secret. Still, some of them, including authors, are less tentative than Dostoevsky; they are either less susceptible to intellectual issues, or better able to solve them. Dostoevsky writes as one finding himself, not out of the fullness of a completed experience. And it is because he is so self-critical and self-discovering that he can express himself both polyphonically and experientially at the same time. Only a believer constantly wrestling with his unbelief could speak with both voices with the same strength of conviction. As we shall see, the sense of utter disharmony diminishes when, in *The Brothers Karamazov*, he begins to discern the difference between theoretical and practical thinking. In the meantime, we can be grateful for a personal discomfort which has so powerfully stimulated the modern novel. And his predicament was an extreme case of the Christian predicament in general. It is not Christians, but their detractors, who expect them to step into the world ready-made.

The Cellar and the Garret

I. RUMBLINGS IN THE CELLAR

There are few documents in literature which look less Christian than *Notes from Underground.* The sick self-consciousness of the writer, his exasperated cynicism, his withdrawal from the world of action (for which he has nothing but contempt), even his exquisitely nasty brand of humour, put him in the category of repudiators and unbelievers. Yet as an introduction to the developed world-view of one who confessed and called himself Christian, they are indispensable. They are precisely the muck in which his Christian flowering has its roots.

Notes from Underground (literally 'from beneath the floor': the analogy of the futile scurrying mouse is repeatedly called upon) is the confession (or the boastings, or both) of a retired civil servant of forty, living alone on a small private income, hating the world and all that is in it, and alienated from its obviousness by what he calls a typically nineteenth-century intellect and sensitivity. He does not consider himself peculiar; on the contrary he is the real man of his time: the others just strut around on the surface. Listen to his peroration: 'I have only in my life carried to an extreme what you have not dared to carry half-way, and what is more, you have taken your cowardice for good sense, and have found comfort in deceiving yourselves. So that perhaps, after all, there is more life in me than in you . . . we are oppressed at being men – men with a real individual body and blood – we are ashamed of it, we think it a disgrace and try to contrive to be some sort of impossible generalized man . . . Soon we shall contrive to be born somehow from an idea.'[1] *We*, that is, all of us, as long as we face our age and generation. We *have* to be like that, unless we are to be cogs in a machine: the great machine of nature and reason. And this makes the utterances of Underground Man something half-way between self-congratulation and a general confession of original sin: the sin which makes him futile and the protest which makes him human are indistinguishable. To this we shall return.

In the meantime, what is he protesting about? First, the belief in the goodness of the natural man, *l'homme de la nature et de la vérite*, a phrase repeated in the text to the point of satire. What is wrong with this paragon is his 'innate stupidity': it is convenient, for it enables him, for example, to represent revenge as justice; whereas the 'mouse' with his 'acute consciousness' knows better.[2] He triumphs merely because he lacks sensibility; not because of any excellence, innate or acquired. The innately superior person (the mouse) is not good, but the bull is no better, only less aware. Second, the belief in action as a way of life; action inevitably contracts consciousness, the expansion of which is the great nineteenth-century achievement.[3] When it meets a stone wall it accepts it: the man of consciousness, not troubled by having to act, does not accept it, even if he knows it is there; and he keeps his emotional range at the proper level of universality. Third and consequentially, the belief in the finality of science, especially mathematics.[4] Why should two plus two make four, if I do not like it? Why should we be reconciled to impossibilities?[5] They are impossible all right, but why should I add my approval or withhold my disaffection? Fourth, the appeal to self-respect. Nobody with any subtlety of consciousness can have any. The 'mouse' will be ashamed, but will forget nothing, and even take pleasure in contemplating what he is ashamed of.

---

[1] Tr. Garnett. *White Nights and Other Stories*, pp. 154–5.

[2] *Notes from Underground*, ibid., p. 57.

[3] 'The legitimate fruit of consciousness is inertia', p. 62.

[4] Dostoevsky had always hated mathematics: see a letter to his father quoted by A. Steinberg, *Dostoevsky*, p. 23.

[5] P. 75: a theme which haunted Dostoevsky's imagination all through.

But it is just in that cold, abominable half despair, half belief, in that conscious burying oneself alive for grief in the underworld for forty years; in that acutely recognized and yet partly doubtful hopelessness of one's position, in that hell of unsatisfied desires turned inwards, in that fever of oscillations, of resolutions determined for ever and repented of a minute later – that the savour of that sharp enjoyment of which I have spoken lies (pp. 57–8).

All these protests are significant of more to come: positive as well as negative. But the two main intellectual preoccupations are, fifth, Utilitarian morality, and sixth, psychological determinism. It is accepted that the *Notes* are primarily directed against Chernyshevsky's *What's to be Done?*[6] The rumblings in the cellar are intended to shake 'the palace of crystal'. Chernyshevsky believed that an ideal society could be created out of the rational adjustment of self-interest: as Bentham had put it, less lyrically but more concisely, 'golden conduct out of leaden motives'. Dostoevsky, knowing all about irrational perversity in himself and in his Siberian fellow-convicts, speaks with the Underground Man when he writes: 'Oh, the babe! Oh, the pure innocent child! . . . When in all these thousands of years has . . . man acted only from his own interest?' (pp. 64f.) He knows that men are neither as rational nor as selfish as they appear in the Utilitarian calculus. It is on this point of psychology that Dostoevsky first embarks on an open confrontation with the Western liberals; that it is put into the mouth of an angry mouse is neither here nor there; the mouse is recording an universal, and particularly a contemporary experience, and no amount of Utopian theorizing can be allowed to silence it. That people always follow their own interest is simply not true; and if society were scientifically planned so that everybody's interest coincided, the mouse would still scuttle for his hole and squeak his defiance.

This, it will be observed, is put forward as a statement about the facts of the case, and so far it carries no connotation of value. Nevertheless, one can discern a value judgment in the making. 'What man wants is simply *independent* choice, whatever that

[6] Textual affinities are adduced by K. V. Mochulsky, *Dostoevsky: his Life and Work*, p. 251.

independence may cost and wherever it may lead' (p. 69). If a man's choice is tied inevitably to his interests, it is not a choice at all; so it might even be a duty to choose stupidly, by way of thumbing one's nose at the 'palace of crystal'. Various analogies are introduced to drive the point home; the ant-hill, the piano-key for theorists to play on, the stop of an organ to be pulled out as they choose. 'All human actions will be tabulated . . ., mathematically, like tables of logarithms up to 108,000, and entered in an index; or, better still, there would be published certain edifying works of the nature of encyclopaedic lexicons, in which everything will be so clearly calculated and explained that there will be no more incidents or adventures in the world' (p. 68). And that is the end of human freedom. The mouse speaks for the dignity of the whole human species.

As so often, Dostoevsky accepts the view of reason propounded by his opponents, and attacking them, attacks reason with them. 'You see, gentlemen, reason is an excellent thing, but reason is nothing but reason and satisfies only the rational side of man's nature, while will is a manifestation of the whole life, that is, of the whole human life including reason and all the impulses. And although our life, in this manifestation of it, is often worthless, yet it is life and not simply extracting square roots.' He thus prepares the way for the reinstatement of religion on anti-rationalist terms. But, for the moment, the 'will' is paramount; and here the successors of Underground Man are the total voluntarists, Svidrigaylov and Stavrogin. The mere refutation of rationalism, even if successful, does not settle how will is to operate. Indeed, the translation of *volya* by *will*, though not positively incorrect, is too specific; *volya* also means freedom, not in the democratic sense of self-determination but in the anarchical sense of the absence of limits.[7] But Underground Man has a point; he knows all about perversity; he has tasted the bitter pleasures of biting off his nose to spite his face, and he sees that no account can be given under the Utilitarian formula of a phenomenon more common than superficial good sense is prepared to admit.

[7] It is one of the cases in which no translator could do any better.

The sheer writing of *Notes from Underground*, especially Part One, is a masterpiece: the undertone of spite, irritability, helplessness and self-congratulation is brilliantly conveyed in the harshly turned sentences, the copious disconcerting parentheses, the blending of colloquialism and abstraction, the broken and persistent dialogue of the writer with himself, mainly in the form of mocking exchanges with an imaginary interlocutor. But our concern with it is: how much of what Underground Man spits out through his chattering teeth is seriously to be ascribed to Dostoevsky? And what light does it throw on the nature of his religious pilgrimage?

1. The first question, which has its analogue throughout his great fiction, is here more than usually difficult to answer. At times Underground Man turns round and calls himself a liar. But his recognition of himself as a liar enters into his final expression of triumph. What, then, is Dostoevsky's own attitude towards him? The ironical tone of the writing suggests that it is clinical: whether autobiographical or not, the material is distanced and even judged. Dostoevsky certainly does not identify with his anti-hero. When he forces himself on a party of schoolfriends, is insulted, and walks up and down in front of them from eight o'clock to eleven between the table and the stove, extracting with satisfaction the last bitter drop from his humiliation; when, much more abominably, he raises the hopes of a recently recruited prostitute, and, when she comes to him in pure love, humiliates her and offers her payment 'from spite', because anything like love threatens his mutinous underground posture, the whole tone of the writing is hostile – even the Underground Man himself shows his abhorrence – the point of the episode is to show that this kind of thing can happen, and that the cycle of insult and humiliation is not in the same universe with the palace of crystal. The whole exercise is directed against the simpleminded one-track analysis of human nature issuing from the French Revolution and the English bourgeoisie. Yet something of the Underground enters into the world-view of Dostoevsky himself. His anti-rationalism, his antipathy to scientific and particularly to mathematical paradigms, his sense of freedom as

unlimited opportunity for good and for evil, his emphasis on the evil which in the absence of some antidote to humiliation is certain to prevail – all this is pure Dostoevsky and helps to explain his tensions and improvisations. Underground Man is not only affirmed as a fact against the psychologist; he has hold of something which in any possible synthesis must remain intact. That is why he exclaims at the end to his 'audience': 'There is more life in me than in you.'

2. To explain fully the religious implications of his mutterings from the cellar, we should have to follow the theory of humiliation through the whole of his major fiction. But there are right from the start some indications which we must make the most of – both in the text and in contemporary writings outside it.

(*a*) In the reflections introductory to Part Two (p. 85) Dostoevsky returns to his theme of 'broad natures', 'who never lose their ideal even in the depths of degradation; and though they never stir a finger for their ideal, though they are arrant thieves and knaves, yet tearfully cherish their first ideal and are extraordinarily honest at heart'. Here is one of Dostoevsky's most persistent themes: there is for Russians no cut-off point for good and evil, as, it would seem, there is for the more legally minded Catholics and Protestants. There is, however, another side to it. The possibility of their co-existence depends on the duality of the nature concerned. Duality is a disease consequent on 'consciousness'.[8] 'Tell me this: why does it happen that at the very, yes, at the very moments when I am most capable of feeling every refinement of all that is "good and beautiful", as they used to say at one time, it would, as though by design, happen to me not only to feel but to do such ugly things, such that . . . Well, in short, actions that all, perhaps, commit but which as though

---

[8] *Sozdaniye*: the elements of the word are exactly those of the Latin; and both are slanted towards 'self-consciousness', i.e. a conscious being sees himself in everything else. It could be argued that insofar as it casts one's own personal, or even one's own human, shadow over the world, it is self-destructive; and an enforced acquaintance with the Underground has at least the merit of showing up the doubleness (not to say duplicity) of the various German Idealisms. The remedy, of course, is to go on and not back: to show that there is a consciousness which is not self-consciousness, because it is others-consciousness.

purposely occurred to me at the very time when I was conscious that they ought not to be committed. The more conscious I was of goodness and all that was "good and beautiful", the more deeply I sank into my mire and the more I was ready to sink in it altogether. But the chief point was that all this was, as it were, not accidental in me, but as though it were bound to be so.'[9] The 'good and beautiful' are conceived as *ideals*; they are *entertained*; and they have no power.

We have noticed in Part One of this work the affinity of 'doubles' and 'ideals'; here we have it again. In the letter to Fonvizina, Christ is an 'ideal'. It is interesting to note just how Dostoevsky's Siberian experience had affected his attitude to ideals. In his 'Schiller' period he had actually thought 'ideals' could be realized. In *The House of the Dead* he learnt how little this intellectual prattle amounted to. Salvation, if available at all, would be a long and difficult business. He now does not think ideals can be realized; the most they can do is to light up the darkness and make it more evident. Properly speaking, this should mean that Christ can illuminate but cannot save. The change effected by Siberia was that this world is not the place to expect ideals to flourish in. The document in which the position is most clearly set out is to be found in Dostoevsky's notebooks for 1864; in an entry amounting to a funeral meditation immediately after the death of his first wife. It is also important as containing material far more explicitly Christian than anything he had written for more than twenty years.

(*b*) *Notes from Underground* was written in Moscow while his wife was dying, and Dostoevsky, who had not been conspicuously loyal or attentive to her, was at her side with the utmost consideration and devotion. The meditation, therefore, belongs to the same period of development as the *Notes*. It is spontaneous and confused, as one might expect under the circumstances. It starts from the assumption that no one here and now can love another as oneself – Christ commands the impossible. The 'law of personality' ties us down to earth. Only Christ could achieve

[9] This sentence is not only revealing, it is, in its scapegrace scattered parenthetical intensity, a stylistic *chef-d'oeuvre*.

it. Now Christ is the 'ideal' to which, according to the law of his nature, man tends. (So far he is simply ideal.) But then, he is also 'the incarnate ideal of man', and this means that man's full development is in following him. That he can only do by using the whole force of his 'I' to annihilate this 'I', 'and to make himself over to all and to each, individually and unconditionally. So that way the dialectic is achieved'. The law of the 'I' blends with the law of humanism, and in the fusion both (the 'I' and the all) are mutually annihilated to the advantage of both, and the highest end of each man's individual development is attained. 'That', he adds, 'is Christ's paradise'. But if that is the final end of man, to achieve it would put an end to man as an earthly being. It makes no sense to suppose that he must expire at the moment of achievement. Therefore, there is another life. We know little about it, but it has been predicted and foreshadowed by Christ, 'the final and ultimate ideal of man's whole development' who has 'presented himself to us in flesh and blood according to the law of our history'. Then follows a passage about the world in which there is no marrying or giving in marriage, poignantly relevant to the occasion, but we need not follow it. Then comes a parenthesis marked N.B., in which it is explained that Christianity cannot prevail here and now, because it is the ideal for our future development, and on this earth man is in a state of transition; as Christ himself said, to the end of this world there will be struggle and development ('doctrine of the sword'). Another N.B.: 'the nature of God is directly opposed to the nature of man'. This bears on the status of 'love everything as oneself'. It is in contradiction with the law of human development. And – a very important sentence – 'that' (i.e. the law of human development) 'is not an ideal law, as the anti-Christs say, but the law of our ideal'. This (super-worldly) ideal is mainly shown on earth by the impact of its negation. 'When a man does not offer his "I" in sacrifice and *in love* for man or for some other being (Masha and I) he experiences suffering and calls it by the name of "sin": and the terrestrial condition is one of balance between that suffering and the paradise of joy procured by the fulfilment of the law, i.e. by sacrifice.' Without that it makes no sense.

It will be seen, even from this *précis*,[10] that Dostoevsky, at the time he wrote the *Notes*, was engaging in theological speculation in a definitely Christian sense; and this is enough to show that Underground Man is brought on the stage not as a mouthpiece for the author, but as an alarming indisputable fact. But the content bears examination. (1) In describing Christ as an 'ideal', Dostoevsky keeps his options open; he might very well not be Lord of the World. (2) In describing him as an ideal incarnate, he does something to dissipate the suspicion of dualism. (3) In emphasizing, for the first but not for the last time, the importance of personal immortality (the only official dogma of the church which he embraces unequivocally), he seems to edge away again from the world; it is because what has to be accomplished cannot be accomplished in the world that he so cherishes it; (4) thus slightly moderating, but not retracting, the appeal to eliminate the special 'I' here and now. This remains when all the 'Idealism' is pared off, and it is the basis of Dostoevsky's later Christian anthropology. There is already an oscillation between Christ the impossible and Christ as presence.

How far this should be read back into the *Notes* we should know better but for the imperial censor. That insensitive official took out a large portion of Part One, Chapter 10. Dostoevsky comments to his brother in a letter dated 5 April (26 March) 1864: 'It would have been better not to print the last chapter but one at all (it is the most important, where the essential idea is expressed), than to print it as it is, i.e. with cobbled-up sentences and full of self-contradictions . . . Those brutes of censors, – where I made a mock of everything and sometimes blasphemed *for form's sake*,[11] that is passed, but where I deduced from all this the necessity of faith and of Christ – that is suppressed.[12] Dostoevsky never restored the excised passages, nor, as far as we know, were they preserved, to be published after his death, like 'Stavrogin's Confession'. So we can only guess at

[10] Part of the entry is translated into English in Magarshack, *Doestoevsky's Occasional Writings*, pp. 305–6, and the whole of it appears in French in *Dostoievski*, by Pierre Pascal, Text V, pp. 114–18.

[11] That is, verisimilitude.

[12] Letter 74 in J. Coulson, *Dostoevsky: a Self-portrait*, p. 124.

their contents.[13] But in this context Christ could only have been a projection of an ideal out of the depths.

If, then, it is asked, how is *Notes from Underground* a preparation for the struggle for God in Dostoevsky's inner experience, it may be said: (1) that it excludes the tacit compromise with Utilitarianism which was the fashionable religion of nineteenth-century England; (2) that it sets a sharp line between 'reason' which is *ex hypothesi* irreligious, and religion which, if permissible, will be unreasonable; (3) that the way of nature is not in the least godlike, and the average man's secular virtues lead him nowhere; (4) that the first and last enemy of religion is the experience of humiliation; (5) that 'ideals', being both the cause and the consequence of human doubleness, cannot save – even if they are presented as incarnate, for they are still not presences but presentations. A good deal of rubbish has been cleared away. But there is one issue on which Dostoevsky's clinical sympathy is at odds with his reflective judgment. Underground Man commends a life of consciousness as the only life possible for a man of modern sensibility: he has no use for the vulgarities of action. At times Dostoevsky will be found accepting this dichotomy, with the plus and minus signs reversed.[14] At other times he proffers a Russian version of 'practical reason'. In view of his increasing emphasis on 'active love', culminating in *The Brothers Karamazov*, this issue, unresolved in *Notes from Underground*, is one for which we must watch carefully in his later work.

That is as may be. What is certain is that *Notes from Underground* contains the basic psychological introduction to Dostoevsky's whole study of man, including his Christian study of Christian man.[15]

[13] The only place in the existing Ch. 10 for the excised section is nearly at the end. 'Can I have been constructed simply in order to come to the conclusion that all my construction is a cheat? Can this be my whole purpose? I do not believe it.'

[14] Especially in *Crime and Punishment*, which is the story of an intellectual who takes his ideas over-seriously. Cf. the advice of Porfiry Petrovich: 'fling yourself straight into life . . . and the flood will bear you to the bank and set you safe on your feet again' (p.412).

[15] It is underplayed by post-revolutionary Russian critics. In that admirable collection, *Tvorchestvo Dosteovskogo*, Moscow 1959, which deals with other works at great length, it is mentioned only in passing. Its offence is that its effective interest

II. BROODINGS IN THE GARRET

Crime and Punishment is structurally Dostoevsky's best novel. It moves fast, it is free from digression, it abounds in striking characters, it is socially and introspectively observant, and it holds the reader breathless by its sheer concentration. Yet it is intellectually puzzling. The reason is a change in mid-course from a projected Utilitarian murder to a definitively 'Napoleonic' murder – intended to establish the murderer as a 'great man' to whom alone such transgressions are allowed. Either version is in conflict with the Christian anthropology which Dostoevsky is now far enough advanced in his pilgrimage to introduce. Moreover, it is his deliberate view that Utilitarian self-interest expresses cautiously the same egocentric attitude which in sheer self-will is expressed courageously and without reserve. For both these reasons he could plead that the change does not affect his main purpose. But to take the finer points we have to consider the difference between the original and the final versions as well as the continuity.

In the first sketch of the novel, as outlined by Dostoevsky in a letter to his editor, M. N. Katkov,[16] Raskolnikov is programmed as an Utilitarian. Concerning his intended victim he is to ask: 'What is she living for?' 'Is she any use to anyone?' He puts it to himself that if he had the money, he could make his mother more comfortable, and extricate his sister from her position as governess in the household of the predatory Svidrigaylov. In the text as we have it, there are traces of this Utilitarian motivation but they have been submerged.[17] The argument that the world would be well rid of its human vermin is no longer put in the mouth of Raskolnikov; he overhears it being propounded by a fellow-student. The intention of rescuing his sister is also dis-

---

is not social but psychological and metaphysical. The contributors have a mid-Victorian distaste for mental quirks and oddities, and the only cause of behavioural malformation which they admit is social malformation.

[16] *Pisma* I, p.418.
[17] 'I've only killed a louse, Sonya, a useless, harmful, loathsome creature' (p. 373).

carded: before committing the murder, Raskolnikov believes
that she will be amply provided for by marrying the unpleasant
but undoubtedly affluent Luzhin. And as for using the money
philanthropically: he misses most of it and buries the rest under
a stone. The question is now mainly not what good it will do but
whether great men with an original contribution to make have
greater freedom from common obligations than the common
average. The problem raised by Chernyshevsky finally dis-
appears under the horizon. Henceforward Dostoevsky is to be
concerned not with individualism in its prudential form,[18] but
with its grimmer manifestation of arbitrary self-will.

Now *Crime and Punishment* was written to show that even in a
desocialized intellectual there is an in-built revulsion against
murder, a sense of guilt in its presence, which will outweigh his
intellectual convictions to the contrary, and make him confess.
But what sort of confession will it be? The Utilitarian, as Dostoevsky understood him, need not feel guilty at all; if he fails, he
will merely exclaim: 'I'm a fool.' (This is how all of us feel in
Utilitarian situations, that is, in situations in which moral issues
are not involved.) For the 'Napoleonic' character the case is
more complicated. If he fails, it is not merely his plans which are
at fault but he himself; he has shown himself to be merely
average, and therefore not entitled to moral immunities, by the
bare fact of his failure. His self-criticism must take the form: 'I
am personally inadequate.' And this is not so far from the
Christian formula, 'I have sinned.' Later, on Dostoevsky is to
insist that the man who is way-out and hell-bent is nearer home
than the mere malingerer.

In the Epilogue to *Crime and Punishment*, Raskolnikov avoids
the Christian formula (a point to which we shall return), but
he used both the others, and indiscriminately. He is made to
remark that all he was guilty of was a 'simple blunder' (p. 486).
This is appropriate in a failed Utilitarian, but not in a failed
'Napoleon'. The 'Napoleon' in him goes further: 'Those other

18 Or in what he believes to be its derivative socialist form: cf. Raskolnikov's
remark: (the Socialists) 'work for the common good. I have only one life: I don't
want to work for the common good' (Part III, Ch. 6).

men succeeded and so they were right, and I didn't, and so I had no right to have taken this step.'[19] *No right*: not a mistake, but a transgression. He slides so easily from the one formula to the other that we must conclude that Dostoevsky was not greatly concerned about the difference. To us, nothing seems less 'Napoleonic' than Utilitarianism – that intellectual representation of the feelings of those described by Napoleon as a 'nation of shopkeepers'. Nevertheless, Dostoevsky had a way of looking beyond historical combinations to intrinsic resemblances; and prudential Utilitarianism has this much in common with arbitrary self-will: that both deny in the individual any motivation and/or obligation other than self-concern.[20] It is this feature of Raskolnikov's ethic (and it can be read either way) which is up for judgment.

But we are concerned to collect from *Crime and Punishment* hints of a *Christian* viewpoint; and neither stupidity nor failure to be a superman is matter for a Christian conscience. That being so, we must look beyond Raskolnikov; for, right to the end, Raskolnikov shows no sign of Christian repentance. True, he is driven, by an obscure horror of isolation, to confess;[21] and having chosen Sonya to confess to he is impelled by her sheer strength of personality to confess also to the authorities. But at no stage does he admit Christian arguments or act for Christian reasons. His theory travels with him to Siberia, tormenting both Sonya and himself. More than once, the author, in the third person, says of him that he does not know what is happening to him; for example, when he did not jump into the canal, 'he could not understand that his decision against suicide arose from a presentiment of a future resurrection and a new life'. Any action conforming to Christian expectations he attributes to other

---

[19] P. 487. The quotation concludes a piece of sophisticated dialectic beginning with 'my conscience is easy'. In that case why 'no right'? Nietzsche might have told him.

[20] Razumikhin speaks for his author when he tells Luzhin that the crime-wave among educated people is simply the putting into practice of his 'scientific' principle, 'Love thyself above all.'

[21] Again, Dostoevsky is telling us that togetherness is the first step in religion, just as religion entails togetherness. Both socially and religiously, individualism is the enemy.

causes: weakness, for example. Dostoevsky's approach is wholly and deliberately anthropological, as if he were pledged to defend Christian values anonymously – it was perhaps the way he accepted them himself at the time. Much of his pleading is to be found in the secular observations of the worldly-wise and kindly examining magistrate, Porfiry Petrovich, who sees that what is struggling for expression behind Raskolnikov's protestations is a genuine sense of guilt, and observes that, for one who needs to expiate, suffering may well bring release and prison pacification.[22] This is pure analytical psychology, depending on no religious assumptions; but it fits readily enough into Dostoevsky's Christian pattern. Where Porfiry leaves off, Sonya takes up. Nevertheless, as so often with Christians, Sonya is the catalyst releasing the healthier forces of nature. Immediately after the murder, finding that memory and prudence were forsaking him, Raskolnikov was asking himself: can this be the punishment already beginning? The way forward to the Christian dispensation is so far solely through the failure, in his hands, of his preferred alternative. For the moment, the Christian in Dostoevsky sits on the sidelines and watches.

As the novel ends, his premonitions look like coming true. Raskolnikov, loner and dissenter,[23] once described by his friend Razumikhin as a man who had never loved anyone, falls in love with Sonya at long last. Only then does he begin to see the possibility (no more than that) of a Christian future. He does not envisage a Christian frame of reference and then love: he loves first, and it so changes his own frame of reference that he asks himself whether he might possibly come to share Sonya's 'convictions'. At that point his intellect interrupts him, and he hastily adds: 'or at least her feelings and impulses' (*stremleniya*).[24] Even in anticipation he is doubtful about the dogma; if ever he gives up his own driving idea, it will be

[22] This is not to be read as general social theory, and still less as theology; it is directed to Raskolnikov and expresses Porfiry's estimate of him. As such, it is accurate enough.

[23] This is what his name means in Russian.

[24] 'Aspirations', which is Garnett's translation, is too much in the air: 'impulses' is better, but too instinctive. 'Strivings', understood dispositionally, might be nearer the mark.

because 'life has stepped into the place of theory': being in love is incompatible with being a loner. And if there are no concessions to orthodoxy on the side of theology, there are no concessions about repentance either. Raskolnikov never repents; even falling in love and reading the Gospels do not produce that effect. On the contrary, they submerge his whole dismal history in such a tide of gladness that he literally forgets the past and begins to look only forward. One has a preview of Tikhon telling Stavrogin that there is no forgiveness for those who cannot forgive themselves. This is not orthodox doctrine, and one can understand the dismay of stricter and sterner believers like Leontyev. But it is authentic Dostoevsky.

To return. *Crime and Punishment* leads to a Christian anthropology. But what kind of Christian anthropology? To examine the problem, we have to collect the explicit religious references in the text.

1. As the above references show, there is no theology in the novel, and particularly no theodicy. When Raskolnikov, in a persecuting Underground mood, tells Sonya that her sister might have to follow her into prostitution, Sonya exclaims:

'God would not allow anything so awful!'
'He lets others come to it.'
'No, no! God will protect her, God!' she repeated beside herself.
'But, perhaps, there is no God at all,' Raskolnikov answered with a sort of malignance, laughed and looked at her (p. 290).

It is true that Raskolnikov is moved to ask her to read him the story of the raising of Lazarus, but for the moment the only effect is to make him repeat himself and to call senselessly for violence: 'Freedom and power, and above all, power!' (p. 298). The issue is joined and then left open. So, when the priest attempts the conventional words of consolation to Marmeladov's widow ('God is merciful; look to the Most High for succour'), the subsequent dialogue leaves us with the feeling that it is hollow mockery (pp. 168–69). At this stage in the story, God is not evident: he has to be dragged out from behind the despair of the innocent and the trepidation of the guilty; and argument about his existence has nothing to do with it.

2. If theology counts for little, so does the church. The priest at the bedside performed the conventional offices, but he had nothing to offer the widow and family – not like Raskolnikov, who contributed his last twenty roubles. In the end 'he bowed his head and said nothing' (p. 169). And Dostoevsky does not utter the pietistic truism: 'There is nothing to be said.' He just finds the priest and his offices inadequate.

3. Even within the limits of anthropology, Dostoevsky's Christianity is selective and, to those attuned to Puritan notions of moral deserts, peversely selective. The main carriers of the Christian message in *Crime and Punishment* are a drunkard and a prostitute. Marmeladov's outburst, gorgeously decorated with fragments of Church Slavonic, is so fundamental for the understanding of Dostoevsky that it must be quoted at length. He says to the tavern-keeper,

'Do you suppose, you that sell, that this pint of yours has been sweet to me? It was tribulation I sought at the bottom of it, tears and tribulation, and have found it, and I have tasted it; but he will pity us who has had pity on all men, who has understood all men and all things, he is the One, he too is the judge. He will come in that day and he will ask: "Where is the daughter who gave herself for her cross, consumptive stepmother and for the little children of another? Where is the daughter who had pity upon the filthy drunkard, her earthly father, undismayed by his beastliness?" And he will say, "Come to me! I have already forgiven thee once . . . Thy sins which are many are forgiven thee, for thou had loved much . . ." And he will forgive my Sonya, he will forgive, I know it . . . And he will judge and will forgive all, the good and the evil, the wise and the weak . . . And when he has done with all of them, then he will summon us. 'You too come forth', he will say. "Come forth, ye drunkards, come forth, ye weak ones, come forth, ye children of shame!" And we shall all come forth without shame and shall stand before him. And he will say unto us, "Ye are swine, made in the image of the Beast and with his mark, but come ye also!" And the wise ones and those of understanding will say, "O Lord, why dost Thou receive these men?" and he will say, "This is why I receive them, O ye wise, this is why I receive them, O ye of understanding, that not one of them believed himself to be worthy of this." And he will hold out his hands to us and we shall fall down before him . . . and we shall weep . . . and we shall understand all things' (pp. 20–21).

This is spoken character, but it is also innermost Dostoevsky. The only version of Christianity which appeals to him at all is that which includes the wastrels and scoundrels and leaves no one outside.

And then there is Sonya. Seeing how sacrificial is her attitude to her profession, one might feel that she is not as guilty, for example, as Raskolnikov, and that the comparisons which he allows himself to draw between their misfortunes are not only malicious in intent but also in themselves unfair. But Sonya does not feel like that. She feels that she has sunk to the depths, and it is only God who keeps her going. Again, only a God who is present in the depths is the slightest use; but if he is so present, he may work miracles – the moral equivalents of the raising of Lazarus, which is a symbol throughout the novel.[25]

Because of her strength and single-mindedness, she in turn can keep Raskolnikov going, and finally urges him into the confession which, as Porfiry Petrovich kept telling him, his nature would insist upon. But her conviction is based not on the facts, but on defying the facts: God does not order things for the best, but is with her though she is gripped by the worst.

4. Finally we must re-examine certain references to religion which concern Raskolnikov himself. It is clear that his mother gave him an adequate religious upbringing which, amidst the excitement of Western ideas, he 'almost lost'.[26] When he is directly questioned by Porfiry on his religious beliefs, he says 'Yes' to belief in God, and also to the raising of Lazarus. Considering his later description of himself, ironically, as 'atheistical vermin', considering the instinctive reaction to him of his peasant fellow-prisoners in Siberia as the atheist among them (though he had never talked in this strain), considering his bitter interjection to Sonya: 'Introduce divine providence and there is nothing more to be said', his reply to the questions may appear to be hypocritical and even false; but it is more probably Dostoevsky's way of showing that his 'advanced' convictions

[25] Merezhkovsky doubted Dostoevsky's belief in the miraculous. Cf. D. Grishin, 'The Beliefs of Dostoevsky', *Twentieth Century*, p. 259. Yet this most formidable of all miracles is called in to redress the desperateness of the human condition.

[26] Dostoevsky's phrase about himself leaps to the mind.

had a good education to contend against; which comes out when
he has to label himself for official purposes. It is this residue
which produces conscience-reactions very soon after the murder,
and which, in the end, renders Raskolnikov susceptible to pressure from Sonya and Porfiry Petrovich. As Razumikhin testified
at the trial, Raskolnikov was good and generous-minded before
he took to ideas: he conspicuously failed to illustrate the thesis of
his own magazine article. His rudeness to Sonya is due to the
same cause: he had identified himself with his big idea, and the
threat to it was too much for his self-esteem: so he had to exag-
gerate it and take precautions against those who threatened it.
The fact of the matter is that Raskolnikov was fit material for
redemption: his egotism and his atheism were mainly theoretical;
because he had staked so much on his theoretical adventures, he
found it difficult to withdraw, and the issue is in doubt till his
feelings take charge in the last three pages. But he is worried and
concerned: he has not achieved the arctic indifference of Svidrigaylov; and Dostoevsky, for whom consistent development of
character was more important than intellectual tidiness, gave
the novel the right ending.

   That has frequently been denied. Mochulsky, for example,
referring to the return of Raskolnikov to the 'stream of life', observes that we know Raskolnikov too well to believe it.[27] Our
answer is that we know Sonya too well not to believe it. Sonya
is the most constant and one-piece character in Dostoevsky's
gallery. Critics of the 'social realist' variety complain that she is
unreal; humility and meekness are practically ineffective. It is
true that she cannot change the social order; but that is not what
the book is about. She can help the man she loves: to 'social
realists', is this a matter of complete indifference? It is true that
her arguments do not amount to much; it would be out of character if they did; and in any case no one was less likely than Dostoevsky to turn to argument for salvation. Look not at what
Sonya says, but at what she does. She meets Raskolnikov's first
overture[28] by confronting him with Lazarus raised from the

<hr />

[27] *Dostoevsky: his Life and Work*, p. 812.
[28] The demeanour of Raskolnikov in this first visit is masterfully portrayed

dead; she knows by looking at him that the lesson will sink in. Naturally, it exasperates him, and he is rude and explosive; but the seeds have been sown. At the second interview, when she guesses his secret, she throws her arms around him and exclaims, 'How you must be suffering!' How could the social realist improve on that? She guides him towards the inevitable confession. She has to contend with his haughty and obstructive defence of his 'idea', but she is wise enough to wait till he can stand no more, and all the time stands by him despite his resistance and his rudeness. She follows him when he goes out to confess to the authorities, and it is her look of despair when he comes out of the office with his mission unaccomplished that sends him back to his destiny. She follows him to Siberia, where she finds him still unresponsive and unchanged at heart, and proceeds to make herself indispensable both to him and to the whole community in exile – they have no one to do their sewing. For sheer strength of purpose, this undersized young woman with the undistinguished face and the remarkable blue eyes could hardly be surpassed. Just because she is all concern and does not wrestle with his intellect, she triumphs.[29] That is what comes of humility and meekness; and that, given the characters in question, was what was bound to happen.

But not only is the ending right in itself; the whole novel prepares the way for it. Raskolnikov's pride and obstinacy are

---

(Part IV, Ch. 4). When he finds that Sonya is suffering (he has made her suffer, by his inconsiderate atheist chatter when she was deeply distressed about her family) he is genuinely moved, and bends down and kisses her feet. But he is too intellectual to make a properly personal response. What he says is: 'I did not bow to you personally, but to all suffering humanity.' By way of honouring her, he treats a woman as a symbol. Humanists have gushed over this confession. Edward Wasiolek, more discerningly, calls it 'an expression of the self-willed and rationalizing Raskolnikov' and 'self-deceptive humanitarianism' (*Dostoevsky: the Major Fiction*, p.72). Actually, it is a modest step forward; the nearest approach to personal concern which his abstract theoretical way of being will allow. Dostoevsky presents it both as an advance, and as still stilted and inadequate. In both ways it is completely in character. It is just how a self-centred intellectual would express an unexpected and genuine concern. It is, in fact, a masterpiece.

[29] In thinking of her as a 'gentle, dove-eyed creature', Raskolnikov showed his usual lack of human understanding (Part III, Ch. 6).

directed against what he knows to be a weakness in himself; he is never a good exponent of his theories, and in the end his 'weakness' takes over, as we should have expected. But it is true that in him his theories do not get a fair test. That is why, as the novel grew, the alarming figure of Svidrigaylov began to loom over his shoulder. In the early drafts, Svidrigaylov plays only a small part; in the completed novel, he is only just prevented from stealing the show. Several times he suggests to Raskolnikov that they are spiritually akin, and so, up to a point, they are. The difference is that Svidrigaylov has travelled much further along the same path. He has achieved in practice the complete omnivolence which Raskolnikov merely believes in. He has only one human feeling left: his passion for Dunya. When he deliberately, not out of magnanimity, but as an act of self-conquest, lets her go, he has cut his last link, he is utterly and unreservedly out in the cold (the Arctic myths and metaphors which surround him are very significant); he can will everything, that is to say, nothing in particular; and his last victory is to go out and shoot himself. This was the logical conclusion of their common theory that Raskolnikov could not rise to.[30] So it is true that Svidrigaylov takes over the role of representing the 'idea', but that does not mean, as John Middleton Murry avers, that 'Svidrigailov is the real hero of the book'.[31] To suppose thus is to assume that the novel is not about Raskolnikov, but about Raskolnikov's 'idea'. Despite certain pronouncements to the contrary, Dostoevsky writes about people, and about ideas because the people he is interested in usually have them. But the emergence of Svidrigaylov into the foreground of the novel shows that Dostoevsky is indeed aware of Raskolnikov's problem, and of the failure of Raskolnikov to see it through.

As a Christian document, therefore, *Crime and Punishment* is only a prelude. It shows how with a morose but sensitive intellectual with a decent background, in the hands of a woman who was both infinitely patient and deeply in love with him, Christian anthropology may vindicate itself in practice. But two points

---

[30] It is worked out in detail in the characterizing of Kirillov in *The Possessed*.
[31] *Fyodor Dostoevsky: A Critical Study*, p. 113.

remain unsolved. (1) As mentioned above, could it work with case-hardened irresponsible will-power like Svidrigaylov's, or with a deep-seated sense of humiliation, like Nastasya Filippovna's in *The Idiot*? Svidrigaylov as presented in the novel is no fit candidate for redemption: perhaps because nobody loved him, but one has the impression that selfless devotion would have got on his nerves: he had gone too far. As for humiliation: it remains to be studied in *The Idiot*, unsparingly and in detail. In short, Christian anthropology has been shown at work, triumphantly, but in a relatively favourable instance. And, (2) in *Crime and Punishment*, as later in *The Possessed*, Dostoevsky puts the burden of proof on the antagonist. He sets out to demolish an alternative attitude to life by displaying its consequences, and he is not called upon to cross-question his own. In *The Idiot* and *The Brothers Karamazov* the heat is on the Christian anthropology itself; it is subjected, from within, to the same relentless scouring as the various aspects of radicalism receive in his other two main works. If this is not done in *Crime and Punishment* it does not mean that he is closing his eyes. As we shall see, Dostoevsky used the novel to probe what as a journalist he took for granted.

In conclusion, we take up a few specific issues related to Doetoevsky's religious pilgrimage. All of them have been touched upon by F. I. Yevnin, in his learned and penetrating contribution to the volume *Tvorchestvo Dostoevskogo*.[32]

1. Like his fellow-critics in the volume, Yevnin regrets that Dostoevsky, who presented social evils so unsparingly, nevertheless condemned those who were trying to get rid of them by social action and commended the mystical futilities of individual intervention. There is no need to defend Dostoevsky's politics; the most that can be said is that he was gunning, not so much for socialists as for anarchists, and that, just at that moment, the anarchists were the better part of the revolution. What concerns us is the deprecation of personal initiative. What was Sonya to do? She could hardly buck the whole system single-handed. She

[32] Edited by N. L. Stepanov. From a wide reading of the literature of the 1860's, he traces the affinities and sources of Dostoevsky's contemporary comment, including, improbably but indubitably, Napoleon III's *History of Julius Caesar*.

could intervene to help the man she loved out of a predicament which she (and Dostoevsky) knew he would be unable to sustain. Assuming that the cause of Raskolnikov's aberration was the competitive ethic of incoming capitalism (and this is an over-simplification, in which the conditions under which a man acts are taken to be the decisive cause), why must there be no ambulance for the victims? With or without statistics, there is room for personal ministrations; at the worst, they are all the unfortunate have left: at the best, they are better than imposing schemes of assistance in which persons are merely numbers. In insisting that Christian concern is more efficacious with morally displaced persons than politics, Dostoevsky has a point. In any case there is no necessary conflict between them.

2. In the discourse of Porfiry Petrovich (which, as has been noted, is not presented as Christian), much is made of the difference between *razsudok* and *razum*, in the context, theorizing and good sense. Yevnin shows by quotation that it was also invoked by other 'reactionary' writers, including Khomyakov.[33] He objects that it damages the image of reason in the scientific and analytic sense. He is right; it was meant to. He proceeds to describe it as a surrender to obscurantism and to its ultimate source, religion. But it could equally well be described as a more rational way of expressing what Porfiry Petrovich (and Dostoevsky with him) is at other times tempted to present as a distinction between reason in general and 'nature' considered as non-rational. The distinction between *razsudok* and *razum* serves the purpose of bringing practice within the bounds of reason without destroying its distinctiveness as practice. It means that practical reason is not applied theoretical reason, but is none the less reason: that when one stops theorizing, one does not necessarily stop being intelligent. That Dostoevsky should thus have guarded himself against his own, and his opponents', temptation to identify the rational with the theoretical shows that he was more aware of the dangers of irrationalism than he is sometimes given credit for. Incidentally, as he finds in right practice ('active love') the only sure refutation of unbelief, the concept of *razum*

[33] In *Tvorchestvo Dostoevskogo*, p. 160.

may help to blur what sometimes seems to be his too rigid dividing line between reason and religion.[34]

3. Much has been made, by admirers as well as by detractors, of Dostoevsky's 'religion of suffering'; and, sure enough, it is denounced by Yevnin as 'reactionary' and 'degrading to humanity'.[35] It is true that Dostoevsky jotted down in his notes for *Crime and Punishment*: 'Man is not born for happiness', and 'man has to earn his happiness, and always by suffering'.[36] This dialectical way of thinking is typical of him, but his point in emphasizing it is that men have to go through the worst to be safe from it; if they have not outfaced it, sooner or later it will be on hand to outface them. He is warning Utopians, not handing bouquets to quietists. It is true, again, that Mikolka in the story confesses to a crime which he did not commit in order to 'find suffering', but Dostoevsky presents him not as a model, but as a case-history; and when Porfiry Petrovich tells Raskolnikov, apropos of the incident, that 'suffering is a great thing', he is not speaking philosophically, but in character, to wheedle Raskolnikov into the inevitable confession. The 'religion of suffering' is natural to those who see no way out of it, and Dostoevsky himself, in sociological mood, in the *Diary*, observed that 'the fundamental quest of the Russian people is a craving for suffering' (I. p. 36). On the other hand, no one has ever surpassed Dostoevsky in delineating the disastrous effects of suffering. If accepted, it may pacify; if it is dodged, it will return; if it is used, the spirit triumphs. And, certainly, if it is resented, the devil gets to work: that is his great opportunity. But what Dostoevsky never says is that suffering is a good to be cherished.

The same dialectical way of thinking governs his attitude to crime. Yevnin, pure-minded and civically responsible as usual, objects that Raskolnikov is directed through crime to redemption, crime being given in the process a sort of providential

---

[34] *Razum* is present pre-eminently in the character named after it, Razumikhin; probably as good a student as Raskolnikov, and likely to go much further, because of his motivation, and above all, not subject to ideological intoxication. There is no doubt that Dostoevsky approves of him. But he also finds Raskolnikov more interesting. Doubtless he has a fellow-feeling for him; also the best characters do not make the best stories.

[35] In *Tvorchestvo Dostoevskogo*, p. 164.   [36] Ibid.

sanction.[37] Porfiry says to Raskolnikov: 'Perhaps God has been waiting for you in this' (i.e., the crime). This is not to say that it has been providentially planned, but it is to say that it can be providentially worked upon. In this sense, Yevnin is right: Porfiry speaks for his author: and that means that crime may actually bring a man nearer to a moral recovery. This is not the kind of paradox which is favoured by establishments of any kind, and perhaps by communist establishments least of all. But, unpacked, it means simply this: that intellectuals have an irresponsible way of getting hooked on ideas; that engaging in practice forces them to face the consequences of the ideas they entertain; and that then, and then only, will they be driven to reconsider their ideas. A backward glance at Dostoevsky's letter to Todleben from Siberia (p.20 above) will show how deeply autobiographical these observations are. But his object is not to fit crime into a theodicy; it is rather to show how, with difficulty, a not untypical intellectual may be brought up with a jolt by enacting what he believes, and be put in the way of believing differently.

But neither suffering nor crime is thereby commended. What is commended, and that strictly in terms of character, is on the one hand the capacity to use suffering constructively, as with Sonya, and on the other, as with Raskolnikov, the subjection of obsessive ideas to the implacable test of realization. These are good secular counsels, preparatory for Christianity, and to be fulfilled in it; they are not the end of the journey. Till Raskolnikov's defiance, shaken by the love of a woman, is submerged in the love of God, it cannot be known what will come of his pilgrimage; all we are told is that he has turned the corner. But if he had remained spitefully in his garret he would have been as unreclaimed as the anti-hero of *Notes from Underground*. Under God, the proverb is reversed: it is when we fail to go further that we fare worse.

4. Yevnin further objects that Dostoevsky's Christian anthropology leads to a certain unreality in the conduct of the story. In the first place, there is the ending which he says, rightly enough,

[37] Ibid. p.163.

is never portrayed, only announced. The issues thus raised we have already considered, and we need only add that Dostoevsky cannot tell two stories at the same time. Secondly, he makes the more original point that the affairs of the Marmeladov family are put in order, as it were providentially, by, of all people, Svidrigaylov. The literary question is: is it in character? To suppose that it is false or artificial is to disbelieve in the characterizing of Svidrigaylov: certainly not the sort one meets every day, but Dostoevsky does go to a great deal of trouble to explain him. The whole point of him is that he is not limited even by himself: he is the complete nihilist who can do exactly what he likes. Many of his inclinations are purposelessly selfish; but in the man who can will anything that is quite compatible with an equally purposeless benevolence. There remains the theological question: is it not just too odd that the role of Providence should be filled by such a person as Svidrigaylov? Unfortunately, neither Aquinas nor Leibniz nor, it would seem, Yevnin have listed among the divine attributes a delight in the incongruous. The God who can raise up the foolish to confound the wise can raise up the nihilist to confound the unperceptive. God uses some very curious agents indeed – including, by the way, atheists.

To conclude: in *Crime and Punishment* there is a sidelong approach to a Christian interpretation of man. It tells us that ideas without a disposition to act are irresponsible: that when they are acted upon, and not till then, they will disclose themselves as true or disastrous; that individualism in its most cogent and representative form is indeed disastrous; that to stand behind another in patience and humility, but insisting absolutely that he accept his own integrity, is the only way to change him; and that the change will occur when he gets round to loving instead of wasting himself in defiance. In Raskolnikov's case, it is not the love of God which takes hold of him; yet from the moment of the change even his fellow-convicts seem kinder; because he has turned from cosmic protest to accept one of the world's primary dispensations. That is only an introduction to religion; but the rest may safely be left to time.

This is Raskolnikov's story, and it does not probe the depths.

He has a new future some way ahead of him, but even he offered a long resistance and, as has been noted, he is not the most effective embodiment of his 'idea'. Supposing he had been tougher and more relentless, determined to accept nothing? The issue might well have been different, and in *The Idiot* it *is* different. Here, along with a fuller understanding of what Christianity means, there is a fuller appreciation of the difficulties it has to face. Instead of a foreseeable though unenacted Christian recovery, we are confronted with that contradiction in terms, a Christian tragedy.

xⓔ FOUR ⓔx

A Christian Tragedy

I

Of all his major works, *The Idiot* gave Dostoevsky the greatest trouble. As the notebooks show, draft upon draft was discarded, and in the end he confessed that he had only communicated one-tenth of what he had to say. But there is one constant feature from the first draft to the complete novel in its final form. That is the figure who emerges eventually as Nastasya Filippovna. Here is the plan for an early version of her: 'an original, frivolous, capricious, provocative and poetic nature, superior to her environment'. As Edward Wasiolek remarks in his introduction, 'in all the plans and into the final version, we have a proud, vengeful, sometimes hysterical woman, fatally compelled to provoke and reject love, to punish and be punished'.

Here is a challenge for the emerging Christian in Dostoevsky: how could such a personage be restored to her right mind? There is no doubt that Myshkin is a test case. There is also no doubt that Dostoevsky presented him with fear and trembling. Prophetically, he complained that he had to bring him onto the scene before he was ready. The 'Idiot' of the early drafts was a 'double' of the first order. 'His passions are violent, but he has a burning need of love, a boundless pride, and out of pride he means to dominate himself, to conquer himself. He takes delight in humiliation.'[1] He was intended to find his way towards the

[1] This reads more like a programme for Stavrogin. Dostoevsky had a way of projecting his intentions from one novel into the next.

light, but his doubleness appears to have proved unmanageable as fiction, and from the seventh draft onwards Myshkin appears as 'the perfectly beautiful human being'. At the same time Rogozhin takes on a personal identity. The original Idiot is divided into two. Dramatically, this is an improvement: the reactions of the two characters towards each other, and of each of them towards Nastasya Filippovna stand out in a classic parallelism and contrast. Moreover, we begin to understand the remarkable mutual attraction between Myshkin and Rogozhin: they belong together because they were once part of a single personality. But there are inconvenient consequences.

In the first place, Myshkin is deprived of a material base. Having decided on this point, Dostoevsky set about it thoroughly. He gave him no social experience; he fetched him from a Swiss sanatorium; he allowed him only one very distant relation; he endowed him with his own malady, epilepsy, and an accompanying nervous frailty which was likely to prevent him from seeing material issues through; he was particularly ill equipped to cope with women, unless, like Marie in the Swiss village, their position required of him only compassion: he was alone in his sweetness and light, except for a remarkably clear perception into the intricacies of humiliation in others. He was an *ideal* character, a God's fool,[2] a senior contemporary of Parsifal (1882), a spiritual compatriot of Don Quixote (who always fascinated Dostoevsky) and, despite his author's repudiation of 'Schillerism', a sort of Christian sequel to it. He is the product of a confusion in his author's mind between the ideal and the spiritual.

But, secondly, Myshkin *requires* a material base. For he is determined not only to *understand* people, but to help them. Myshkin's technique is humility (*smireniye*): a willingness never to take offence and, if need be, to take the blame when he is not responsible – the habit which infuriated Aglaya, and in the end, also her mother. It has to be remembered that Dostoevsky was not reared on Roman rights or mediaeval chivalry – those filters through which our Western Christianity has trickled through to us. He took his Christianity neat at the source – if

---

[2] *Yurodivy*, mentioned prophetically in the third draft.

there was any filter it was the devotion of a submerged people. As we have seen in our general introduction, the only cure he could see for conflict and domination was that everyone should assume responsibility for everyone else. Now this is a very positive and demanding belief. Soviet critics, even acute and scholarly ones like Fridlender, assume that meekness is equivalent to backing down. The same mistake is made by pacifists who talk of 'non-resistance'. Actually, it takes a great deal of insight and initiative to practise it effectively; Myshkin has to be ready for anything. He has the insight, and he can take the initiative; he makes a considerable impression from the start on the Yepanchins, on Ganya, even on the servants, by his sheer unforced friendliness and sense of equality, and he handles the affair of the 'son of Pavlishchev' with shrewdness as well as humanity, producing a marked effect on the undergrounders and off-beats who cooked it up. On the schoolboy Kolya and the selfless Vera Lebedeva he produces an effect little short of idolatry. And of course there is that singular friendship-in-rivalry with Rogozhin.

But in none of these cases, not even the off-beats, does his meekness arouse hostility. In the social set it falls flat, and in the two crucial cases it fails. The first is Ippolit Terentyev: not the first in time and conception, for the notebooks show that he was a late addition to the story: but in the story as it stands he introduces for the first time the complication that a man who lives with a fixed grievance will resent any attempt to remove it. Ippolit is dying of consumption at eighteen and he will not be reconciled to the scheme of things: and he is particularly incensed when Myshkin's sympathy causes him to break down. 'You drove a dying man to shame' (p. 299). It is true that towards the end he was beginning to think differently, but he has raised the issue: how can humility help the humiliated? And this is the problem which faces the all too perfected Myshkin in relation to Nastasya Filippovna.

The Idiot is the only novel of Dostoevsky's which is centred on women. Berdyaev claimed that his gallery was almost exclusively masculine,[3] the women being there merely to help him to

[3] *Dostoevsky; an Interpretation*, p. 112.

delineate the men. There is a strong case for this view of *The Possessed*, of *The Brothers Karamazov*, and even of *Crime and Punishment*: but Dostoevsky had practised, in *Netochka Nezvanova*, the difficult art of writing as a woman in the first person, and he had, in the years immediately preceding, been through four experiences: keeping vigil over his dying first wife, travelling around with the brilliant and merciless Apollinaria Suslova, being rejected by the beautiful and strong-minded Anna Korvin-Krukowska, and being happily married to the cool, competent and devoted Anna Grigoryevna. Whether it was experience or imagination, he created in *The Idiot* not one, but three, female characters fit to take their place with those of Flaubert or Stendhal or even Tolstoy. Aglaya Ivanovna Yepanchina and her mother Lizaveta Prokogyevna are superbly delineated and enter very much, as we shall see, into any estimate of Myshkin's tragedy and the author's purpose in creating him. But the central figure is Nastasya Filippovna. It is she who provides the acid test for the 'perfectly beautiful human being' and his gospel of compassion. Nastasya was an orphan, taken under the protection of Afanasy Ivanovich Totsky who seduced her in her 'teens and kept her in style in an apartment, but on having reached the fifties wanted to marry and settle down, and proposed to General Yepanchin for his eldest daughter, so soon as Nastasya could be conveniently married off. This is the marriage-market manoeuvre which sparks the story off, and incidentally Dostoevsky, who was consistently a liberal on the 'woman question', makes it clear how he detests the worldly Utilitarianism of the whole proceeding. Nastasya shows some indignation with the avaricious young man Ganya Ivolgin who is to take Totsky's money for her (witness her scandalous irruption into his parents' household) but her grievance is deeper. She cannot get over having been 'Totsky's concubine', though in fact she had not only been kept by him, but kept him off, for five years. If her sense of guilt seems out of proportion (it certainly would to Utilitarians), we must remember not only the official though unregarded ethos of the period, but also that Totsky had been as it were *in loco parentis*, and that Dostoevsky had originally ascribed the seduction to her real father: the shadow of an incest which could not have been admitted to Katkov's domestically oriented periodical continues to overhang the definitive story. Nastasya's implacability probably derives from the early draft. But, whatever its cause, it is the mainspring of her life: she cannot bear to be deprived of her guilt; and neither can she bear the forgiveness which will cancel it out, and her with it. She will not compromise on a marriage of convenience, and has already arranged to be abducted from her own party by the wealthy and passionate Rogozhin. In her clearer moments, she sees what will come of it: Rogozhin's knife, if not the four jars of Zhdanov's disinfectant. But with everything that is in her, intelligence, initiative and remarkable strength of will, she will pursue her destiny, identified with the innocence she has lost and the guilt which she carries, and utterly indifferent to comfort or self-interest.[4]

This is the situation when Myshkin arrives on the scene. From the moment he sees her portrait, he is deeply moved by her air of pride and suffering; when he meets her in the Ivolgin apartment, he looks behind her contumacious raillery: 'Surely you are not what you are pretending to be now?' He sees, there as elsewhere, the hidden goodness, and cannot rest till he has gate-crashed on the party at which she was to announce her decision about Ganya. He begins by telling her 'everything is perfection in you'. Appealed to as the one disinterested person present, and in reply to her direct question, he says, 'No, don't marry him.' This suits her very well: she is waiting for Rogozhin. It is at that point that Myshkin, overwhelmed by a pity which in his inexperience he believes to be love, makes an offer of marriage himself. Nastasya has already been attracted by his simplicity and goodness of heart, and she vacillates, acting as if she had accepted but in an ironical tone which bodes no good. She is moved by being taken as better than she is or will allow herself to think she is. It almost, as Sartre would say, changes her 'fundamental project'. But Myshkin plays it by ear and plays it wrong. 'You want a lot of looking after, Nastasya Filippovna. I will look after you . . . I shall respect you all my life, Nastasya

---

[4] Psychologically, she serves as another refutation of the Utilitarian analysis.

Filippovna.' These are the words of a protector, a psychiatrist, a social worker, perhaps a priest; they are not the words of a lover. For a lesser woman, for Nastasya herself before she had been driven to extremes, they might have been efficacious: but the injury has gone too deep. She cannot believe that Myshkin would not reproach her afterwards; more importantly, in Totsky's presence she cannot submit to a happy ending. The sensible Ptitsyn[5] cites the ancient Samurai custom of ripping open one's stomach before the enemy as a way of avenging oneself upon him. And she would probably be right to veer away from a marriage unequally combining the looked-after and the after-looked. The situation called not merely for humility, not merely for a recognition of goodness hidden behind the evil; it called for masterful handling, such as the original Idiot, including as doubles both Myshkin and Rogozhin, might have been able to exercise. As it was, Myshkin, a too angelic nature, rushed in where angels, of all people, should have feared to tread.[6] The absence in him of any trace of Rogozhin drove her straight into Rogozhin's arms: and it provoked her into complaining that he needed a nurse. Yet in the very desperation there was a tribute: a suggestion that the temptation to fold up and give in was almost too much for her. She knows that she needs help, but her self-will forbids her to accept it. That is why, in the rest of the story, she goes to such extreme lengths to keep Myshkin out of her life and to deliver him over to Aglaya.

Myshkin, then, fails in his task as a redeemer, because he is not sufficiently incarnate: and it is hard to believe that Dostoevsky did not arrange it so. That holds in any case, irrespective of the other woman: Aglaya. But in the six months of his absence in Moscow, Myshkin had acquired more of a grip on Russian customs and society, and felt the need of more positive contacts with less extraordinary people. So he wrote immediately to Aglaya, a short and incoherent note reminding her, rather too

[5] The sensible people have the last word in *The Idiot*: Ptitsyn in Part I, Radomsky in Part V. Nothing could more pitilessly put the 'perfectly beautiful human being' back into perspective.

[6] Angels do not marry nor are given in marriage; nor, for that matter, do psychiatrists or social workers marry their cases.

warmly for ordinary discourse, of his existence, adding: 'I need you very much.' In effect, he needs to borrow from the normal to help the abnormal: but he does not see it. All he feels is the need. But from that point on the tragedy is inevitable. For Aglaya is well-connected, good-looking, disposed to be unusual and romantic, but fundamentally healthy-minded, unconventional enough to be attracted by him, but not to share his compassion for the 'insulted and injured'. And Myshkin? He is much clearer now about Nastasya: 'I don't love her with love, I love her with pity' (p. 206). Even though Nastasya in Moscow runs away from Rogozhin and asks for his protection, he begins to be afraid of her (p. 239) and, being humble, he begins to ask himself, miserably, 'Am I the cause of all this?' But, first, it is not so certain that Nastasya does not need him; Rogozhin thinks she does, and even says that she is in love with him. And, secondly, knowing that he must face towards the world, he gets himself installed at Pavlovsk, with the scheming parody of humility, Lebedev, and is involved on the worldward side of him with Aglaya. At a crucial moment (recorded pp. 307–8) the thought occurred to him that he could withdraw altogether and go back where he came from; but he dismissed it, and once again, 'he put on the harness of necessity'.[7] It has been said that Myshkin's feeling for Aglaya is represented as purely aesthetic. This view understates the sadness of the situation. Myshkin feels for Aglaya as a man, as far as he is able. But he has his doubts. Confronted with her mother's direct question, 'Are you in love?' he replies, 'N-No', and refers back to his feelings at the time when he wrote his original letter from Moscow. Moreover, he asks for her hand, in reply to her own challenge 'with a sinking heart' (p. 515). He knows he is emotionally inadequate, but he cannot cut his main link with the ordinary world. Of course it goes wrong. He cannot do what both Aglaya and her mother beg him to do: leave behind the motley crowd of undergrounders collected round Lebedev's villa, to cut something of a figure, above all to stand up for his rights. They have reason and experience on their side: merely passive saintliness will not serve,

[7] Aeschylus, *Agamemnon*, 217.

as Myshkin would have had to learn but for his legacy. On this issue alone, there was bound to be trouble. Myshkin did not fit into the Yepanchin mould; and he should never have allowed Aglaya to fall seriously in love with him, The absurdity of the betrothal party, Myshkin's inappropriate oration and his breaking of the valuable Chinese vase with his awkward gesture, all emphasize the incongruity. Just as he cannot live apart from the world, so he cannot become one with it: and this quite apart from the intervention of Nastasya Filippovna. Put the two factors together, and disaster is inevitable.

From the beginning, to lighten her own load Nastasya tries to throw Aglaya in Myshkin's way. She discredits a rival suitor; she writes to Aglaya the letters which precipitate the tragedy: and finally intrigues through secret messengers to procure an interview. Up till then she had been ready to surrender; Aglaya to her was 'perfection'; the moment they met, ordinary human jealousies upset the poses of renunciation and respectability; they tell each other home truths, and Myshkin is forced to choose. As a man of compassion, he cannot leave Nastasya helpless and swooning, and he attends to her while Aglaya runs away in a rage. When it comes to the point, passion and compassion are at odds and compassion wins. But, as the worldly-wise Yevgeny Pavlovich Radomsky points out to him later, in the attempt to reclaim the irreclaimable (Yevgeny's estimate) he has driven to distraction an eager and thoroughly wholesome girl who loved him like a woman; one who suffered just as much as her more spectacular but deranged rival. As a rejected suitor he is indignant on Aglaya's behalf, and his fears are confirmed when Aglaya marries on the rebound a bogus Polish count and becomes a convert to Roman Catholicism – and to anyone who knows Dostoevsky's prejudices about Poles and Catholics that is a supremely unhappy ending. As for Myshkin himself: his link with the normal world being cut, he prepares to marry Nastasya in a condition of fatalistic dejection, and, sure enough, she is spirited away by Rogozhin's agents on the way to the wedding. Myshkin accepts the situation with what can only be called an appalling tranquillity, and seeks out Rogozhin. He has killed her, as she knew he would. Their reconciliation over the corpse is a superb piece of writing, but it ends in Myshkin's reversion to sheer idiocy. Purity has been tried out in the world and has broken under the strain.

The story has been told in some detail, because it looks like a failure of the Christian hope in the face of humiliation. Myshkin is marked as a Christian, in inverted commas, both by Ippolit and by Yevgeny Pavlovich; and if that is so, his failure is a Christian failure. He says very little about it himself: on his own telling his reflections on religion are the fruit of very recent experiment, and he lets slip, when attending General Ivolgin's funeral, that he had never attended an Orthodox funeral before (p. 589). He is not a *practised* Christian nor, as far as the evidence goes, a *practising* Christian; that deadly phrase of Radomsky's about his 'innate inexperience' applies to his Christianity as much as to anything else. But *The Idiot* deals directly with what Dostoevsky held to be the principal problem of Christian anthropology: the problem of pride and humiliation. Nastasya is proud, or she would have conformed; she is humiliated and so cannot humble herself. On the Christian assumption which Dostoevsky accepted, it ought to have been possible by humility to get humiliation right. As it did not happen one has to assume either that Myshkin was an insufficient embodiment of the Christian idea or that the Christian assumption is through and through mistaken.

The Soviet critics and their precursors draw the latter conclusion. Gorky described Myshkin as a 'half-dead fatalist' and blamed it on his religion.[8] Gorbachov[9] observed: 'the precept of the individual is powerless and even ludicrous in the face of real life with its wild human passions'. 'The Idiot is bowing to the mystical intercession of Christ.' The theory is developed by Fridlender:[10] 'feeble, lifeless and reactionary': 'the beautiful is in profound contradiction with life'. Myshkin's method of dealing

---

[8] As he included Alyosha Karamazov in the same condemnation, one needs to be careful, but there are passages which almost justify him: his acceptance of the course of events is sometimes almost inhuman, as for example, after the interruption of his wedding.

[9] Seduro, *Dostoevsky in Russian Literary Criticism 1846–1956*, p. 165.

[10] 'Roman Idiot', *Tvorchestvo Dostoevskogo*, pp. 191ff.

with evil is based on religion, i.e. superstition; all the more regrettably because Dostoevsky's analysis of the bourgeois marriage-market is particularly penetrating. One would like to ask him the one question which he does not guard against: in the absence of social reform, can *nothing at all* be done to help individuals in trouble? He is right, and so are his fellow-critics, in finding Myshkin inadequate: but the trouble with him is not that he is socially unaware (though he is), nor that he is a Christian (on the contrary, he is insufficiently Christian). If he is to be a Christian, he must nor merely react compulsively to suffering; he must grapple with the turbulent actualities of his situation. He is aware of it; that is why he is unhappy. Because he has too much sweetness and light he cannot give the course of events the handling they require: at least, not so far as concerns the object of his compassion, Nastasya Filippovna. In his attempt to adjust, he reverts to the condition of a 'double': as a one-piece man must do when he is not suited to his task. Making excuses for Keller, he remarks: 'all people are like that . . . it is awfully difficult to struggle against these double thoughts' (p. 310). And Dostoevsky comments, as it were editorially: 'the problem of double ideas had evidently occupied his mind for some time'. As we know, it had occupied Dostoevsky's *all* the time.

The trouble, then, is that Myshkin, divided in mind, rooted in the saintly simplicities but confronted with worldward complications, though he can shed light for those who can be brought to see (Burdovsky, for example), cannot carry the strong-willed self-accusing Nastasya to the point of safety; even the vulgar Utilitarians who were arranging a marriage of convenience for her would have served her better.[11] But neither can he pass over

[11] In one way, his innocence was against him; it gives her a noble excuse for resisting him – she will 'ruin' him. Contrast the situation in George Eliot's *Scenes of Clerical Life* ('Janet's Repentance') when the clergyman is able to say, and not merely formally or figuratively, to the unhappily married female alcoholic who consults him, 'in speaking to me you are speaking to a fellow-sinner'. It is out of his *guilt* that he can save. One should not wish such guilt upon Myshkin, but it could have put him on the necessary terms of moral equality. Dostoevsky saw later that the vicious circle of pride and humiliation can be broken only when each person assumes responsibility for the guilt of every other. He is curiously reticent about appealing to the original act of atonement; but what he in the end and in effect commends is its piecemeal recapitulation by all men.

to the world and leave the disinherited behind him, as the world, and Aglaya and her mother, insist: 'If you don't throw up these nasty people at once', Aglaya announces, with understandable exasperation, 'I shall hate you all my life' (p. 300). In fact, he makes the worst of both worlds. But not because he is a Christian. It is the mark of a Christian to get busy and do things: 'Why call ye me Lord, Lord, and do not the things which I say?' 'By their fruits ye shall know them.' By this highly uncontemplative and pragmatic standard Myshkin falls short, not because he does not try, but because his equipment is lacking; his 'innate inexperience' leaves him improvising his techniques: the intuition is Christian, but the practical responses are unreliable. Of course, if Christianity is merely a resigned acceptance, a mixture of mysticism and fatalism, to attribute his failure to Christianity is fair enough; and that is the way that Soviet critics, aided and abetted by the Russian word *smireniye* in which humility is slanted towards submergence, choose to understand it. But the failure, to the extent that it is one, is not a failure *of* Christianity; it is a failure *in* Christianity. Rather surprisingly, Myshkin tells Ippolit that he has always been a materialist. It is not quite true; but it is clearly what Myshkin thought he had to be. He knew that he needed material control to achieve his ends. And that Dostoevsky should ironically have given him this sentence shows that he, at least, knew what was wrong; for a Christian, Myshkin was not materialist enough.

The point may be illustrated by comparing Myshkin with Sonya in *Crime and Punishment*. Sonya's concern was undivided: she had compassion for Raskolnikov but she was also in love with him. That is why, so far from humbling herself before him, she could take him in hand and give him unequivocal moral advice. Myshkin's love for Nastasya was three-quarters pity, and she was quick and intelligent enough to see it. As he learns his way round, he begins to notice the difference and turns his human love towards Aglaya, but again, because he is insufficiently incarnate, he unintentionally but none the less cruelly deceives her. He vacillates and in the ensuing crisis is ruled by pity. Because he is drawn both ways at once, he can neither save nor satisfy. If he had been both sacrificially and passionately in love with Nastasya, as Sonya was with Raskolnikov, he could have swept her from the mercenary clutches of Ganya and the savage sincerity of Rogozhin alike. Being sacrificial and not passionate, except in his sacrifice, he failed, and the result is a Christian tragedy.

But was this Dostoevsky's intention? On the balance, it is difficult to believe that *The Idiot* is a deliberately clinical exercise. There seems to be a gap between the confident programming ('N.B. The Prince *is* the Christ', he wrote in his notebooks, in big letters) and Myshkin's final fatalistic submergence in the stream of events. Even in the novel, from his early successes we are led to believe that Myshkin is sent into the world as the best possible emissary of humanity. But, in working out the story in terms of human character, Dostoevsky finds him cracking under the strain. Being a novelist and not a theologian, he cannot interfere, and the story runs to its predestined conclusion. There is about *The Idiot*, more than in any of Dostoevsky's other novels, the tragic sense of inevitability. One does not find oneself saying at any point 'this could have happened otherwise': not even when Myshkin stays behind soothing the prostrate Nastasya and allows Aglaya to run away. He does not *exercise* compassion; if he did, he would have some to spare for Aglaya. He *is* compassion: he is drawn inevitably to the greater weakness and the greater need. The 'perfectly beautiful human being' is predestined to fail. No wonder Dostoevsky wrote to his niece that he had not succeeded in conveying the tenth part of what he had intended. He added, it is true, 'I still love the unsuccessful idea': a hint that the theme will be stated again, with a hero strong enough, rooted enough, to take the strain – a foreshadowing of Alyosha in *The Brothers Karamazov*. But, for the moment, the character on which he lavished so much affection relentlessly took his own way, and failed, for the best artistic reasons, to embody his author's dearest convictions.

II

That being so, three particular problems call for attention. The first is how to read the observations of Radomsky to Myshkin the day following the scene between Nastasya and Aglaya (pp. 581ff.). The second is to situate Myshkin's remarks about religion when Rogozhin asks him bluntly, 'Do you believe in God?' (pp. 217ff.) The third is presented to us by the title of the book.

1. Calling on Myshkin after Aglaya's refusal to see him (which he is still simple enough not to understand), Radomsky puts it to him, courteously but with understandable indignation, that his compassion for Nastasya has made him unjust to Aglaya; that on that first hectic day in Petersburg ending with his proposal to Nastasya, he had rushed himself off his feet and lost control of the sequence of events; that there was in his over-reaction an element of 'conventional democratic feeling' for a 'lost' woman, just because she was 'lost'; and finally that torn between compassion for Nastasya and a human affection for Aglaya, he had 'never loved either of them'. And Myshkin, over-wrought and perplexed, though he does not commit himself on the 'conventional democratic feeling', admits his guilt on all counts. This is Radomsky's estimate: is it Dostoevsky's last word? It is objected by Edward Wasiolek, in his introduction to the notebooks for *The Idiot*, that Radomsky is the worldly sensible conventional type which Dostoevsky most disliked, and that his valuations should not be ascribed to his creator.[12] But Dostoevsky goes out of his way to give him all the necessary credentials. He becomes Kolya's confidant; that intelligent adolescents like Kolya should trust a man is always, for Dostoevsky, a point in his favour. He goes to visit Myshkin, now returned to Switzerland and his original idiocy, every few months; and he corresponds on terms of affection with the one character who had silently loved Myshkin for himself and without qualification, Vera Lebedeva. It is even hinted that they might marry; and anyone who might marry Vera must, we feel, have Dostoevsky's general approval. And, finally, the narrator (in effect Dostoevsky) says explicitly: 'We are in complete

---

[12] He adds that in earlier drafts Radomsky, then called Velmonchek, was programmed as 'an odd mixture of cunning, subtlety, calculation, mockery and vanity'. But Dostoevsky could have re-shaped him: the Radomsky of the text has all these characters, transformed by honesty, good sense and humanity.

sympathy with some forcible and psychologically deep words of Yevgeny Pavlovich's'; and then follows an account of his conversation with Myshkin already discussed (p. 581). We have noted above (pp. 71f.) that Dostoevsky frequently stations a normal and neutral character on the edge of his stories as a point of reference, and this is the pre-eminent instance. His creator stands right behind Radomsky, and that means that he sees, clearly and miserably, that, and why, Myshkin broke under the weight of their common theme. At the same time, Radomsky speaks in character, and his testimony has to be sorted out. When it concerns Aglaya, whom he understood and loved, he is revealing: no one better than he can judge the wrong that has been done to her. In the main, he is also right about Myshkin: he is right about the packed sequence of events during his first day in Petersburg which led to his first declaration to Nastasya; he is right about his 'innate inexperience' (he is credited with a gift for words, and this shows it); he is right in pointing to the doubleness in Myshkin, and the division in his mind between pity and love; and when he asks, 'What will compassion lead you to next?' we feel like breaking out in applause. But on the evidence of the novel he is wrong about the 'mass of intellectual convictions' and the 'conventional democratic feeling'. He naturally looks for explanations to ideas and ideologies, and it would be wrong in Dostoevsky not to exhibit him as so doing. But if we hark back to Part One of *The Idiot*, he ascribes no intellectual convictions to his hero. He sees Nastasya merely as a sufferer, never mind from what cause: 'in that face there is so much suffering'. His compassion, though perhaps out of proportion (as Radomsky accurately and remorselessly insists), is not in the least intellectual or social: it is as purely personal as anything can be. The point has to be stressed because it bears upon Myshkin's interpretation of Christianity. 'Where was your "Christian" heart?' Radomsky asks, referring to his neglect of Aglaya in the split second of decision (or indecision).[13] He thinks

[13] The inverted commas indicate a turn of Radomsky's voice. But at the very least, they show that Dostoevsky was capable of seeing the situation through Radomsky's eyes, and therefore of standing in judgment on Myshkin.

that Myshkin's sacrifice of the normal to the abnormal is a lapse of Christian feeling. But the version of Christianity which Myshkin represents, and which Dostoevsky does not disdain, commands a disproportionate concern with the afflicted, and Myshkin even believed that if only he had been allowed to see Aglaya, she would have shared it. In *The Idiot*, Dostoevsky did not solve his problem, and his hero paid the penalty.

2. Myshkin's longest explanation about religion is in reply to a direct question from Rogozhin: 'Do you believe in God?' (p. 217.) His response is surprisingly evasive. At first he does not answer at all: he asks Rogozhin why he asks him, and just as he has said good-bye he returns to 'the question of faith', indirectly and by aid of a series of stories. It would have been so easy to say Yes, if that was what he meant. Instead, he almost says, 'It depends on what you mean by God.' His four illustrative stories run as follows. (*a*) He recalls an encounter with a well-bred, well-read atheist of whom he observes that 'he was talking about something quite different'. Evidently the standard atheist arguments seemed to him to be not so much wrong as irrelevant: in the modern jargon, they were category-mistakes. (*b*) He comments on the murder of a comrade by a peasant for the sake of his watch; the murderer drew his knife, and said 'God forgive me for Christ's sake', as he proceeded to slit his throat. Are we meant to suppose that this is more like religion than are, say, the proofs of the existence of God? (*c*) Also an equivocal case: that of a drunken soldier who sold Myshkin his 'silver' cross (it was only tin) for twenty kopecks, and hung it round his neck, delighted to have found someone he could cheat; and Myshkin puts off judging him: 'God knows what is hidden in these weak and drunken hearts.' The soldier may have been distressed at parting with it: anyway, it plays a solemn part in the friendship between Myshkin and Rogozhin. (*d*) The perfect instance: the peasant mother crossing herself when she sees her baby's first smile; and saying 'God has just such gladness every time he sees from heaven that a sinner is praying to him with all his heart.' In this case 'all the issue of Christianity finds expression', i.e. Christianity is where the sinner is. But the mixed bag of experi-

ences, taken together, show that 'the issue of religious feeling does not come under any sort of reasoning or atheism, and has nothing to do with any crimes or misdemeanours'. There is something else here (in Russian, more incisively and idiomatically, *tut chto to nye to*), and there will always be something else – something that the atheists will always slur over – they will always be talking about something else.

It would not be just to say that on this account of the matter Christianity is reduced to mere feeling. It is taken for granted that the mother's reaction to her baby's smile tells us, figuratively, something about the nature of God. It is because the atheist is embrangled in abstract concepts that he cannot see the point. What he denies (e.g. perhaps 'necessary being') is irrelevant in the face of the basic human experiences. All the same, Dostoevsky himself knows this will not do: he brought Ippolit in to say so. If the basic human experiences are to count, what about an intelligent and rebellious youth, dying of consumption at eighteen? Experience is matched against experience: and then, what? There has to be some hard theological thinking. Neither Myshkin or anyone else in the novel can supply it; neither at this stage could Dostoevsky. His religion, like Myshkin's, is non-theological: as already remarked, it is the atheists in his novels who do most of the theological talking. What Dostoevsky is asserting, almost to the point of identifying himself with Myshkin, is that Christianity is a transaction between God and sinners, and that philosophers had better keep out of it – unless they confess themselves sinners, and then they will come into it as sinners and not as philosophers.[14]

3. At this stage the thought may occur to us that Dostoevsky never intended the 'Idiot' to be victorious. There is a certain bitterness in the very title: idiot Myshkin was and idiot he will be again when the world has proved too much for him. Perhaps Dostoevsky thought it enough that the evil in the world should be *confronted* by the good, and so shown up in its true colours. Such an interpretation fits well enough with the description of

---

[14] Intellect and morality are religiously irrelevant because they make no call upon the focal point of religion, namely, compassion.

the good, and of God, as 'ideal': the gist of his highly personal confession of 1864, after his first wife's death. Perhaps he thought that the good could never be more than a lodestar. In that case Christian behaviour in this world is simply not viable. That the best should inexplicably be laid low was clearly a possibility entertained by Dostoevsky at this time. His imagination was powerfully affected by seeing Holbein's version in the Bâle Gallery of Christ's descent from the cross. No hint of resurrection: no hint of anything but the obliteration of the best thing that had ever happened. There is a replica hanging in Rogozhin's house, of which Myshkin observes that it might cause people to lose their faith. Ippolit (p. 410) saw it there and was overcome by it. 'It suggests the conception of a dark, insistent, unreasoning and eternal power to which everything is in subjection.' The hopelessness of it all – might not this have inspired this unnatural masterpiece, a Christian tragedy? Even the passionate interest in personal immortality which Dostoevsky displayed at this time[15] might be read as the reverse side of a this-wordly despair. If Myshkin is the perfect man, then the perfect man after a few promising minor achievements, when he meets the historic obstacles of pride and self-will, is programmed to relapse into idiocy. There is a streak of Satanic desperation in Dostoevsky, but it is rarely as iridescent as that.

Before accepting this interpretation, we should look at the other side. And let us be clear what the question is. Is the perfect man hopelessly inadequate, or is Myshkin never presented as the perfect man?

There is something embarrassing, for Anglo-Saxons, in the phrase 'the perfectly beautiful human being'.[16] It suggests ineffectiveness from the start. It does not suggest, even incidentally, strength of mind or logical stringency. It is linked, even by Dostoevsky, in his letters, let alone by Aglaya in the novel, with the figure of Don Quixote. Indeed, he says that Don Quixote is the best example of the perfect human being in fiction, and adds, as a writer, that he is acceptable because he is slightly ridiculous.

---

[15] Again, see his meditation on the death of Marya (cf. pp. 84f. above).

[16] Russians, apparently, respond with less sense of shame to the word *prekrasny*.

Is there a clue here to the creation of Myshkin? He is never ridiculous, but he is set apart by his oddities, distanced from the institutions which type the individual – family, country, and not least profession; and he has that natural simplicity and guileless-ness which can at times dazzle the world, but can never encom-pass it. He has no feeling for rights; he would rather be cheated than produce bad feeling; and he seems to have a positive prefer-ence for the undeserving. Is this how Dostoevsky thought a Christian should operate? At times it seems so; if so, he will have achieved perfection at the expense of power. But it should be noted that 'the perfectly beautiful human being' is not the 'perfected human being'; the hard edges required to perfect him might detract from his 'beauty'. And Dostoevsky alludes so often and so deliberately to defects in his equipment that it is hard to believe that he thought him 'perfect', even if 'perfectly beautiful'. He is impulsive to a degree; though penetrating in matters that he understands, he is not particularly sensitive to environment – his long stories are at least odd, and are regarded as such by the Yepanchin girls at their first meeting; and his disquisition on Catholicism and Socialism at the betrothal party is completely out of proportion. He loathes the thought of facing the questions that were surging in his heart and mind (p. 222). He subsides easily into 'shame and extreme distress' (p. 275). He is 'morbidly sensitive' (p. 298). And his nervous system hangs on a thread. All this direct from the narrator, without drawing on Radomsky's analyses or the motherly anxieties of Lizaveta Prokofyevna. The conclusion must be that the 'perfectly beautiful human being' is hardly fitted for the world and cannot change it: in particular, he cannot stand up to what is after all the greatest test a Christian can be put to: a strong-willed neurotic without concern for her own advantage.

The fact is, Myshkin is physically and psychologically un-equal to the task; despite his odd remark to Ippolit, he is not sufficiently a materialist. It is not his 'Christian heart' which is lacking; it is the equipment and the expertise which Christians in the various spheres are expected to draw upon. The 'Christian tragedy' might have been avoided, but only on the following conditions:

(a) If Myshkin had been physically more robust and normal, and less of a *Yurodivy*, a God's fool.[17] (b) If he had had the support of an integrated religious community. Myshkin is anthropologically Christian, but shows no sign anywhere of corporate affiliations. Neither did Dostoevsky, as late as 1867. The tragedy of *The Idiot* is the tragedy of a natural-born but non-participating Christian. Human compassion needs roots to nourish it and affiliates to work with. That Doestoevsky came to see the point, and indeed through observing the fate of his own creature, is shown by his later creation of Alexey Karamazov, who is both physically robust and rooted in the Orthodox community. (c) A third condition: If he had been a determined celibate, or if he had found, not a romantic like Aglaya, with a normal portion of human egoism, but someone as selfless as himself. Dostoevsky provided such a woman in Vera Lebedeva, but Myshkin does not look her way – at one stage he says to himself, 'What a jolly girl!' and promptly forgets all about her. This hint from Dostoevsky can hardly not be deliberate. Vera, who loved him deeply and silently, could even have entered into his compassion for Nastasya, as Aglaya could not; she was built that way. Once again, Myshkin was unobservant, both of another and of himself.[18]

---

[17] Murray Krieger in his essay on 'The Curse of Saintliness', in *The Tragic Vision*, University of Chicago Press 1960, takes note of the disasters following Myshkin's major interventions, and attributes them to the clumsiness of saints as a class. The trouble, however, is not the saintliness, but the lack of physical backing. Even the physiognomy ascribed to Myshkin is that of the standard Russian *ikon*. He is *too much* an *ikon*: if that is what Krieger means, perhaps there is no conflict after all.

[18] Berdyaev (*Dostoievsky; an Interpretation*, p. 36) draws attention to the tendency of the Orthodox Church to 'relegate spiritual life to another and transcedent world', and praises Dostoevsky for bringing it back to earth. He is right; but he misses the agony at the cost of which the result was achieved. Myshkin is the test for this distanced kind of spirituality; and after Dostoevsky's disillusion with Utopias this was the avenue he had next to explore. It led him nowhere, and he had to try again, with a better estimate of this world, and even a foretaste of a new and Christianized Utopia. See Ch. 4. It remains to be said that Dostoevsky never fully resolved the doubleness. Who can blame him? The most we can ask is to be aware of the alternatives pulling us apart: especially if there is in each of them something too good to lose.

To conclude: there are previews in *The Idiot* of the road by which Dostoevsky was to travel back from an 'ideal' religion to a religion with roots. Anna Grigoryevna gives the clue when she records in her diary that 'that long isolated life (abroad) had a good effect on the growth and manifestation in my husband of his Christian ideas and feelings'.[19] Living abroad, she meant, made him more Russian, and it was through his Russianness that he made his way back into the Orthodox Church. Myshkin is on the way to discovering it when he tells Rogozhin that a something which is not something else will be found more quickly and clearly in the Russian heart than anywhere else. 'There is work to be done, Parfyon! There is work to be done in our Russian world, believe me!' (p. 220.) It is not merely that, belonging to a corporate body, he would be able to work forward with the strength of others as well as with his own, but also and mainly that within a religious unity to which the 'alienated' inalienably belong, the task of reconciliation is already in part accomplished. The Soviet critics have maintained that *The Idiot* is a study in the bankruptcy of individualism. They are right; but the remedy lies, not in socialism, which is merely self-interest on a large scale, but in the unforced union of minds and hearts immemorially practised in Orthodox Russian communities. With some prescience of what he might discover in this region, Myshkin 'was beginning to have a passionate faith in the Russian soul' (p. 227). And, right at the end of the novel, Lizaveta Prokofyevna, rightly acclaimed by Krieger as one of Dostoevsky's most magnificent creations, breaks out in the same strain. To the civilized and sceptical Yevgeny Pavlovich, who has declared himself superfluous in Russia, and in the presence of Myshkin who can no longer even recognize them, she exclaims: 'All this life abroad, and this Europe of yours, is only a fantasy . . . remember my words, you'll see it for yourself' (p. 620). Dostoevsky had already seen it for himself as, freed for the first time from money troubles, he and his wife set out for home. It was through Russia that he was to recover the sense of organic unity in church and state, in the absence of which Myshkin's

[19] Quoted by Miriam Šajković: *Dostoevsky: his Image of Man*, p. 80.

chivalrous but stumbling Christian initiative had been submerged in Christian tragedy.

But it is to be expected, from Dostoevsky's habit of using his fiction to probe his public certainties, that in his next novel this new source of assurance will be relentlessly scrutinized. The expectation is fulfilled in *The Possessed*.

xҳ FIVE ҳx

The Assay of the All-man

I

In *The Idiot* it is a version of the Christian style which is under scrutiny. Another version is similarly scrutinized in *The Possessed*, but as it were incidentally: for the most part, Dostoevsky turns his attention to the alternative. For a struggling Christian who is still exploring, it is easier to think it negatives; especially when he is Dostoevsky, who was not an *anima naturaliter Christiana*, and indeed almost stumbled into faith through disenchantment with the contemporary substitutes. His examination of these in *The Possessed* takes him some distance towards the goal which he was already beginning to see ahead of him. There were other factors, external and specifiable: his wife, who saw it coming and had the sense not to hurry him; his passion for Russia which, in the contradictory way habitual with him, grew greatly when he was abroad from 1867 to 1871, and predisposed him to the one influential force in Russia with no Western counterpart, namely the Orthodox Church: and finally the conviction that to write about these things he would have to advance his hitherto unsystematic theological education.[1] But we have come to see that his personal progress was not always reflected in his art, and in *The Possessed* we have an *imaginative* study of the atheist generation. It is quite pitiless, not only to his opponents but to himself; for in the heat of inspiration he puts in question as an atheistic derivative the

[1] Letter to his niece, Sofya Ivanova, 23 January 1869 (*Pisma* II, p. 161).

religious assurance which in the prose of his public existence he claimed to have attained; and despite the unusually strong element of comedy and satire, the whole piece is flooded with darkness – a darkness in which one can just discern the gesticulation of the demons.[2] But the object is not to accept the darkness still less to exult in it; it is to expose it and to force us back to the Christian style by displaying atheism in all the horror of its variegated consequences. It is a tribute to Dostoevsky's unflinching honesty that he includes among them his own favourite stand-by, Russian religious nationalism.

Like its predecessors, *The Possessed* (*Besy*, literally, 'devils' or 'evil spirits') underwent modifications in the course of composition. Its first orientation was political. The murder of Shatov by the local revolutionary circle on the orders of Pyotr Verkhovensky is modelled on the actual murder of the student Ivanhov by the terrorist Nechayev. Not that the characters correspond, or were even meant to: on this very episode, Dostoevsky observed: give me the crime, and I will create the criminal.[3] But the Nechayev case set his inspiration moving; and it activated his memories of an international gathering of rowdy radicals which he attended at Geneva in 1867, which, together with more distant recollections of the Petrashevtsy, supplied him with a model for the theatrical extravagances, the rhetorical *cliché*, the absurd points of order, the interruptions and the crossfire so brilliantly and, as every ex-radical knows, not so inaccurately depicted in the conspiracy scenes of the novel. And not only was the political aspect the first to emerge, but it continues, in the definitive version, to dominate the plot; practically every move which keeps it going is initiated by the original political 'hero', Pyotr Verkhovensky. Finally, the great speech of Stepan Trofimovich, which gives rise to the title – the evil spirits entering into the revolutionary swine and leaving the exhausted country in its right mind, sitting at the feet of Jesus – was planned from the start for a political context; it is foreshadowed

---

[2] The darkness is enhanced by the oblique and almost reluctant manner of narration.

[3] To Katkov, 8 October 1870 (*Pisma* II, p. 288).

in very similar words in a letter to Maykov of 9 October 1870.[4]

But the political message of the novel is not its central purpose. Dostoevsky introduced, almost as a latecomer, a second hero: one from whom Pyotr was to be derivative: Nikolay Stavrogin. In taking him as the chief character, we have Dostoevsky's explicit statement behind us: 'Stavrogin is ALL': 'everything else moves kaleidoscopically around him'.[5] But as Dostoevsky's creation was apt to outrun or revise his intentions, we shall proceed to show it from the internal structure of the novel. The matter is of some importance for our main theme, for by throwing the emphasis back from Pyotr onto Stavrogin, Dostoevsky also throws the emphasis back from politics to religion. The projected novel on *Atheism* is superimposed on his pamphleteering.

Here, again, we must allude to a circumstance of composition, or rather of publication. As editor of *Russky Vestnik*, Katkov declined to publish the chapter entitled 'At Tikhon's', which contained Stavrogin's 'confession' to the old monk: he had allegedly seduced a twelve-year-old girl who later committed suicide. Dostoevsky evidently thought the episode significant for he pleaded for its retention and re-wrote it in a less circumstantial form:[6] but Katkov, with his domestic readers in mind, refused to budge. So the story was issued without a chapter which many critics regard as central, and it was not published till after the Revolution: Dostoevsky did not restore it when the novel appeared in book form. That would seem to suggest that he found the work to make sense without it. And so it does: but it makes a different kind of sense from that which it carries with the chapter included. To anticipate our further discussion: Stavrogin stands out on the one hand as the great all-willer, and on the other as the embodiment of a sort of death-wish. As the work stands, the emphasis is on his will: as it was originally written, the emphasis is on his feelings of guilt. Both themes are eminently Dostoevskian, and both are present in either case: it

[4] *Pisma* II, p. 291.

[5] Quoted from the notebooks by Yevnin, *Roman Besy*, in *Tvorchestvo Dostoevskogo*, p. 244.

[6] Stavrogin was made to withhold the 'second sheet'.

is a matter of degree, but degrees are significant. Here we merely note: (1) that the all-willer is bound to fail anyway for lack of a positive objective; (2) that his motivation is more obvious, and less remarkable, if he is saddled with a sense of guilt; (3) that there are survivals in the final text of the original intention; and (4) that the excluded chapter is of capital importance to students of Dostoevsky's religion.

To proceed: on any showing Stavrogin is intended to be highly contemporary. He is of noble birth; he has been through a period of debauchery; he is, of course, unemployed despite his talents; he suffers from an *ennui*, which in the 1860's, had ceased to be romantic and had become cynical; and, naturally enough, he is an atheist and always has been.[7] He has been tutor-educated by that *fainéant* liberal, Stepan Trofimovich Verkhovensky – by presenting whom as the teacher of Stavrogin and the father of Pyotr, Dostoevsky means to suggest that the liberals of the 1840's, including himself, have a good deal to answer for. But beneath this fashionable disguise there is something more formidable. He is not only one of the 'evil spirits': he is acknowledged by the others as their chief. He has no aims, no illusions, and hardly any affections, together with the strength to will anything, quite irrespective of reason and self-interest. His great asset is the charisma which enables him to influence his dependents, as it were experimentally, to different and incompatible styles of behaviour; but of that later. In the meantime, there are the deliberate absurdities to which, as exercises of perverse self-discipline, he commits himself – because, for whatever reasons, he does not care what becomes of him. Thus he marries a half-wit for a bet; bites the ear of the governor of the province; fights a duel he does not believe in, and throws his shots away; accepts a blow on the face from Shatov with a deadly calm; and finally (though here he is anticipated by local scandalmongers) comes home to announce his preposterous marriage to his friends and townsfolk. The core of all these incidents is sheer will, with the overtones of arbitrary unboundedness suggested by the Russian word *volya*; and it can

[7] His admission to Shatov, *The Possessed*, p.231.

hardly be an accident that he is given the patronymic *Vsevolodo-vich*: we are surely prompted to disengage from it the notion of 'all-willing'.

But the 'all-willer' is human. To be *everything* is to defy human limitations. Hence (and quite apart from any feelings of guilt) he is also a sufferer. After his fruitless feat of ear-biting (pointless, except to show that he can do what is pointless, that his will is not limited by reason) he has an attack of 'brain-fever' – Dostoevsky's usual way of describing nervous prostration. It was not a natural absurdity such as might have been put on by a clown like Lebyadkin; it was the uncongenial effort of a sensitive spirit who neither spares nor deceives himself. It has been suggested that the name *Stavrogin* is a construct from *stauros* (in Byzantine Greek, *stavros*), meaning a cross. If so, it is in the suffering of one who transcends and is bound to human limitations that the resemblance is to be found.[8] But, unlike the unrepeatable exemplar, he transcends humanity only in idea. In actual life, for one man to be exhaustively universal is impossible, and the result must be tragedy. The black angel is no more able to cope with the world than the white angel, Myshkin. He cannot shake off the loyalties of his dependents; he is pinned down by his random commitments (his marriage, for example) and tempted by ordinary human weakness, which is the best way of describing his attraction to Liza. Because he spurns limitation and cannot escape it, he must suffer and, what is more, he can achieve nothing – achievement depends on the contraction of will to a definite object. The most understanding of his dependents, Kirillov, tells him he is 'not a strong character' (p.271); and he himself says the same thing in that splendidly economical scene with Darya Pavlovna (pp.272–74):

Dasha seized his hand.

'God save you from your demon and . . . call me, call me quickly!'

'Oh! a fine demon! It's simply a little nasty scrofulous imp, with a cold in his head, one of the unsuccessful ones.'

[8] The all-man is not the man-god; the man-god is what happens when one of his constituents escapes from the others. The preacher and would-be exhibitor of the man-god is Kirillov, who is only one of Stavrogin's spiritual *protégés*. But the man-god is a product of his omnivolence. And as his will cannot encompass the god-man, he is almost by definition an atheist.

In the end, after the breaking of his last life-line (with Liza), realizing that 'nothing has come from me but negation' and indeed 'not even negation' (p. 635), left alone with a will broken by its aspiration to be independent of binding objectives, he wrote, as a last resort, to Darya Pavlovna, asking her to go to Switzerland with him 'as his nurse' and without illusions: but before she could act on it he had seen the impossibility and had hanged himself. He had kept his commitment to non-commitment right to the end, and 'the doctors emphatically and absolutely rejected all idea of insanity'. What Kirillov did for an idea, he did for lack of an idea or of anything else. The love which could have encompassed he could not return. Darya Pavlovna is Sonya without the urgency; she will sacrifice anything for him, she will spend her life looking after him; but to be nursed by Darya would be the end of the all-man. Either way he is caught; if he stands out, he will break down; if he submits, he will be broken down. This is the inescapable dilemma of the omnivolent *I*.[9]

It must have cost Dostoevsky something to pursue this dialectic to its conclusion. He admired the unlimited man; he admired the Russian for being an unlimited man; and never at any stage could he tolerate the compartmental rigidities which he alleged to prevail in Europe, and in Germany in particular. The man who could take contradictions in his stride and *live* them through, the man with a contempt for those who out of respect for logic or dislike of personal inconvenience restrict themselves to one thesis of a paralogism, has his whole-hearted approval. Indeed, the lure of the unlimited was his most constant temptation. The fascination exerted on him by the 'double' was that the 'double' can encompass polar opposites while respecting their polarity. In crucifying Stavrogin he is crucifying something precious to him. But, having worked out the all-man in flesh and blood he saw that he could not sustain the burden: the burden which nevertheless, as Stavrogin had to admit to Kirillov, he

[9] This is the straightforward reading of the text as it stands. In the context of the *Confession*, Stavrogin's behaviour is less arbitrary; his pointless acts are traced back to his sense of guilt, and interpreted as self-punishing. See pp. 145ff. below.

was compelled to seek (p. 270). Negatively, Dostoevsky did not
change his mind: he continued to dislike the specialist rigidities
of particular I's (or We's) as much as ever. He continued to
defend Russians as unlimited and unspecialized; as being able to
enter simultaneously into attitudes and situations which Europeans could only appropriate separately one by one. But,
positively, the attempt to synchronize the polarities turned out
in his hands to be a failure: one of the many cases in which
Dostoevsky the theorist found himself corrected by Dostoevsky
the artist. When he came again to consider the problem, he took
the bolder step of challenging the premises from which the all-
man and the compartmental rigidities alike descended: the
doctrine of the separate I.[10] He discovered what it was in
Russian Christianity which impressed him: *sobornost'*, and 'the
responsibility of each for all', the separate and identifiable I
being merged in the totalizing charity of the religious collective.
But that does not impress itself on his fiction till *The Brothers
Karamazov*. What he does in *The Possessed* is to embody and,
with love and agony in his heart, to dispose of, a long cherished
alternative.

There is one sphere, however, in which there is no limit to the
all-man: the sphere of imagination. It is possible for the totally
uncommitted man, with all his strength and for him only, to
develop out of himself different and incompatible possibilities
and to try them out on other people. That is what, in the period
before the action begins, Stavrogin appears to have done with
Pyotr Verkhovensky, Shatov, and Kirillov. They could hardly
be more different, but each of them looks up to Stavrogin as the
author of his own particular enterprise. Into Verkhovensky he
instilled an unscrupulous ardour of revolution; into Shatov a
sort of religious nationalism; into Kirillov (who perhaps understood him better than any of them) the cult of the man-God.
'Instilled' is perhaps too strong a word, except for Kirillov;
what Stavrogin did, out of the utter emptiness of his heart (and
the heart of the all-man must needs be empty) was to feed his
associates with what they would be likely to fall for anyway, but

[10] Cf. the meditation after the death of Marya, pp. 84f.

in such a manner as to make them revere him, to the point of embarrassment. Having no convictions whatever, but a multiplicity of imaginings which he has willed and transmitted but never himself enacted, he hates being identified with, or responsible for, any one of them: but, mesmerized as it were by his variously refracted charisma, none of them can let him go.

The first of them is the revolutionary leader, Pyotr Verhovensky. Astute, dapper, relentless, merciless, and cynical, and moreover an egoist of the first order (this last touch is perhaps unfair to the genuine article), explainable, if hardly excusable, on the score of neglect by his father who sent him as a baby to distant relations from Berlin by parcel post; he is nevertheless utterly devoted to Stavrogin, dedicates to him as it were his revolutionary agitation and actually proposes, when he has destroyed all existing institutions, to install his idol – 'Ivan the Tsarevich' – as the sole authority. By devising it so, Dostoevsky intends to show that revolution, with its inevitable sequel of tyranny, is just a function of the religious blackout. Or, to express it in terms of literary technique, he is able to absorb the political subplot (as it then becomes) into the new metaphysical dimension in which Stavrogin moves. Most of the moves in the novel are set going by Pyotr to save Stavrogin from himself; especially the move to kill his imbecile wife and set him free to marry a woman who will be both more congenial to Stavrogin, and more acceptable as the consort of a Tsarevich. Of course he misunderstands Stavrogin completely; he has no notion that the bearing of unbearable burdens is part of his demonic dedication; but he succeeds in exposing his weakness. Stavrogin knows that the murder is being planned, but indirectly and by inference, and he fails to interfere. The result is that when Liza comes to him, and he almost hopes to find happiness (which, in his role as the emptied-out all-man, he must not do), because he is incapable of emotional attachment, he tells her the truth – he knows that if he did not she would 'follow him like a dog' – and she goes cynically but unhappily away. The black angel rejects the temptation, and Pyotr is astounded. He has given his idol all he thought he wanted, and everyone suffers, no one more than the black angel himself. It is thus that the political dimension of the novel is swallowed up in the metaphysical afterthought. Stavrogin has created Pyotr from part of his nature only. The all-man is dispersed into compact fragments, dependent on the centre but independent and conflicting in respect of each other.[11]

It is appropriate, before leaving the political foreground, to add the following comments. (1) Dostoevsky ridicules the revolution, but he has nothing to say for the establishment. The Governor is a solemn fool, governed by a stupid wife who likes to be thought clever, and if the story had been written to show that provincial administration was a shambles, it could hardly have been more effective. (2) The general picture of the gentry, male and female, is anything but complimentary; Gaganov *fils*, Yuliya Mikhaylovna and Varvara Petrovna herself, Stavrogin's mother, suggest that it will neither exert itself or reform itself. (3) Being an artist as well as a propagandist, Dostoevsky is genuinely sympathetic with the one member of his revolutionary gang who is utterly honest and really means business. Among the rogues and pretenders, the decent fanatic Erkel stands out as a shining light. (4) He does not neglect the political background of Stavrogin himself. He was educated by the egregious Stepan Trofimovich; his Russian style is imperfect (p. 633, illustrated in the Russian letter which follows); he treats his estates merely as a convenience and has lost touch with the people (p. 238). His failure is partly at least that like so many Russian aristocrats, he does not belong in his own country. His fatal omnivolence is the end-point of a training in detachment from local and ordinary values. (5) Dostoevsky takes every opportunity to belabour the liberals of his own generation. Not only is there the unkind parody of Turgenev as Karmazinov;[12] there is the

---

[11] If it were our business to examine Pyotr Verkhovensky as a sample of the revolutionary world, there would be more to be said, and writers who have inherited the revolution have said it. But, except for his atheism, he is outside our scope: and his atheism is modelled on Stavrogin's. And yet how different! – as different as it must be, if the one is a highly specialized practitioner and the other a *vsechelovek*. It is not accidental that Stavrogin is made to protest to *all* his spiritual offspring that they have misrepresented him. By limiting him to one concept when he incorporates the polarities they *must* misrepresent him.

[12] E. H. Carr has suggested that the naming of this character is significant:

characterization of Stepan Trofimovich with its inevitable sequel: old liberals father young nihilists. This is the unspoken conviction of conservatives the world over. (6) The attack is primarily on the nihilists. Socialism figures ambiguously; Dostoevsky states explicitly that Pyotr Verkhovensky is not a Socialist;[13] and Pyotr Verkhovensky himself is made to say that he is using socialism merely as a lever (p. 393). Yet he foreshadows the joint triumph of the International and the Pope, and he approves of Shigalev whose formula is: starting from unlimited freedom I arrive at unlimited despotism. Dostoevsky seems to be saying (a) that nihilism inevitably turns into despotism, (b) that this despotism is what is ordinarily called Socialism, but (c) that Socialism has a deeper meaning which is not despotic and is not so much the dialectical development of nihilism as the prior denial of its assumptions. He is keeping the word clean in case he should want to appropriate it himself. Along this road he proceeds to the religious collectivity adumbrated in *The Brothers Karamazov*.

II

The next dependent is Kirillov. He is Westernized, inarticulate in Russian and an engineer. Like Pyotr Verkhovensky, he is an atheist: indeed, he claims to be the first atheist to live up to his convictions. Like Pyotr, he is swayed by a single idea – kindled in him by Stavrogin in his passage through a succession of ideas. The thesis (which is also an obsession), set out in three conversations at different turns of the novel, with the narrator, Stavrogin, and Pyotr Verkhovensky respectively, is, briefly, that if a man is to be completely free (and here we note an *internal* connection with Stavrogin's own wilfulness – Kirillov is more *like* Stavrogin than are his other dependents), he has to kill himself: not for a reason, but precisely because there is no reason (p. 581). (If there were a reason, the act would not be un-

French, *cramoisi*, 'Mr Pink', Carr translates: the dictionary suggests a deeper hue, 'Mr Crimson'.

[13] Commenting in the *Diary of a Writer*, p. 146: cf. Pyotr's own confession to Stavrogin, *The Possessed*, p. 393.

equivocally a determination by the will.) In the past, people have missed the point because they thought there was a God; that would indeed limit the compass of the will. But then God is merely an idea; possessing, no doubt, a sort of subjective being ('he does not exist, but he is', p. 105), but in reality entirely incorporated in my own will. In this sense, there is no God; therefore, for the first time, *I* am God: I have taken over this attributes and am a man-God (p. 221).[14] 'All will has become mine (p. 580); but unless I kill myself, there is a challenge to my will which my will has failed to answer.' 'There will be full freedom when it will be just the same to live or not to live' (p. 104). So the logical outcome of my being man-God, and 'the highest point of self-will', is that I commit suicide. Here, indeed, is the ambition of 'all-man' focussed to a point.

Kirillov is more than usually an ideological character. He helps the plot, of course: his intention to kill himself, being known to Pyotr Verkhovensky, is used to throw the blame on him for the murder of Shatov; and he comes in handy as a second for Stavrogin in the duel. But in the high argument of the novel he is more than useful: he is the focus. He is the high-water-mark *reductio ad absurdum* of the kind of atheism he professes. It is not scientific atheism: as Berdyaev has pointed out, in the formation of Russian atheism science plays only a small confirmatory part: in the 'death of God', science is merely an accessory after the fact. The sequence of thought is along the lines of Nietzsche's exclamation: 'If there was a God, how could I bear not to be God? Therefore there is no God.' But Kirillov is the more relentless: his version is: 'If there were a God, I would not be God; but in virtue of my will, I *am* God; therefore there is no God.' The conclusion depends on his experimental enlargement of his will; like the traditional believer, he must take death in his stride.[15]

14 A distinction is here made between the man-God and the God-man: a contrast which contains a compact summary of Dostoevsky's religion. It contains also his final answer to Feuerbach, of whose doctrine Kirillov's thesis is a slightly subjectivized but still recognizable version.

15 And not merely because he feels he has to. That is why Kirillov is made to express his love of life and his belief in the goodness of things. In this respect he differs from the later version of atheism portrayed in Ivan Karamazov.

Among Kirillov's utterances are several which, while utterly apposite to him, and in no way intrusions, seem to reflect Dostoevsky's own intellectual history. (1) He is given lines about Christ which recall, tangentially, the famous letter to Fonvizina. 'That man was the loftiest of all on earth. He was that which gave meaning to life . . . and if the laws of nature did not spare even him, have not spared their miracle and made even him live for a lie and die for a lie, then all the planet is a lie' (p. 582). If Christ is one thing and the truth is another, he remains an inexplicable intruder, and he cannot win. This utter separation of fact and value, while just intelligible at the far end of the Protestant decline, is wholly opposed to the Orthodox emphasis on Easter, and to Dostoevsky's own vehement protestations about immortality in the *Diary*. Kirillov does not represent Dostoevsky's official opinion at the time of writing: he represents only too well a slice of his past, perhaps continuing to haunt him in the more rational (i.e. untrustworthy) moments of his present. (2) There is the same kind of tension in Kirillov's conclusion: 'God is necessary and so must exist; but I know he doesn't and can't; surely you must understand that a man with two such ideas can't go on living.' 'Necessary' in this context means 'not to be lived without', 'practically necessary'; 'Doesn't' and 'can't' refer to the hard facts of the case. The separation of fact and value, carried to its legitimate extreme, makes action impossible – except for the enacting of the conclusion, which is not to go on living. Incidentally, Kirillov is a criticism of Stavrogin, who still wants to encompass the polarities. To decide at all is to limit the range of the will. With some penetration, Kirillov remarks to Pyotr Verkhovensky, 'If Stavrogin has faith, he does not believe that he has faith: if he hasn't faith, he does not believe that he hasn't' (p. 579). If he is to be an all-man, he has to entertain, and even to enact, both faith and doubt. That is why he achieves nothing: though, as we shall see, he goes Kirillov's way in the end.[16] (3) It is to Kirillov that Dos-

---

[16] There are intrusive impulses of kindness and respect in this black angel. Thus he is reported as saying of his half-demented wife, 'I really do respect her, for she's better than any of us' (p. 173); and particularly if we anticipate the *Confession*, he suffers the continual hangover of a bad conscience.

toevsky gives the lines about the man-God and the God-man. It is essential to his religious stance that the two concepts are utterly opposed; and he deftly arranges that the opposition should be announced from the other side of the fence. 'God is man' arises out of his existence: 'man is God' arises out of his non-existence. When he affirms the man-God, Kirillov speaks as a consequent atheist; and Stavrogin, who has put the idea into his head, cannot object with any conviction.

This, then, is what Stavrogin's most understanding associate makes of his life and conversation. He owes it all to him: 'Remember what you have meant in my life, Stavrogin' (p. 222). It is not Stavrogin's natural medium; he seeks not a fantastic and definitive deliverance, but a continuing burden. But if he has to act? He cannot go with the 'iconoclasts'; he might envy their simple-mindedness, but that very envy would make him angry with them: he would have liked to commit himself, but he is true to his demonic contract, and keeps a rod in pickle for those who can (p. 635). Still less can he identify with Shatov, though he is inclined to accept, and to turn against himself, Shatov's conviction that 'the man who loses connection with his country loses his gods, that is, all his aims' (ibid.). When his hand is forced and his wife murdered without his approval, it is true, but with his foreknowledge, when Liza, faced with the truth, turns away from him and closes his last approach to the world, when nothing is left to him but Darya Pavlovna, to whom he appeals as a last resort but then repents of it, it was Kirillov who supplied the model. He did not think he could match Kirillov's 'greatness of soul'; it would only be another item in an interminable list of deceptions. 'I shall never, never shoot myself.' Yet before Darya could reach him, he had hanged himself (significantly enough, so did Matryosha) and without Kirillov's obsession to help him through. We are not told what happened between his writing of the letter and his final decision; but he was certainly not playing at 'greatness of soul'. He was keeping it as rational and matter-of-fact as he could. Nevertheless, it was Kirillov's way that he went; and Dostoevsky means us to infer that is the appropriate way, not only for the logically consequent atheist who enacts his convictions, but also for the uncommitted all-engendering atheist who inspired him. Infinite of purpose or extravagantly single-minded, both assert will over every kind of limit. It is in this respect that Kirillov is more *like* Stavrogin than the others: Shatov and Pyotr Verkhovensky at least have something definite to live for.

That brings us to Shatov: the most unlikely and, for the public Dostoevsky, the most compromising of all the dependents. Shatov, a former serf on the Stavrogin property, joined the local revolutionary association, with all that that implies: detachment from God, country and the soil. Later and apparently under the stimulus of Stavrogin, who at that time was trying out something different, he retracted and became an espouser of Russian religious nationalism. In the original draft of him, as in his name, there is a hint of unsteadiness (the root *shat* – signifies 'shaky', 'loose', 'tottering'), and though in his final shape he is out-wardly sure and definite, there remains in him, behind his confident nationalism, a religious insecurity. His outward allegiances seem wholly alien to what we know of Stavrogin: but that only shows that we underestimate Stavrogin's versa-tility: he can turn up at any point of the compass. That Shatov himself acknowledged his dependence (unwillingly and despair-ingly) there can be no doubt:

> 'Stavrogin, why am I condemned to believe in you through all eternity? . . . Shan't I kiss your footprints when you've gone? I can't tear you out of my heart, Nikolay Stavrogin!' (p. 237.)

and that Stavrogin himself planted the seeds of a doctrine he did not believe in, trying it out on a likely subject and out of his own utter emptiness, is conveyed to us by both parties. And this is of capital importance for us in weighing the evidence for Dos-toevsky's religion at the time of writing.

Consider one by one the content of Shatov's beliefs, (pp. 231ff.). 'An atheist ceases to be a Russian.' 'Announcing to all the world that Christ without an earthly kingdom cannot hold his ground upon earth, Catholicism . . . proclaimed Antichrist and ruined the whole Western world.' 'Didn't you tell me that if it were mathematically proved to you that the truth excludes Christ, you'd prefer to stick to Christ rather than to the truth?' And finally, the great torrent of prophecy: 'The people is the body of God.' 'Every people is only a people so long as it has its own god.' 'But there is only one truth, and therefore only a single one out of the nations can have the true God.' 'Only one nation is "god-bearing", that's the Russian people' (p. 234).

The significance of these confessions is that every one of them is part of the creed of the public Dostoevsky. They are mostly to be found in the *Diary*, the third has been lifted bodily from the letter to Fonvizina of 1854. Yet they are attributed to Shatov who is the dependent of Stavrogin and is, on his own confession, an atheist. That is to say, the Russian Christ (perhaps even the Russian God) is somehow spun out of an atheist's imagination. Stavrogin points out to Shatov that he 'reduces God to a simple attribute of nationality'. He is right: the coupling of God with soil and homeland condemns the proletarian or the traveller abroad to unbelief. There is perhaps a dark prognostication here: for most people God *does* have roots in the soil, and the movement of masses of people into towns or into new countries quite often *does* have a distracting effect on their faith. But a religion which is *exclusively* agrarian or national is not directed wholly to Christ or God. Shatov does little to meet the difficulty when he replies, 'on the contrary, I raise the people to God . . . the people is the body of God'. Which people? The Orthodox congregation? The Orthodox Church as a whole? Or the Russian people as such? Shatov fails to make the distinction. Stavrogin proceeds to pin him down, just as the reader longs to pin down Dostoevsky in many passages of the *Diary*:

'Do you believe in God, yourself?'
'I believe in Russia . . . I believe in her orthodoxy . . . I believe in the body of Christ . . . I believe that the new advent will take place in Russia . . . I believe . . .', Shatov muttered frantically.
'And in God? In God?'
'I . . . . I will believe in God' (p. 235).[17]

---

[17] The dots do not represent omissions; they are copied from the text.

The Russian expresses not a resolve, but simply futurity (*Ya budu verovat' v Boga*): behind it lies uncertainty rather than desperation. But even so, Shatov is saying that he believes all that the public Dostoevsky believed without exactly believing in God. He adds 'I haven't told you that I don't believe'; and whether one underlines *told* or *don't* is a matter of interpretation. If Dostoevsky is crucifying his public image, it would be more natural to underline *don't*; and the prose of the passage seems to point the same way. Shatov is not confessing a hidden unbelief: he is leaving the issue open. But as long as it is open, he cannot, on his reckoning, be said to believe.[18]

There are several points here which need disengaging.

1. In doubting Shatov, Stavrogin is applying a strict sense of 'belief', and Shatov, when he doubts himself, shares it. They both have in mind belief in a God who is more than his manifestations. This is what Shatov does not see his way to, though he lives in hope. Neither of them, however, pays much attention to 'reason' and 'science'. Shatov declares that they count for little in the life of nations and quotes Stavrogin (and Dostoevsky) on 'preferring Christ to the truth'. We have noticed this emphasis in Dostoevsky all through and we shall refer to it again. Belief in God, if it is to be achieved, is not to be achieved by reason.

2. The conversation throws light on Stavrogin – as much light as Dostoevsky wants, for as a matter of style and exposition he needed to keep him in the dark: it enhances his demonic quality.[19] It shows Stavrogin not simply as a denier, but as an experimenter among the positive and negative components of his all-embracing character. He tells Shatov: 'In your words I recognize my word of two years ago' (p. 235): that is, he really

[18] There is the same ambiguity in the conversation between Shatov and his wife Marya (p. 544) after her return. Marya says:
   'What are you preaching? You can't exist without preaching, that's your character!'
   'I am preaching God, Marie.'
   'In whom you don't believe yourself. I never could see the idea of that.'
Are we to take Marya's word for it? After all, she has been away from him for three years. But why did Dostoevsky make her say it, if there was no doubt about it?
[19] See Yevnin, in *Tvorchestvo Dostoevskogo*, p. 261, on 'the aureole of secrecy around the principal enigmatic characters'.

did imagine for himself a Russian religious-nationalist phase, as well as a revolutionary and a nihilistic phase. He is even as likely to love God as to love evil: 'Is it true', Shatov exclaims, 'is it true that you saw no distinction in beauty between some brutal obscene action and any great exploit, even the sacrifice of life for the good of humanity? Is it true that you have found identical beauty, equal enjoyment, in both extremes' (p. 236)? *Equal* enjoyment: not merely 'the bad equally with the good', but also 'the good equally with the bad'. If Stavrogin is an 'evil spirit', he is none the less a fallen angel, homesick for heaven: 'I wasn't lying when I spoke as though I had faith' (p. 232). The all-man is strictly 'beyond good and evil', and the demonic man merely *turns* good into evil. It is the tragedy of Stavrogin that he cannot *in practice* fulfil his whole nature: and the commitments to absurdity which he makes to assert his will rebound fatally to the side of evil. In a world which survives only by the observation of limits, 'good' can be achieved only by limitation; and that is the one thing of which an 'unlimited' man is incapable: it is the *reductio ad absurdum* of the *vsechelovek*. It is also a tragedy for Dostoevsky, who hated limitations and, as a novelist, expounded characters by recording their internal inconsistencies. The failure of Stavrogin is a victory for Germans, compartmentalism, punctuality and other major aversions of his author.

3. The characterizing of Shatov, in particular, shows how the growth of Dostoevsky's art is related to the growth of his experience. We have noted that during the period of composition Dostoevsky was undergoing a significant religious development. Not only is *The Possessed* a first attempt to cope with the problems raised by the unmanageable plans for 'Atheism' and 'The Great Sinner' but the little things show a shift to the religious dimension. For the first time in his fiction, Dostoevsky locates a major scene in a church; he is speaking of a world in which people naturally do go to church, and the chronicler has to follow them there if he is to understand them. Marya Timofeyevna's invasion of the sanctum, manipulated for his own purposes by Pyotr Verkhovensky, triggers off the series of explosions which ends with riot and murder and suicide. There

is nothing specifically religious in the church attendance of provincial notables, but it forms a background; there is nothing comparable in *Crime and Punishment* or *The Idiot*. (It is noted in passing that the priest was a popular character.) It is just in this period that his correspondence shows increasing signs of pious and even pietistic diction, not merely with his conservative friends Maikov and Strakhov, but with his favourite niece and *confidante*, Sofya Ivanova. Yet (to return to the novel) he never allows the picture to be disturbed. He records faithfully the absurdities of the prophet, Semyon Yakovlevich (who is taken by Yevnin to be one of the instances of the 'pure religion' which Dostoevsky is seeking). And there is at least some ambiguity about the 'confession scene' with Tikhon; at no stage is one more tempted to be sorry for Stavrogin than on his encounter with this sick erratic sharp-eyed monk who seems to take up his imperfectly good intentions systematically in the wrong way. Of that later; here it can only be said that Tikhon's handling of a potential penitent was not particularly skilful, and Dostoevsky shows clearly enough, by incidental comment, that he sees it. Our immediate concern is with the Shatov-Stavrogin dialogue; and of this we can only say that it shows us Dostoevsky ruthlessly probing into his own recent religious advances, and finding them hollow. As the same thing has happened in *The Idiot*, we are forced to recognize that Dostoevsky's fiction stands in a relation to his personal life as a corrective, operating spontaneously and immediately, as soon as he has had time to express his new ideas in flesh and blood. Dostoevsky's insight was neither political nor philosophical; it was directed to character; and if character will not stand the weight of the idea that is put upon it, sooner or later the idea has to be remodelled. We have seen how the ideal God breaks down in *The Idiot*; he is insufficiently incarnate. Taking Shatov as representing the contemporary religion of Dostoevsky, the Russian God breaks down in *The Possessed*; he is too narrowly incarnate: and that in spite of the fact that the Russian God is what Dostoevsky set out to defend. It was easier for him to slip in this instance because, for the greater part of the novel, it is atheism and its derivatives that are under attack, and Dostoevsky conducts this part of the operation efficiently enough. But the moment he starts to present a positive alternative, that, too, breaks down, even though it was to be successfully defended at the prose level in the earlier numbers of the *Diary*. What we learn from these misadventures is that Dostoevsky's works are, among other things, contemporary, unsparing examinations of his religious condition for the time being; and only in *The Brothers Karamazov* is there any degree of coincidence between them.

Before passing to Stavrogin's *Confession*, there is one general feature of Dostoevsky's analysis, bearing on his religious prepossessions, which requires attention. That is his relation to Russian sectarianism. There is not much on this topic in his public writings or his correspondence; but the general psychological resemblance between the revolution and *Raskol* ('schism' first and 'dissent' afterwards) was noted by Berdyaev in his study, *The Russian Revolution*,[20] citing Dostoevsky as a principal witness, and has recently been documented in a fascinating study of Dostoevsky's name-choosing by Richard Peace.[21] The implications of the name 'Raskolnikov' have often been canvassed: Peace has added Pyotr Verkhovensky's references to the 'Castrates' (p. 395), and the fact that the house where Shatov and Kirillov and Lebyadkin and his sister (Stavrogin's wife) have their quarters is called the house of Filippov in the street called Bogoyavlenskaya ('Epiphany Street'). Danilo Filippov was a seventeenth-century schismatic, a seceder from the schism of the Old Believers, who claiming that divine inspiration can dispense with authorities threw all the books on religion he could find into the Volga and was imprisoned in the Bogoyavlensky monastery. The coincidence is certainly remarkable, and it suggests that Dostoevsky saw a historical connection between the old sectaries and the new nihilism.[22] The line of descent was clearly stated by Berdyaev:

---

[20] Especially pp. 5–11.

[21] *Dostoyevsky: an Examination of the Major Novels*, esp. pp.170ff.

[22] Perhaps Dostoevsky had been studying the sects in preparation for 'The Life of a Great Sinner', as he had promised in his letter to Maykov (see above, pp. 39ff.).

Russian nihilism and the apocalyptic strain in the Russian character are connected, and this connection shows itself in the extreme form of the schismatic spirit. Nihilistic and apocalyptic tendencies, hankering after spiritual nakedness, refusal of the processes of history and of cultural values, expectancy of some final catastrophe, are deeply rooted in the psychology of the *Raskol* . . . and these tendencies remain as psychological forces, but in a secularized form, in movements which are divorced from the Christian religious consciousness . . . A schismatic and eschatological disposition is the fundamental psychological fact of the Russian nineteenth century . . . The Russian *intelligentsia* of the nineteenth century was a class of intellectual schismatics, an intellectual *Raskol*.[23]

It is not contended that Dostoevsky was concerned with the contemporary influence of the sects, though they make a significant appearance in *The Idiot* in the background of the 'passionate' Rogozhin. But he was concerned to note the deep roots of the contemporary nihilism which he deplored, and he undoubtedly did want his readers to take note of the historic parallels. It should be added that the same tendencies are to be found within the Orthodox Church (e.g. Father Ferapont in *The Brothers Karamazov*) and within Dostoevsky himself (his dislike of the intermediary, his incapacity for scepticism, his delight in polarities, and an apocalyptism by no means restricted to a vision of the Last Judgment). In general, he both glories in this schismatic unlimitedness, and crucifies it: Stavrogin is the outstanding example.

Something of an answer is to be found in the last days of Stepan Trofimovich. This romantic scholar and self-deceiver dies in an odour of sanctity, repenting of his worst sin (*j'ai menti toute ma vie*) and setting out, in his high-flown fashion, some of Dostoevsky's deepest religious convictions; 'God is necessary to me, because he is the only being one can love eternally' (p. 623): 'the one essential condition of human existence is that man should always be able to bow down to something infinitely great': yet with a hint of German Idealism which is exactly right for him: 'hail to the Great Idea'. And he is chosen to apply, magnificently, the story of the Gadarene Swine to the contempor-

[23] *The Russian Revolution*, pp. 6, 7–8.

ary Russian condition. Dostoevsky did look for light at the other end of the tunnel. Finally, he introduces as a late-comer the Bible-selling widow, Sofya Matveyevna; the single-hearted un-complicated kindly woman whose only idea was to spread the Gospel and to help others: a striking contrast to the tortuous complex protagonists of the story.[24] Again, that there should be such people is a pin-point of light in the novel; but she appears only on p. 600, after all the main characters have been destroyed. Perhaps we are being asked to believe that it is from her likes that the new Christian society is to be built on the ruins. She is free from the spiritual agonies of self-mortification and the apocalyptic expectations which Dostoevsky's atheists inherit from the sects. But she is still only on the margin. She was able to bring peace and happiness to a dying sentimentalist, but she never had to cope with a Stavrogin. For that, as we shall see, even the resources of a trained and saintly Orthodox Christian monk proved to be insufficient. To the end, *The Possessed* is flooded with darkness.

III

There remains to be considered Stavrogin's 'confession', ex-cluded from the novel by Katkov as editor of *Russky Vestnik*. As we have seen, it makes a difference to the interpretation of Stavrogin and contributes much to our understanding of Dos-toevsky's religion. It is a common view, stated by Andrey Kozin,[25] that through its omission 'the whole construction and meaning of the novel is destroyed'. It loses its one effective con-frontation of light and darkness; with the removal of Tikhon, there is no religious character remaining to exhibit the religious stance to which Stavrogin testifies only negatively by his failure. It is left to some stray remarks by Shatov and the narrator and, by a sublime inspiration, to the insight of the dying Stepan

[24] Sofya, recalling the Heavenly Wisdom, is the name given to three selflessly Christian women in the course of the novels: the others are in *Crime and Punishment* and *The Raw Youth*.

[25] In the introductory article to his annotated edition, Inter-Language Literary Associates, New York 1964, p.17.

Trofimovich, to develop the theme on the positive side. If that were all, we should have to conclude that in failing to reinstate the chapter in the completed book version, Dostoevsky was sacrificing literary values to save trouble. It is possible, but it would be untypical. He might have thought that darkness could be left to its own condemnation; moreover (and this is the theme it is proposed to develop) he might have come to see that there was something wrong with the chapter itself, and that it might be better to omit it, whatever the consequences, rather than let it stand as a conspicuous failure of the Christian witness.

First of all, the story. Meditative and perturbed, Stavrogin goes to the monastery on Shatov's advice to see Tikhon who is something of a local celebrity though, characteristically, Stavrogin had not previously heard of him.[26] His reputation in the monastery is not unmixed; everyone recognizes his power and his penetration; but in the course of the narrative he is described as 'sick', 'half-queer', 'off-beat'; his health is bad (he collapses during a testing interview with Stavrogin); he is 'remote', on his own confession, and, on any showing, sudden and imperious; and despite his sympathy and his self-enforced patience he ends, not with absolution, but with the prophecy of worse to come. If he was intended to be a redeemer (and there is evidence that at one stage Dostoevsky meant Stavrogin to be saved)[27] he falls down on the exercise. Is it possible that Tikhon is a prolongation of Myshkin: uncommonly quick of understanding but, in the face of the pride-and-injury syndrome, powerless? Is it also possible that Dostoevsky, re-examining the episode some three years later, found that it could no longer serve his now stronger purposes?

To continue with the story. After some uneasy sparring during which Stavrogin, half sincere and half sarcastic, raises questions about the reality of devils, and chaffs Tikhon about the

---

[26] Tikhon was named for Tikhon Zadonsky, an eighteenth-century monk who stood up to the ecclesiastical unbelievers appointed to episcopates by Catherine II. Dostoevsky had a great veneration for him, but there is in fact little resemblance; Dostoevsky's Tikhon is very nineteenth-century and an expert on Dostoevsky's own problems.

[27] Cf. Kozin, op. cit. p. 7.

moving of mountains,[28] they develop a certain mutual respect and come together over the passage in the Book of the Revelation about the Church of Laodicea: 'because thou art neither hot nor cold, I will spew thee out of my mouth'.[29] It provides Tikhon with the opportunity to enounce one of Dostoevsky's cherished convictions, that 'plenary atheism is more to be honoured than worldly indifference';[30] the atheist has only to take the final jump and he is home, while the indifferent worldling will never make home, unless he is badly frightened. But the real subject is 'devils'; Stavrogin leads up to it, because he has one of his own. Finally he puts down on the writing table five 'sheets' of badly printed Russian characters containing his 'confession'; his motive is so far not revealed.

Some years before, while he was living riotously but unhappily in Petersburg (incidentally browsing in theology) he had allegedly seduced a twelve-year-old girl. The episode is veiled: Stavrogin will not allow Tikhon to read the 'second sheet'.[31] But the lead-up is mean and sad enough: the girl has been unjustly treated by her mother and is ready for anything. And the after-effects as described in the remaining sheets are, as Katkov observed, 'intolerably realistic'. Stavrogin goes off and enjoys himself with the gang; but it is not long before he is warned by an unprecedented fear that something must be wrong. He tries to banish the unease by planning in one way or another

[28] Is he himself thinking of that major impossibility?

[29] That passage was after Dostoevsky's own heart. When the chapter was suppressed he included it in the scriptural readings of Sofya Matveyevna to the dying Stepan Trofimovich, pp. 613–14. It fascinates Stavrogin because he knows he answers to the description.

[30] Kozin, op.cit. p.40.

[31] It could be argued that the confession is fabricated; Stavrogin, when concealing the 'second sheet', jeers at his host's monkish suspicions, and says 'it wasn't my fault that the girl was stupid', followed by the enigmatic *nichego ne bylo*, the most obvious translation of which is 'nothing happened' (p.52). And the narrator says oddly: 'I advance no proof, and by no means affirm, that the document is spurious.' On the whole it is better to give the episode the fullest interpretation, and to treat the device of the 'second sheet' as Dostoevsky's attempt to placate Katkov – there is a mischievous sally about the 'censorship' on the previous page. If 'nothing happened', it is hard to account for Stavrogin's extreme feelings of guilt. On the alternative translation 'it wasn't all that important', there is room for a reversal of feeling after the event. It would be just like Dostoevsky to leave the matter obscure, even apart from difficulties with his editor.

to take it out of the person who caused it. He returns to the house where Matryosha, the girl, lives: the first time she flees from him headlong upstairs, the next time, finding her alone, he sits down and does nothing, just to torment her. Finally she gets up and faces him with a white face, feverish eyes, and an emaciated little white fist. She goes off to the storeroom; when twenty minutes later, he looks through the chinks, she has hanged herself.[32] His first wild guilt reaction was his legal marriage to the half-wit Marya Timofyeyevna, sister of his boon companion Lebyadkin; the motive, to express his utter contempt for himself. The ceremony was witnessed by Kirillov and Pyotr Verkhovensky, and the secret is already sizzling in the provincial town where the action of the story opens. Soon afterwards, still saying, and to all appearances, caring nothing, Stavrogin sets out on four years of world travel, in which, as in later years, he shared quarters with Shatov and Kirillov and, out of his utter boredom, fired them with their respective enthusiasms. In a German hotel he has his first visitation: the girl appears before him, between his sleep and his waking, shaking her little fist. The 'devil' has begun to work on him; it is this that eventually takes him to Tikhon. In the meantime, he makes the acquaintance in Switzerland of two Russian young ladies, the Liza Nikolayevna and the Darya Pavlovna of the main novel: though by this time incapable of real affection, he seems to have turned both their heads, and there passed through his mind a wholly disinterested evil intention; he is so weighed down that another crime would make no difference: why not marry Liza and commit bigamy, just for the devil of it? But he escapes and goes back home, to find Liza in the same town: their mothers, scenting a match, have seen to that. Unable to settle, ill at ease, with the web of Pyotr Verkhovensky's conspiracy already being thrown around him, and beset by devils inside him, he takes Shatov's advice and consults Tikhon. It is with 'devils' what the conversation naturally commences: and Stavrogin proposes his own plan for dealing with them. He will publish to the world the confession that Tikhon has just finished reading.

[32] This is no stuff for pleasurable family reading. Katkov had a point.

Here we interpolate. The question is asked: why does Stavrogin, on everyone's testimony a man of great power and persuasiveness, *do* so little with his abilities? We now have an additional explanation: not only is the will of an all-man inevitably divided and frustrated, but this all-man is shackled by a sense of guilt. Stavrogin is not all darkness: he is a 'double', as indeed an all-man has to be. He is afflicted by a light which humiliates him: something is struggling in him against his spite and his wickedness: something which so troubles him that he has to engage in more spite and wickedness to deaden the suffering. It is often said that Dostoevsky preached suffering as a way to salvation. But the recipe works only if the suffering is consciously accepted and dedicated; otherwise it exasperates and destroys – look at Nastasya Filippovna, and now at Stavrogin.[33] Stavrogin is tormented by the angelic streak in him; the chief of the 'evil spirits' looks back at the heaven which overhangs him. That is why he suffers from hallucinations and goes to consult Tikhon. And it is because he hopes to be rid of the suffering without surrendering to its meaning that the consultation is a failure. Even so, he misses salvation by a whisker.

To return. To his surprise, Tikhon does not agree to his proposed publication of his confession. It would certainly be a noble and a Christian act, if it were inspired by a genuine repentance. But is it? The pages have been written not humbly, but defiantly; their author is not submitting to the judgment of his readers, he is challenging them. (Stavrogin knows this to be true: Tikhon's psychological analysis is never once at fault.) He will excite their hatred or, worse, their laughter; and either way he will react against them and do worse things yet just to spite them. It is then that Stavrogin has his moment of illumination. Putting the subtleties on one side, he exclaims: 'I want to forgive myself: that is my chief aim, my whole aim.'[34] He knows that crucifying himself will only enlarge his 'I', and what he

---

[33] As Berdyaev observes at the end of his masterly essay on 'Russian Religious Psychology', in *The Russian Revolution*, p. 49, with specific reference to Dostoevsky, the experience of suffering without the experience of the meaning of suffering, that is, of the Cross, will lead to unbelief and despair.

[34] Kozin, op. cit. p. 80.

needs is to forget it.[35] Tikhon welcomes this revelation with delight: 'If you believe that you can forgive yourself and are trying to obtain only this forgiveness, by your own suffering, then you already believe all the rest of it. What did you mean by saying that you don't believe in God . . . God will forgive your unbelief, for you honour the Holy Spirit in the truth, though you do not know him.'[36] Here there seems to be a basis of agreement; and it is easier to understand Tikhon's unorthodox reputation in the monastery than Kozin's comment that Stavrogin is rebuffed for refusing to accept his forgiveness by faith alone. On the contrary, Stavrogin's truly Pelagian discovery is welcomed by Tikhon as the solution of the whole problem. Those who hate themselves will take it out on themselves by hating others. Stavrogin, it is true, flinches when he finds scripture stacked against him: 'Whosoever offends one of these little ones . . .'; but Tikhon reassures him: 'Christ will forgive, if only you get to the point of forgiving yourself.'[37] And 'who embraces him, the immeasurable, will understand the All, the illimitable.' He is right with Christ and he is right with God.

On this note Stavrogin proposes to leave; he asks for Tikhon's prayers, and thanks him for his help. But Tikhon pins him down about the publication of his confession. He knows it will lead into the vicious circle of hurt and pride; what is needed in the situation is less 'I', and publishing will exhibit and produce an excess of 'I'. By putting aside his intention, Stavrogin will 'shame his pride and his devil' and will 'attain his freedom'. He 'awkwardly' (the phrase is Dostoevsky's) mixes it up with worldly language about 'spoiling his career' (Stavrogin's death-wish is virtuously up in arms on this issue), and moralistic talk about the 'inexorability'. But, even so, Stavrogin finally consents not to publish, and he listens attentively as Tikhon gives him the best possible advice: to attach himself secretly to an elder of acknowledged sanctity in the neighbourhood, living in the world but in constant touch with spiritual help. One might feel that the

[35] This is Dostoevsky's criticism of the sectarian legacy in Russia; his remedy is the new orthodoxy: each is responsible for all.
[36] Kozin, op.cit. p.81.   [37] Ibid.

interview was about to produce results. But Stavrogin has been struggling uneasily in its later stages, and Tikhon, in the last stages of exhaustion, seeing that he is about to do the right thing for the wrong reasons, allows the precognitive psychologist in him to take precedence over the spiritual adviser. In something between a trance and prophecy, he sees Stavrogin embarking on another crime; if he does not publish, he will draw attention to himself in another manner, possibly *because* he has decided not to publish. He has no doubt by now that it will somehow concern Liza. In the heat of prophecy, he forgets the suppliant. 'Damned psychologist', Stavrogin remarks as he leaves the room in a rage: it is hard not to agree with him. The monk's insight lets the devil slip through; as we have been told before, it is from the best ingredients that his tastiest triumphs are compounded.

As noted above, the whole novel reads differently when this episode is excluded. The sense of guilt being removed (though it is presupposed in the passages when Stavrogin deplores his failure in achievement), it reads primariiy as the exercise of a formidable will directed against taste and interest. *Stavrogin's Confession* supplies a motive, an effective and convincing motive, for behaviour which otherwise looks just arbitrary. It makes the whole work richer and at the same time more confused: for omnivolence should not be inspired by anything but itself. Once again, as in *Crime and Punishment*, Dostoevsky conflates two themes which have something in common: in either case, the fatal obstruction is concern with the 'I'. But we are concerned with the bearing of the episode on Dostoevsky's understanding of religion; and in this connection it is most illuminating. It stresses again the knife-edge balance between plenary atheism and total belief; it shows how pride in a good intention may wholly subvert it; it takes the new and startling point that the sinner must forgive himself if God is to forgive him; but perhaps the most illuminating touch of all is Tikhon's failure to restrain his justifiable forebodings, with the result that a patient (penitent might be too strong a word) goes out with the spiritual night he was trying to escape. He correctly identifies the patient's condition, but by blurting it out ranges the patient's pride and perversity behind it. He continues to find fault with his motivation, even when he has agreed not to publish. Publish or not publish: either way Stavrogin can't win: and therefore Tikhon can't win either. Like Myshkin, he is a protagonist in a Christian tragedy. The irony of it is that the advice which Tikhon has been giving right up to his disastrous outbreak of clairvoyance, and which Stavrogin has at least not rejected, was wise, gentle and sensible: to station himself as a sort of out-patient in a living Christian community, sharing in the joys and griefs and everyday concerns of others, would have helped to erode his besetting and formidable 'I'. What Tikhon learnt to his cost was that the accusing finger, no matter how well directed, is not an instrument of rehabilitation. Dostoevsky prepares the way for his failure by continued remarks about his awkwardness and his bad health; the ending is not an author's accident. But it does mean that on the likes of Stavrogin – a 'loner', without roots, without affections, without a society: a nihilist *par excellence* – even a highly trained and disciplined Christian may work in vain. And perhaps this is why Dostoevsky, then three years further ahead in his pilgrimage, did not trouble to reintegrate the excised chapter in the published volume.

Of course, what Tikhon prophesied happened. Without his intention, but with his foreknowledge, Stavrogin's legal wife was killed to clear his way; because he was too honest, or by this time too indifferent to be dishonest, he admitted it to Liza, who might otherwise have followed him 'like a dog'; in the end he could not consent to fall back on the ministrations of Darya Pavlovna; and he died by hanging himself, like Matryosha. Kirillov staged his final metaphysical experiment; the 'devils' claimed Shatov; deserted by their rogue of a leader, they wrecked themselves by their great stupidity: the administration was saved despite its even greater stupidity; and the only hope remaining is that the devils have plunged into the lake along with the swine. Even so, there are plenty more of them. Neither the way of wilfulness nor the way of self-punishment, neither the way of Western liberalism nor the inheritance of the sects, has any light to throw on the all-pervading darkness. The only alternative, we shall see, is the way of religious consentience, in which the 'I' is infinitely enhanced and its exclusiveness totally eliminated. Before that perspective *The Possessed* stops short. There is just a hint of it when Tikhon suggests, as an antidote, an unostentatious attachment to a religious community. But in the novel as published even this is obscured, and we are left with the spectacle of evil devouring its own children. Perhaps it is the darkness before the dawn.

Variations on the Earthly Paradise

Between the appearance of *The Possessed* in 1872 and the first instalments of *The Brothers Karamazov* in 1878 there is comparatively little *artistic* evidence for Dostoevsky's religious development. There is factually no doubt about it: he was home, he was happier, he attended church services, and had even taken steps to strengthen his theology. Also, there was journalistically no doubt about it: as we have seen, there are emphatic confessions of his politico-religious faith in the *Diary*. Artistically, he was absorbed by *The Raw Youth*; a curious work, prolix, over-complicated, narrated in the first person by a youth so raw as to be somewhat tiresome, and though revealing incidental religious glimpses, mainly concerned with the depicting of an aristocratic 'double'. Versilov is the most deliberate of all Dostoevsky's experiments in this *genre*, and if only he were not obscured by the oblique stop-go method of narration, the most strikingly successful. That the work should somehow fail to reach the level of his major fiction shows that the greatness of Dostoevsky lay not in pure psychology but in his capacity to register metaphysical insights and apprehensions in narrative form.

The lack of religious enquiry has been various ascribed to a political move leftwards, a return to Utopia, and/or romanticism, a treaty of peace between religion and the world. The political motive can be briefly disposed of. It was the creation of Dostoevsky's right-wing friends, Maykov and Strakhov. They were disgusted with him for submitting *The Raw Youth* to his old radical crony, the poet Nekrasov, editor of the liberal journal *Sovremennik*. If Dostoevsky had been a traditional conservative, he would not have done it: but Katkov was running *Anna Karenina* as a serial in *Russky Vestnik* and had no room for a second ambitious project, and Dostoevsky, as an ex-radical, had personal contacts and certain sympathies in the liberal camp. He had always favoured the liberation of the serfs; he believed in judicial reform; he advocated the freedom of literature from the censorship; and on one issue he was further to the left than many liberals: he hated, as much as any socialist, competitive individualism. He was also intensely patriotic and by now a committed Christian; but if Nekrasov was prepared to accept him, he was prepared to work for Nekrasov.[1] Incidentally, Nekrasov gave him a free hand; and though Dostoevsky may have exercised a certain self-censorship (he always wrote with his readers in mind) there is much more religion in *The Raw Youth* than is sometimes allowed; characters are apt, in character, to quote scripture as they never did, for example, in *The Idiot*: two of them, the narrator's nominal father, Makar Dolgoruky, and his real mother (another Sofya) are cast in a religious mould,[2] and in a memorable monologue Versilov, though ambiguously, as befits a 'double', speaks of the Golden Age, past and future, as a possibility on earth, in a context full of Dostoevsky's known formal opinions. The fact is that Dostoevsky had a cross-bench type of mind, and while vehemently national and absolutely distrustful of competitive co-existence as a way of living, had nothing of the traditionalist in his character. The traditionalists saw it and reacted accordingly. Their verdict was that of Dr Johnson on David Hume: 'Sir, the fellow is a Tory by chance.'

The other characterizations of the new emphasis – a return to romanticism and Utopia, and a reconciliation of Christ with the way things go – are more to the point. This is the stage of

[1] Eventually he pronounced a formal eulogy at Nekrasov's funeral in 1878.

[2] True, they are both old-fashioned long-suffering peasant-type Christians, with great powers of endurance but without initiative – the standard Christian of the Soviet critics – and without 'the thirst for swift achievement' of Alyosha Karamazov. But they are depicted with deep sympathy, and Dolgoruky, at least, in his role as a populist pilgrim, gives expression to a Christian romanticism which had seemed to be extinguished in Dostoevsky in 1849.

Dostoevsky's writing at which he produces, in a puzzling variety of contexts, visions of the earthly paradise. The first, which is already behind him, occurs in the course of Stavrogin's confession. The second and third are in *The Raw Youth*; Dolgoruky's simple hymn of glorification to nature, and Versilov's sophisticated forecast of a possible non-theistic paradise with nostalgic Christian undertones; the fourth, which we take out of sequence, is in the youthful poem on *The Geological Cataclysm* by Ivan Karamazov, of which his devil double embarrassingly reminds him; and the last, and in many ways most significant, is in *The Dream of the Ridiculous Man*, contributed to the *Diary* in 1877. These diverse versions of a persisting vision are distributed, in Dostoevsky's usual way, over a variety of voices; but their content remains stable, and must be taken seriously, for they are absorbed into the religious panorama of Father Zosima in *The Brothers Karamazov*. It is expressed cautiously, as a dream, as a working vision, as a personal utterance in character for which the author cannot be held responsible; but the cumulative effect is unmistakable. However, we must let the documents speak for themselves.

1. We recall that Stavrogin, in a hotel in a small town in Germany, dreamt of a halcyon scene in the Greek islands, the cradle of European humanity, when gods came down from the heavens and mixed with people, when everyone was happy and innocent, and a great abundance of inspired forces went out into love and simple-minded happiness; so different from the world of sacrifice and crucifixion that it brought happiness into his own heart even to the point of pain. In a way, in the dream he knew he was dreaming; so it seemed to be part of the dream that he woke and saw, in the light of the setting sun, a little red spider on a geranium leaf.[3] It was then that he awoke properly, sat up in his bed, and *saw* (repeat, saw) Matryosha on the threshold, frightened and feverish, and shaking her little fist.

There can be little doubt here. The Greek islands are a European Garden of Eden. The terrestial paradise is definitely

---

[3] That spider, the sure sign in Dostoevsky of an approaching metaphysical obscenity.

lost and is only a dream. Nor has the dream, as far as we can see, any 'latent content' other than a sense of guilt in Stavrogin himself. It is located in the past, at a distance and separated off from the world he lived in. And it ended in the waking spiritual horror which disabled him for the rest of his life. There is no temptation to take it for anything but what it claims to be: a fugitive and retrospective glimpse of what now at least is unattainable.

2. By way of contrast, in Dolgoruky's paean the vision is not only not unattainable, it has been attained.

In the summer in July we were hastening to the monastery of Our Lady for the holy festival. The nearer we got to the place the greater the crowd of people, and at last there were almost two hundred of us gathered together, all hastening to kiss the holy and miraculous relics of the two great saints, Aniky and Grigory. We spent the night in the open country, and I waked up early in the morning, when all was still sleeping and the sun had not yet peeped out from behind the forest . . . Everywhere beauty passing all utterance! All was still, the air was light; the grass grows – Grow, grass of God, the bird sings – Sing, bird of God; the babe cries in the woman's arms – God be with you little man; grow and be happy, little babe. And it seemed that only then for the first time I took it all in. Life is sweet, dear . . . And that it's a mystery only makes it better; it fills the heart with awe and wonder, and that awe maketh glad the heart: 'All is in Thee, my Lord, and I, too, am in Thee, have me in Thy keeping' . . . (pp. 354–55).

Here we have a nature-mysticism unexpected in so inveterate a city-dweller as Dostoevsky; one in which God is brought infinitely near, without doctrine, without even Christ – the saints and the festival are only the occasion. There is a quiet rejoicing about it which does not demand action or responses; only that awareness should be expanded to the utmost. What inspires the awe is the mystery; but there is no doubt that but everything is in God. There is no question of time: the blessed moment is here and now. And there is no attempt to meet the counter-evidence from evil and suffering; what is here and now is utterly decisive. That is undoubtedly one pole of Dostoevsky's experience: the other concerns other people, and that is something that Dolgoruky's lyricism does not touch. But it does reveal the personal angle, later to be adopted by Zosima, and in surprisingly naturalist terms. How far the mode of expression so appropriately devised for Makar Dolgoruky would have been used by Dostoevsky in his own person, it is hard to determine:[4] but it is presented, at least, not as the prelude to a bad dream, but as a living reality.

Our third sample, also from *The Raw Youth*, is by contrast subtle and complicated. It is the main part of Versilov's long explanation of himself to his natural son, the 'raw youth' of the piece, and it begins with the account of a dream, described in exactly the same words as Stavrogin's: they had not appeared in *The Possessed*, as printed, and were at Dostoevsky's disposal for his next venture. Like Stavrogin, Versilov claims to have seen the picture by Claude Lorraine, *Acis and Galatea*, in the gallery at Dresden;[5] like Stavrogin, he has an overwhelming experience of delight in the climate and society of 'the Golden Age' in the Greek islands of long ago. There are even the same plants flowering on the window-sill. But there is no spider, and no apparition: only a sense that the setting sun which woke him marked the end of European civilization. There follows a long disquisition, which could equally well have figured in Dostoevsky's public *Diary*, on the universality of Russians and the particularism of Germans, Frenchmen and Englishmen; who are doomed for their exclusiveness to 'pass through fearful agonies before they attain the Kingdom of God'. Arkady takes him up: he is determined once and for all to understand him. 'Did you believe so much in God?' He has said that he is sad about atheism in the West, but 'they are strong in logic, and in logic there is always sadness'. They will go their way, and Versilov continues, in answer to the question, 'Supposing I did not believe very much, yet I could not help grieving for the idea.' He cannot

[4] In an article on Dostoevsky and Nekrasov, in *Dostoevsky i ego vremya* (Dostoevsky and his Time), Nauka, Moscow 1965, p. 178, V. A. Tunimanov quotes from the Ms. project for *The Raw Youth*, to the effect that the 'Makarovy', as they were at that stage, were planned to represent 'Old Holy Russia'. They are quite deliberately archaic.

[5] Dostoevsky knew that gallery very well: cf. the diary of Anna Grigoryevna: *The Diary of Dostoevsky's Wife*, ed. René Fulop-Miller and Dr Fr. Eckstein, tr. Madge Pemberton, Victor Gollancz 1928, pp. 35f., 39f., 199f.

imagine the world without God, but he foresees that somewhere, somehow, it will happen. And then: 'I always imagined a different picture' (p. 466). Without their God, men would feel like orphans, but for that very reason would draw more closely and lovingly together. With the disappearance of immortality, the great abundance of their love 'would be turned upon the whole of nature, on the world, on men, on every blade of grass'.[6] In their metaphysical sadness, men will stand together, working for each other and sharing all they have, and only so will they be happy. 'They would be in haste to love, to stifle the great sorrow in their hearts.' And then, breaking off, Versilov adds: (1) though it is only a fantasy, he cannot live without thinking about it;[7] (2) as to faith, he has not a great deal: he is a sort of philosophical deist, 'like all our thousand', i.e. the rootless Russian nobility; but (3), surprisingly, he cannot complete his picture without Christ, as depicted in Heine's poem *Christ on the Baltic Sea*.[8]

I could not help imagining him, in the midst of his bereaved people. He comes to them, holds out his hands, and asks them 'How could they forget him?' And then, as it were, the scales would fall from their eyes, and there would break forth the great rapturous hymn of the new and last resurrection (p. 469).

What does it all mean? (1) The picture of the earthly paradise is offered as an alternative to the displaced picture of God. (2) Admitting that he is not quite ready for the change, Versilov believes that the future is with it. (3) He is unable to keep Christ out of the picture, and thinks he will be more than ever necessary in an 'orphaned', i.e. a godless, world. He foresees 'Christian atheism', and with only a passing sadness assents to it in advance. (4) What Versilov says at any one time is no evidence for the total Versilov, and still less for Dostoevsky. In particular, the denial of immortality embodied in the picture is wholly opposed

[6] Here he sees in an atheist context what Dolgoruky saw in the context of God.
[7] Again, that deliberate distancing.
[8] Heine wrote *Nordsee*; whether Dostoevsky was simply inaccurate, or whether he really thought *Nordsee* was German for the Baltic, it is hard to determine. In any case he has appropriated much of Heine's imagery from its Hanseatic context and set it down in the Aegean.

to his stressing of it in his 'prose' writings of the period. (5)
Nevertheless, one can discern a sympathy: the theme of the
earthly paradise had an early fascination for him, and with only
a change of key it enters into the religious discourses of Makar
Dolgoruky and Father Zosima. (6) But since his encounter with
evil in Siberia – not just malpractice, but evil in its full psycholo-
gical-metaphysical dimension – the earthly paradise is represented for the time by dreams and visions and exercises in
dissociation, appropriate enough to 'doubles' like Versilov, but not
enough for the rescue of the whole man. (7) It is a surprise to
see Christ thrown in for good measure; the same kind of surprise
as in Belinsky's letter to Gogol. Dostoevsky in his day had
moved in these regions; he knew that they were unbearable; he
also knew that he had never rejected Christ. Versilov here incapsulates something of his author's history.

If this is a fair estimate, the passage does not support the
ultra-Orthodox contention that Dostoevsky in the mid 70's was
ready to relapse into the humanism of his youth. The earthly
paradise is effectively distanced. But it is entertained, no longer
as the prelude to a nightmare, but as something too good to be
true; putting it together with the nature-mysticism of Dolgoruky, we may anticipate that it has only to escape from its
atheist setting to be accepted as a living reality.

That, however, is not the trend of our next variation: Ivan
Karamazov's *Geological Cataclysm*. It is taken out of its apparent
chronological order, because it was an early composition and
may be regarded as belonging to a more primitive geological
stratum than Versilov's sophisticated presentation of the same
theme. Here there is no wistfulness about the loss of God: on
the contrary, it is the starting-point for the whole development.
'As soon as men have denied God . . . everything will begin
anew. Men will wish to take from life all that it can give, but
only for joy and happiness. Man will be lifted up with a spirit of
divine Titanic pride and the man-God will appear. From hour to
hour extending his conquest of nature infinitely by his will and
his science, man will find such lofty joy from hour to hour in
doing that it will make up for all his old dreams of the joys of

heaven . . . He will love his brother without need of reward.'[9]
And so on. ('Charming', say the devil.) It will not happen all at
once: man is too stupid: but even in the interim, man being his
own God, and there being no law for God, 'all is permitted.'

Here is an earthly paradise with the lid off: will, pride, science,
and the man-God; in fact Feuerbach's metamorphosis of God
into man, as accepted by Dostoevsky in his period of alienation,
1845–46. But it has one thing in common with the populist
mysticism of Dolgoruky: the conviction that the end-product
will be joy and happiness and the love of one's brother-man. To
many of us, and certainly to Dostoevsky, the connection is not
evident; in default of God, human excellence is only too likely
to be corrupted by its own success. What this passage shows is
that in elaborating this theme Dostoevsky passes it through
subtle and significant modulations. There is something here not
observable in any of the three previous variations: the emphasis
on human activity. Without that Dostoevsky could not have
advanced to the association of the earthly paradise with *active*
love which appears in *The Brothers Karamazov*.

Finally there is *The Dream of a Ridiculous Man*. Dated 1877, it
stands just in front of that gigantic masterpiece, and it must be
taken as an imaginative construction of his later period. Once
again, the difficulty is to know how to read it. It is a 'dream', and
the man is 'ridiculous': this suggests, as Wasiolek remarks, that
we should not take it as Dostoevsky's opinion just as it stands.[10]
But neither does it mean, as Wasiolek proceeds to argue, that
Dostoevsky is totally disowning it. But let us see.

The 'ridiculous man' had always been ridiculous. He suffered
from his plight so much that he proposed to put an end to himself. One damp night, on his way home, he was intercepted by a
ragged little girl, obviously terrified. He did not help her, and
she flew across the street to another passer-by. He went home
and decided it was a good time to carry out his intention. He was
worried that he had done nothing for the child, and that worry
meant that something did matter. But what was the use, if one

[9] *The Brothers Karamazov*, pp. 701–2.
[10] *Dostoevsky: the Major Fiction*, p. 146.

was going to be nothing at all in an hour or two? Turning these questions over he unexpectedly went to sleep in his arm-chair, with his revolver on the table in front of him. And he had his dream.

He dreamt that he had shot himself, and was being escorted through the air by an unseen companion towards a visible desti- nation – a star in the far distance. It turned out to be Europe. He was landed and his companion disappeared. He was on, or oppo- site, one of the Greek islands (this visual image is common to most of the 'experiences' of the earthly paradise). Here every- one and everything was united in a sort of 'childish joy'. 'It was the earth untarnished by the Fall; on it lived people who had not sinned.' They had no need of science or progress; 'they did not aspire to knowledge of life as we aspire to understand it, because their lives were full'. They were utterly and instinctively attuned to nature, to the animals and to each other. They knew nothing of jealousy, cruelty or competition. As for religion: 'They had no temples, but they had a real living and uninterrupted sense of oneness with the whole of the universe; they had no creed, but they had a certain knowledge that when their earthly joy had reached the limits of earthly nature, then there would come for them, for the living and for the dead, a still greater fullness of contact with the whole of the universe.' They listened to the stranger without understanding but with sympathy when he spoke of the ambivalences of his former life, and in their presence he seemed to become as innocent as they.

But his very presence seems to have been a contamination. One by one, they learnt all the vices of a civilized and progres- sive Petersburger. They discovered lying, sensuality, bloodshed, strife, shame ('and shame brought them to virtue'), honour, cruelty to animals, individuality, mine and thine, separate lan- guages, and acquaintance with sorrow. They began to say (as Dostoevsky has often been accused of saying) that 'truth could only be attained by suffering'. As they became wicked, they talked humanitarianism, as they became criminal, they invented justice. There followed slavery, war, extermination, suicide. The intruder blamed himself and asked to be crucified,; but they found no fault in him; 'they had only got what they wanted'. And they were just going to lock him up in a lunatic asylum when – he awoke.

But he did not, like Stavrogin, see an accusing apparition; he did not, like Versilov, switch over to political analysis; he felt new life coming to him. He put away the revolver, and resolved to spread the good news everywhere. Clumsily, of course; he is still 'ridiculous'; but now he just couldn't care less. 'I have seen the truth; I have seen and know that people can be beautiful and happy without losing the power of living on earth. I will not and cannot believe that evil is the normal condition of mankind.' If it is said: 'but this is a dream', is not our life a dream? And in any case, it is all perfectly simple: it could be arranged in an hour; on two conditions. The first is to love others like oneself; an old story, but 'it has not formed part of our lives'. The second is to repudiate the civilized sophisticated conviction that 'the consciousness of life is higher than life, the knowledge of the laws of happiness higher than happiness'.

There is a postscript: 'And I tracked down that little girl . . . and I shall go on and on.' That is to say, he has started off by *doing* something.[11]

This summary inevitably loses some of the vividness: Dostoevsky depends here, as elsewhere, on continuous elaboration. But it brings home certain points which, we know, were his constant concern. The theme that scientific knowledge of people is neither a substitute nor a basis for personal relations, the theme that humanitarianism is a sign of inward corruption, to take just two examples, are the writer's waking and constant concerns. But we have learned how Dostoevsky can have his most intimate convictions spoken by alien voices, and, along with them, we find in this dream elements which we might have expected his personal voice to repudiate. Dostoevsky did on occasions lend himself to the view, here deprecated, that truth could only be obtained by suffering. He did not hold that temples and creeds were irrelevant or even secondary. And there is no sign of irony in the writing. The ridiculous man is wholly in

11 *An Honest Thief and Other Stories*, pp. 382–405.

earnest, and Dostoevsky is wholly in earnest about him. He could, of course, be speaking in character; it is difficult to judge, for outside his recital he has no character. What is clear, however, is that Dostoevsky does not proceed, as in the two previous cases, to put him into perspective. The narrator says: if this is a dream, if indeed it will never come to pass, he will go on preaching it, and Dostoevsky does not, as he could so easily have done, take the wind out of his sails.[12] In the absence of any literary indications, we have no option but to examine the alignment of the *Dream* with Dostoevsky's other purposes at that time.

In the first place, there is no question of the earthly paradise being round the corner. Evil preoccupies Dostoevsky in *The Brothers Karamazov* as agonizingly as in *The Possessed*. The world he lives in is a real world, a tough world, in which are unsparingly displayed all the wickednesses exhibited by the dream-islanders after the Fall (as it is significantly called). The picture of the world as fundamentally an harmonious and happy place is not inconsistent with his realistic appraisal of things as they are. The novels, of course, are about things as they are; but it makes a difference when these are viewed against a background of better earthly possibilities. In the *Dream* we are given a picture of things *before* the Fall; and it is not even unorthodox to date the unpleasant realities from the Fall itself. Dostoevsky could not have been expected to study the intra-Calvinist dispute between supralapsarians and infralapsarians; but he is, along with many other Christians of all sorts, infralapsarian: there is no sin in the world before the Fall. It is a state of innocence that the *Dream* depicts, not the achievement of saintliness. Nevertheless, some of its characters are carried over into the saintliness due to emerge on the other side of the disaster. Saintliness, equally with innocence, is in the world and an ingredient of ordinary living. The saint, as well as the innocent, will be moved by love of the neighbour, will have a feeling for all things; he will talk to trees and animals; he will close down on the oppres-

[12] N. I. Prutskov, in an analytic study of the *Dream* (*Dostoevsky i ego vremya*, pp. 88–107) entitled 'Utopia or anti-Utopia', stresses the call to action, and points out that Dostoevsky approved the 'higher comedy' as a means for serious intentions: cf. his admiration for Cervantes.

sive I, in his competitiveness and his isolation; he will be consentient by the grace of God as the innocent is consentient by the
premonitory grace of nature. There is a gap to be crossed. How
vulnerable innocence is can be gauged from the fact that one
visitor who did not share in it involuntarily corrupted the whole
community. But there is also a continuity: it is not irrelevant to
remind those who are about to face, in fictional form, the great
contemporary evils, that they are corruptions of nature, and not
nature herself. It is even more important for those who face the
same evils in real life; for it makes a difference to the whole
mood and manner of our striving whether our challenge is
directed to the distortions or to the whole structure of things.

We shall be reminded of the criticism of Leontyev (cf. p. 6
above), here more than usually relevant, for the *Dream* makes
the intervention and even the definition of God subsequent to the
Fall (this, in fact, was the point taken by supralapsarian theologians). There are signs that he might have viewed the sequence dialectically: to go from innocence to saintliness you have
to pass through the middle ground of sin and morality; and in
fact Dostoevsky is sometimes criticized (as by Carr, p. 20) for
viewing sin as the necessary preliminary to salvation. On this
view, the *Dream* states the thesis and the great fiction the antithesis, facing towards a synthesis, for the first time, in *The
Brothers Karamazov*. That is as may be: what it certainly does is
to remind us that the evil in the world, though threatening and
ubiquitous, is not indelible. It also reminds us that pride is the
substance of the Fall, that morality, law and science are consequences of the Fall, that what saves is fellow-feeling (it was an
irritable sense of unwarranted neglect of the little girl's appeal
which, rankling in the narrator's conscience, saved him from
suicide); and that the 'going on and on' starts with the positive
effort to track her down and help her. So engaged, he sheds his
pride and his shame and does not in the least mind being thought
ridiculous. Not very theological? But neither is a dream and
neither was Dostoevsky. We are not happy, and we were meant
to be: and, with no more than a change of disposition, we can
be. If we combine in this spirit with true consentience, we can

exorcise the devils; and we shall have installed the Russian Christ.

Summing up, we may note the following points: (1) The *Dream*, presenting the prospective suicide with a vision of natural goodness, did literally save him. It changed despair into confidence, self-absorption into self-spending. (2) The structure of the Fall-story remains: the earthly paradise is located in the past and in the distance: it is not in Skotoprigonyevsk in 1878. But that it should ever have been, anywhere, is a challenge; what has been, by sacrifice and togetherness, may be again. The apocalypse feeds upon the golden age. (3) Those who think the world essentially evil (Manichees and other dualists) will disagree. Our only concern here is that Dostoevsky, after long vacillation, finally takes his stand against them. (4) In the *Dream*, God is as it were dissolved into the community. It does not follow that the same situation holds in the world of the Karamazovs. It should be noted, however, that for Dostoevsky, God was in Christ to such a degree that he had difficulty in envisaging the divine transcendence. Merging God in the community of Christ-seekers was a temptation to him at all times. The *Dream* even merges him in a community of innocents. Leontyev had a point here. (5) The convert, preaching to others, is tempted to slur a central episode in the *Dream*: his own performance as an arch-corrupter. He puts this right, thereby acknowledging that only by admitting his failures can be help his fellows. It is a lead-up to Zosima's 'Each is responsible to all'. (6) What is not revealed in the *Dream*, and it is vital to Dostoevsky both personally and as a novelist, is the figure of Christ. Presumably, as these folk are in a state of innocence, it would be an anachronism. The condition which the convert preaches is in fact the Golden Rule: 'the chief thing is to love others like yourself', and when he first woke up from his dream he 'called upon eternal truth'; 'not with words, but with tears'. It looks as if Dostoevsky were setting out to state Christian truth anonymously: to confront us with the content, but to stop short of guiding us to its source. In an admittedly fantastic short story, that is perhaps all that can be expected; but his theological reticence is curious, especially as

the story appeared in his own anything-but-reticent *Diary*. Moreover, much is set aside (e.g. questions of immortality and
institutional religion) to which Dostoevsky at the time is known
to have attached a high importance. It is for these reasons that
critics like Wasiolek have treated the *Dream* as an exposure of
the humanism it expresses, and it is certain that Dostoevsky
would not have vouched for it as it stands. But, taken not so
much as a thesis but rather as a musical theme, it has its significance. Making all allowance for Dostoevsky's gift for ideological
disguises, I can only record my artistic impression that it is
seriously entertained. For one thing, it remarkably resembles
certain utterances of the unquestionably Christian Father Zosima.
For another, it ends with an anthropologically Christian formula.
And, finally, there is a certain playfulness in the writing, which
though it serves to distance the theme, none the less coaxes us to
entertain it. The general effect is that Dostoevsky is building a
bridge back to the world of which the *Dream* is an eloquently
fantastical blueprint.

In this sequence of visions, presented not logically or even
chronologically, but as variations on a theme, we note a persistent emphasis on the natural goodness of things, together
with diverse degrees of and grounds for reservation. For Stavrogin the earthly paradise is wholly a dream, and a prelude to the
permanent nightmare; for Dolgoruky it is a mystical personal
conviction, a call to spiritual separation and not to action; for
Versilov it is both an intellectual diversion and a wishful forecast
of the best that can happen in a godless world; in *The Geological
Cataclysm* it is a planned project backed by the will and the knowledge of the self-appointed man-God; for the 'ridiculous man' it
is again a dream, but a dream which issues in action. There are
wide variations; what never changes is that happiness and goodness belong to the world and that people are in the world to help
and cherish each other. So far (except for Dolgoruky) there is no
explicit reference to God; and both Ivan and Versilov assume
his absence. Again, so far, only Ivan and the *Ridiculous Man*
connect the context of the earthly paradise with action. What we
await in *The Brothers Karamazov* is the linkage of the requirements

of action with an explicit reference to God – a reference which is present in the *Dream*, but concealed by what looks like a deliberate disconnection. That is what the sequence calls for. Of the difficulties of effecting it, *The Brothers Karamazov* tells us abundantly.

SEVEN

Each and All: The Brothers Karamazov

I

The Brothers Karamazov, more than any other work of Dostoevsky's, was consciously dominated by a religious concern. By the time he wrote it, he was publicly committed to the faith – not merely to a growing personal conviction but to the outward observances. For the first time, he felt he was executing some kind of a Christian commission and was responsible to his fellow-believers for its success or failure. For example, concerning the figure of Father Zosima: 'I will compel people to admit that a pure ideal Christianity is not an abstraction, but a vivid reality, possibly near at hand, and that Christianity is the sole refuge of the Russian land from all its evils.'[1] So he worked on him with 'fear and trembling'. But in writing for the Christian community, he was writing against himself. He had a number of scores to settle with his own past. His faith had emerged from 'a cauldron of doubt', and unless he could turn on the causes of that doubt and dispel them, he could not carry out his commission with a clear conscience. He embodied them in Ivan Karamazov, so convincingly that good critics have concluded that artistically at least he failed in his objective: he allowed Ivan to steal the show. We shall offer reasons for thinking this view to be mistaken; but if he had not done everything he could to build up his atheist it would not even have arisen.

The book is not about a single hero, but about a family. It

[1] To Lyubimov, *Pisma* IV, p. 59.

revolves around the fortunes and misfortunes of the Karamazovs:
the lascivious cunning cynical buffoon Fyodor Pavlovich, the
father of the others, whom in their different ways they all recapi-
tulate: Dmitri, the eldest, romantic, lyrical, honourable, but
sensual and impulsive; his half-brother Ivan, subtle, secretive,
intellectual, another sensualist but a disdainful one, and an
atheist from compassion; Ivan's full brother, Alexey (Alyosha),
open-hearted and happy, healthy and realistic; a novice at the
neighbouring monastery, but it is hinted that he is just another
Karamazov, and his turn is yet to come; and their illegitimate
half-brother, known as Smerdyakov ('Stinkers'), a valet in his
father's household, earnest, ambitious, with all his father's cunning, but limited, epileptic, and at the mercy of anyone he admires (as it happens, Ivan). The work as a whole can be read as
the story of Dmitri, or of Ivan, or of Alyohsa: it has in fact been
read in all these ways, naturally with different results. It is best
read by keeping the whole of the family in perspective the whole
of the time.

First, Dmitri. He is the pivot of nearly all the action of the
novel; he is also the one completely original character appearing
in it – the others are re-deployments of characters in earlier
works. It is Dmitri's property that his father has encroached
upon; it is Dmitri's 'bad faith' engagement to Katerina Ivanovna
and his rivalry with his father over Grushenka which trigger off
the events leading to his father's murder; it is Dmitri who is
tried and convicted for the murder; it is Dmitri whose rescue is
being planned when the novel ends.[2] The only outward event
which does not originate with Dmitri, despite appearances, is the
murder itself. From the point of view of the plot, he is the heart
and centre. He has, it is true, views about the world; passionate
and romantic ones, such as: 'God and the devil are at strife, and
the battleground is the heart of man'; and it is he, not Alyosha,
who proclaims the curative value of suffering. But he is not a
thinker; when it comes to the metaphysical issues surrounding
and embodied in the plot, the spotlight falls on Ivan. But Dmitri

---

[2] In a letter to N. A. Lyubimov, Katkov's sub-editor, 16 November 1879, he
tells how the character of Dmitri grew upon him. *Pisma* IV, p. 118.

remains the central figure for those who are more interested in plot, in the ordinary sense, than in the superplay of the *idées-forces*.

Ivan is cultivated, rational and highly educated; he is sensitive and well-mannered, and at times charming; but what lies behind is anyone's guess. Dmitri once described him as a 'tomb' (p. 241) but he himself could hardly be more remote and reserved than Dostoevsky when presenting him. Like Stavrogin, he is kept in the half-light – deliberately, so that the reader will have to make up his own mind about the succession of his 'dissimilarities'. We have to find things out about him behind his back. For example, Katerina is said to be in love with him, but there is no record of a private conversation between them; we first learn of their mutual attraction from the prattle of Rakitin, and in one scene only do we meet them together – in the company of other people. We do not even know why this brilliant graduate and Moscow journalist should have chosen to return to the provinces and settle with his father. Even about his *Weltanschauung* there is a certain ambiguity. He is an atheist, yet he writes about ecclesiastical courts, arguing that church should include state; he argues that 'all is permitted', yet gives evidence against himself at the trial, fruitlessly as it turns out but with complete sincerity; and he produced that literary masterpiece, 'The Legend of the Grand Inquisitor', the purport of which, in relation to his own and to his author's opinions, it is hard to disentangle. Why he should have wished his father dead we have no idea: if we speculate about Oedipus complex, we are merely talking generalities. (He is on record, after the event, as saying: 'he was a pig, but his ideas were right enough'.) He gives Smerdyakov his first introduction to general ideas, and it fascinates him. The poor frustrated lackey with the polished boots and the pomaded hair, puts his whole trust in him 'as in God almighty' and would do anything oblige him. Having heard that 'everything is permitted', he thinks to help him by persuading him to go away and killing his father during his absence.[3] When Ivan finds out that his half-

[3] Dostoevsky explained to his correspondent E. M. Lyebedeva (11 August 1879, *Pisma* IV, p. 117). that Ivan refrained from restraining Smerdyakov from an evil deed which he in fact foresaw and thus permitted Smerdyakov to perform it. Without this 'permission' Smerdyakov would not have done it.

formed wish has been translated into action, he is horrified; when he discovers that it was done in his interest, he takes the blame for the unfulfilled intentions. In doing so he betrays a high-minded scruple very far from 'all is permitted', and it is only because Katerina, to save him, produces Dmitri's damaging letter to her that 'the peasants stood firm' and convicted Dmitri after all. Before his collapse he launches the plan for rescuing Dmitri on the way to Siberia, and Dmitri remarks, 'He is superior to all of us' (p. 823). But the tension leaves him in spiritual disarray. He is an atheist who believes that the consequences of atheism are 'all is permitted', and he never recants; but in practice he finds himself sensitively responsive to points of conscience. Smerdyakov said to him at their last interview that he was more like their common father than any of his children. In subtlety and indirectness, yes: but Fyodor Pavlovich would never have agonized, he would only have posed, and would certainly not have given evidence against himself.

Of Ivan's opinions we shall speak presently; they are the intellectual centre of the story. Here we are concerned to tabulate his actions: and it is by displaying their ambivalence, not simply, as Dostoevsky himself supposed, by exhibiting Zosima, that he makes his point even about the opinions. 'Our Russian atheism', in an honest and self-critical exponent, baulks at the hurdle.[4] Ivan's part in the story, as opposed to his disquisitions and his literary exercises, is far from supporting 'all is permitted' or the beliefs from which it purports to be derived. The best evidence against what he says is what he does.[5]

---

[4] Of course, it could be denied that atheism entails 'all is permitted'. As Belkin remarks (in *Tvorchestvo Dostoevskogo*), it guides some people into self-forgetful public service. So it does. But what Dostoevsky was probing was the anarchist version current in his day; and it is not wholly of antiquarian interest.

[5] Three sidelights on Ivan, and on Dostoevsky: (1) Ivan begins his discourse on God and suffering by saying: 'I could never understand how one can love one's neighbours' (p. 248). If it is only love that enables one to see God among other things, this is his fundamental disability. (2) He is too proud to owe anything to anyone: Alyosha, on the other hand, knows how to receive graciously (p. 16). (3) Alexey is universally known by the affectionate diminutive Alyosha; Ivan is never Vanya. In all these respects Ivan is shown as one who keeps himself to himself and neither gives nor receives. These are the estimable qualities which Dostoevsky does not admire.

Then Alyosha. He is described as the 'chief, *though future*, hero' of the story;[6] that is to say, the hero of the proposed sequel. He plays only a modest part in the structure of the story as it stands. We know that he is told by Zosima to leave the monastery and bear witness in the world; that he experiences his first crisis after Zosima's death, and very nearly falls – and it is deftly hinted that in his capacity as 'future hero' he will be haunted by the Karamazov inheritance; but he recovers, strengthened by a momentous vision, and continues on his path as the friend and confidant of almost everyone in the story – Dmitri, Ivan, Katerina, and later Grushenka; he is the one person who both understands and is not revolted by his father; he is in fact, as Grushenka expresses it, the 'conscience' of these others; he is a prompter and a comforter in the wings; but he is not a main actor in the tragedy. He does, however, initiate the society of boys headed by Kolya Krasotkin, and the novel ends with Ilyusha's funeral which is received by the group, under his guidance, as an occasion for repentance (they had made things difficult for him) but not for sadness.

Dostoevsky is thus able to end with the hope of immortality; but above all he is able to distance Ivan's terrifying case-histories concerning cruelty to children. It is reasonable to surmise that this little society would have figured largely in the career of the 'future' hero as the 'present' hero of the sequel. For the moment, it is the only answer offered in the novel to Ivan's most agonizing argument. It is a dramatic answer to a theoretical problem – and for Dostoevsky only a dramatic answer was possible.[7] For the rest, Alyosha is being kept in reserve. But enough is said and disclosed about his character to enable us to prognosticate. At nineteen he is 'well-grown, red-cheeked, clean-eyed, radiant with health' (p. 21). He is a 'realist' and the term is deliberately contrasted with 'fanatic' and 'mystic'.[8] He is ordered out into the world; he will marry (presumably that

---

[6] P. 350: author's italics.

[7] The drama, etymologically, is something *done*.

[8] Belkin in *Tvorchestvo Dostoevskogo*, p. 278, is at pains to show that Dostoevsky as an *artist* is critically realist and not religious. In the creating of Alyosha he reveals himself as critically realist *as well as* religious.

disordered little girl, Lise Khoklakhova), he is a full Karamazov (pp. 109, 111) and will be tempted to the limit; and Dostoevsky seems to have told A. S. Suvorin that he would actually become a revolutionary and commit a political crime, working his way back in the end to his religious vocation.[9] It looks as if Alyosha was to take over the role of the *vsechelovek*: only through deviation and suffering could he return. Perhaps that is one application of the scriptural quotation on the title-page: 'Except a corn of wheat fall into the ground and die, it abideth alone, but if it die, it bringeth forth much fruit' (John 12.24). But that is all for the future: as presented to us, though conscious of his Karamazov inheritance and destiny, he is a normal sensible youngster, with a natural gift for 'relating' to people and an understanding of their problems beyond his years (p. 28). The contrast with Myshkin is unmistakeable. Alyosha has some of Myshkin's personal mannerisms, but none of his spiritual disconnectedness, and Myshkin's infirmity is diverted from his successor to the unhappy Smerdyakov. It is in a normal and kindly but determined young man that the new incarnation is to be illustrated: an incarnation which shuns nothing, and can be adequately tested only in a Karamazov.

Yet the critics demur: Alyosha is 'thin and puny';[10] he is 'not one of the best drawn of Dostoevsky's characters';[11] he is 'ascetic and mystical', he preaches the old stale doctrine of salvation through suffering.[12] But he is happy and vigorous, with great powers of recovery, he is brought back from his moment of despair through the most joyous of all the miracles, that of Cana in Galilee; he belongs to the Zosima group of anti-ascetics in his monastery; he is happiest when he can engage *actively* in the works of love (hence his dislike of the argumentative approach

[9] Quoted by Belkin, ibid., p. 291. Suvorin (1834–1912) was a journalist, editor and dramatist, and is described in the entry in *Literaturnaya Entsiklopediya*, XI, Moscow, 1939) as a 'reactionary'. He was also a friend of Dostoevsky's favourite editor, Katkov. He would hardly have invented this compromising confidence. It is just possible that he recorded it as a mark of distrust: Dostoevsky struck his really reactionary friends as not quite reliable.

[10] E. H. Carr, *Dostoevsky, 1821–81*, p. 287.

[11] N. A. Berdyaev, *Dostoievsky; an Interpretation*, p. 120.

[12] Belkin in *Tvorchestvo Dostoevskogo*, p. 276.

to life which throws doubt on his primary objectives, p. 22), and he deliberately tells Dmitri that salvation through suffering is not for him (p. 824). 'You don't need a martyr's cross when you are not ready for it. You wanted to make yourself another man by suffering. I say, only remember that other man always, all your life and wherever you go. Such heavy burdens are not for all men. For some they are impossible.' This, I believe, is Dostoevsky's final word on 'salvation through suffering'.

It is through Alyosha that he finally proclaims it: Alyosha, who contained in himself the sensitivity and the normality which Dostoevsky almost to the end treated as irreconcilable; Alyosha, whose final message to his boys was 'Don't be afraid of life' (p. 838); Alyosha, supposedly ineffective, who with 'merciless emphasis' forces Katerina Ivanovna to visit Dmitri in prison (p. 821); Alyosha, supposedly 'mystical', whose power derives entirely from his rootedness in the basic robustness and normality of life. That he should have been undervalued by so many and diverse readers is due to two principal factors. (1) Mere dislike of and disbelief in his Christian profession, fortified by his failure to challenge Ivan in argument. (2) More creditably, a failure to see that the 'future hero' is only in the preparatory stages. As was said on the occasion of his favourite miracle, 'my hour is not yet come'.

Thus any one of the three brothers, from a particular point of view, is the centre of the story. Dmitri commands the plot; Ivan is the ideological centre;[13] Alyosha is the spiritual climax. As the novel has a plot, an ideology and a destination, none of them can be neglected and all must be held together at every turn of the road. But it is a novel in the first instance, even if it daringly encompasses philosophical discussion and the biography of a saint in the making. As such it is well knit, it is exciting, it is psychologically brilliant; it is a splendidly contrived mystery story, with full control of the circumstantial detail; it contains legal disquisitions for the prosecution and defence, examined for Dostoevsky by trained lawyers, and comparable in their range and

---

[13] 'All the ideological passions flare up round Ivan', Belkin, ibid., p. 274.

versatility to the declamations of Browning's Dominus Hyacin-
thus and Johannes-Baptista Bottinius; and several first-rate
Aristotelian *peripateiai*, with Katerina's final appearance as the
grand climax: and all this without any reference to 'Pro and
Contra' and 'The Russian Monk' (Part Two, Books Five and
Six). Taking the story as it stands without those chapters, it is
mainly about two separate assumptions of guilt for the murder
which neither of those concerned committed: Dmitri's and Ivan's.
Dmitri, romantic, muddled, honourable and impetuous, almost
on the spot when it happened and with every reason to want it to
happen, accepts an unjust conviction and hopes to purge himself
by suffering.[14] Ivan, carelessly expounding 'all is permitted' to
the half-brother who would do anything for him, actually triggers
off the murder and also takes the blame for his intentions. In
both cases conscience claims its own. When Belkin[15] says that
'the blasphemy is presented realistically and its refutation mysti-
cally', he does not sufficiently allow for this feature of the narrative.

But for Dostoevsky that was not enough. He had to make his
'ideology' explicit, and that meant prompting the appropriate
characters to state and refute the atheist thesis. His equipment
for this task was indifferent: but by sheer force and sincerity he
changed the face of theology. Since he wrote, it has become un-
fashionable, not to say impious, to contend that all is for the best
in God's world. Henceforward, no justification of evil, by its
outcome or its context, has been possible; Ivan Karamazov has
seen to that. No idealist theophany can transform evil to the
smallest degree.[16] Theoretically, Ivan's criticisms are unanswered: Alyosha, in particular, simply agrees with him: and
Dostoevsky himself held them to be 'irrefutable'.[17] The answer
is to go forward from theory to practice: and Dostoevsky dis-

[14] It is Dmitri, behaving strictly in character, who talks of the curative value of
suffering. It is not a metaphysical observation, it is not accepted by Alyosha, nor
by the Dostoevsky of 1880.

[15] Belkin in *Tvorchestvo Dostoevskogo*, p. 276.

[16] The words 'religion' and 'idealist', uttered as a pair by Belkin and other
Marxian critics, are in fact incompatibles.

[17] To Lyubimov, *Pisma* IV, p. 53.

tinguished in the end between the yearning love which does nothing and submits, and the active love which has power to save. It was not easy for him: partly because he never quite escaped from the shadow of Belinsky, partly because he drew too sharp a line between thought and action, partly because of the linguistic backwash of the word *smireniye* ('humility'), and partly because the way of acceptance and resignation which it embodies has a high survival value in hard times, was deeply rooted in the life of the Russian peasantry and had been his court of appeal from the violence of his own resentments. But against both resignation and revolt he rose to the conviction, expressed in the reminder of Zosima to Mrs Khokhlakova, and in his delineation of Alyosha, that the love to which we are called is a vigorous and active love, very different from the sweet sentiment of our dreams. Here Dostoevsky passes from the 'problematics' of Ivan[18] to the practicalist faith of Alyosha, which gives the novel its sense of direction even without the projected sequel.[19] On the way, however, he gave his intellectual difficulties a final airing, and he did it so well that his challenge has been widely mistaken for his permanent response. No wonder Pobedonostsev was alarmed, and Dostoevsky himself anxious. He was never able wholly to transcend the intellectual plane, or to work out the dialectic of practical reason, and philosophically this is what his programme requires. But through Zosima and Alyosha he presents us with an attitude to life of which something like the Christian view is both the premiss and the conclusion. As a matter of fact, he does refute Ivan, but indirectly, and not at the point where he tried hardest. This will have to be shown in detail by analysis of the chapters concerned.

[18] A favourite phrase of the Russian critics.

[19] Belkin in *Tvorchestvo Dostoevskogo*, p. 277, finds humility wholly 'reactionary'. He cannot sense its revolutionary overtones, because he assumes that the only effective change is social change. That is why he is so perplexed that anyone as hostile to the bourgeois ethic as Dostoevsky should also be hostile to the revolution which was attacking it. He just does not believe that 'active love' can flow in strictly individual channels. Unfortunately Dostoevsky is writing novels, and the novel *must* be concerned with the story of individuals, over and above their social context. If ever they are submerged in it, the novel as an art-form will have been displaced by that notable non-art-form, the treatise on sociology.

II

There are two contributions to literature recorded in the novel from the pen of that promising young writer, Ivan Karamazov: his unlikely and remarkable treatise on ecclesiastical courts (pp. 58–65) and his superb 'Legend of the Grand Inquisitor' (pp. 259–79). Both are in need of interpretation. There are also two episodes in which he figures which bear upon his religious problems; his discussion with Alyosha, which ends with the 'Legend' and in which he does practically all the talking (pp. 240–59), together with the attempted answer in the shape of Father Zosima's life and reminiscences (pp. 302–45): and there is finally Ivan's 'dream' in which he finds himself face to face with the devil, who insists on recapitulating his discarded opinions and shows him to be in a state of doubt far removed from the confident atheism of his formal profession (pp. 685–703). Taken together, these four interludes, amounting to 107 pages, form the intellectual drama of *The Brothers Karamazov*. As we shall see, they show Ivan intellectually victorious, and defeated in action; another demonstration that 'the atheist is always talking about something else'.

We shall take first the episode which Dostoevsky himself regarded as central: 'Pro and Contra'.

In a tavern, the full brothers Ivan and Alyosha have their first intimate conversation, expected also to be the last. They quickly get down to the 'eternal questions' which Ivan thinks so characteristic of the younger generation. The Moscow intellectual and the provincial novice inevitably come round to religion, and Ivan states his position. Previously when his father had quizzed him on the subject, he had said bluntly, 'there is no God' (p. 139). In a more relaxed mood (Alyosha had that effect on people; for Dostoevsky a Christian effect), he gives his brother the details and the qualifications. He is prepared to admit God, and even that he is drawn to him: it is not primarily a question of 'being', it is a question of 'what *kind* of being'. What he cannot and will not accept is the world which he has made – and let us suppose he has made it: it only strengthens the case against him. It is the *world* which is unacceptable. There are too many cruel terrible things in it here and now, and a happy ending will not obliterate them. Covering another popular loophole, he is prepared to allow the freedom-defence, as far as it will go; but if every adult had entirely deserved his own sufferings (and this is a considerable concession), there remain the children: they have not tasted the apple and cannot be held responsible. He then proceeds to tell horrible stories of cruelty to children, all drawn from Dostoevsky's newspaper scrap-book for 1876. Finally he says that their tears being beyond the reach of atonement (p. 257), seeing that there can and should be no forgiveness (p. 258), he doesn't want the final harmony. The price is too high and as an honest man he will respectfully 'give back his entrance ticket'.

It is because the challenge is so moderate that it is so formidable. I first read it fifty years ago, and my theology has never been the same since. It may, I think, be taken to represent Ivan's genuine state of mind; in which case he is not an atheist, but an anti-theist. He does not deny God, he defies him. Moreover, there is something quite Christian about his defiance. That is why Alyosha finds it difficult not to agree with him. Even if we reinterpret divine omnipotence to denote not the manipulation of puppets but the management of free men, it still presses hard on us: why should the innocent suffer? In *The Brothers Karamazov* there is an answer: 'each is responsible for all'; and if we felt that responsibility keenly enough we could abolish suffering – for the future. But what about the atrocities of 1876? We can only say: *if* men had felt their responsibilities instead of wrapping themselves up in their own virtues and passing judgment, the events would not have happened. Ivan goes further: he will have no part in a world in which they *do* happen.

Before proceeding, let us note what he does not say, and what is not said in reply to him. (1) It is nowhere urged that 'the fathers have eaten sour grapes and the children's teeth are set on edge'. This, we have noted, is what Rozanov thought Dostoevsky, as an Orthodox Christian, should have said. Alyosha, the Christian of the new dispensation, does not even contemplate it. Even if it is true, Ivan and Alyosha agree that it is unjust and unjustifiable. In fact, the truer it is, the more necessary it is to hand back one's entrance ticket. (2) It is nowhere proposed to fall back on the doctrine of retribution in another world. Hell for the evil-doer is no more retrospectively efficacious than punishment by the courts. Dostoevsky did, as a matter of fact, attach great importance to immortality, and it is confidently affirmed by Alyosha to his boys' club on the occasion of Ilyusha's funeral. It was vital to his theory of personal existence. But he never appeals to it as a compensation and if he had it would not meet Ivan's difficulty: the happy ending does not invalidate or obscure the abominable here and now. As for hell, Zosima (p. 343) interprets it as meaning the inability to love, whether here or hereafter. Doubtless torturers of children would qualify, but it would not help the children. (3) In one of the most flagrant case-histories, Alyosha admits that the torturer ought to be shot. This normal reaction is seized upon by Ivan and acknowledged by Alyosha, as incompatible with Christian charity. They agree (and Dostoevsky as a Christian agrees) that it does nothing to cancel the record: it only feeds the self-righteousness which Christians are called upon to avoid. 'Judge not, that ye be not judged.' (4) Both Ivan and Alyosha assume that in the end of all the 'universal harmony' means forgiveness for the torturer. Ivan digs in his toes and says 'no forgiveness' and therefore no harmony. A more sentimental Christianity would have said 'all right, no harmony; sheep go one way and goats go the other', and he would find texts to support him. What is interesting, as a revelation of Dostoevsky's mind, is that Alyosha does not suggest such an answer. What he does say is that Christ 'can forgive everything, all and for all, because he gave his innocent blood for all and everything' (p. 259). Unless there is forgiveness for torturers, the Kingdom of God is incomplete. Ivan, a natural moralist, will not have a bar of it. Alyosha is troubled, but trusts and believes that no one is out of the range of redemption.[20] It is

---

[20] Dostoevsky does not use the technical theological term, *iskuplyeniye*; he says forgiveness, *otpushcheniye*, because in the forgiveness, and only in the forgiveness, is the redemption.

in that context that Ivan relates the 'Legend of the Grand Inquisitor'.[21]

The general plan of salvation, then, is for all; and the condition of it is that there should be no breach between saints and sinners. There is in the first Psalm a sentence which expresses everything Dostoevsky detested: 'The sinners shall not stand in the congregation of the righteous.' It is only if all stand in with all, only if the sinner does not feel himself excluded from the congregation, so that he does not have to be first snubbed and then patronized, that there is any hope of a sinless society.[22] The more grimly orthodox regard that prospect as hopeless anyway: they might well ask themselves for what were they redeemed. Dostoevsky, rightly or wrongly, saw a redeemed world as a sequel to the unbroken world of nature. No more than Ivan will Alyosha accept the salvation of a selected remnant: they, and their author, knew their Belinsky backwards. Ivan will have no part in a harmony built out of suffering; Alyosha sets out to create in miniature the kind of society in which it will not occur. Dostoevsky in his own person rejects the analogy of the musical discord. Zosima in his recollections uses language inescapably reminiscent of the Ridiculous Man's dream.

Nature is beautiful and sinless, and we, only we, are sinful and foolish, and we don't understand that life is heaven, for we have only to understand that and it will at once be fulfilled in all its beauty, we shall embrace each other and weep (p. 317).

And Alyosha recovering from his despair:

[21] The question, 'How can I forgive his tormentors?' is raised by Ivan even in his 'preface' (p. 260), apropos of God's judgment on those who crucified Christ. In the Greek poem he quotes, 'The wanderings of Our Lady through Hell', Our Lady begs some relief for them, and is finally granted a respite from their sufferings from Good Friday to Trinity Sunday every year. This touching and very mediaeval compromise would not have commended itself either to Ivan or to Dostoevsky.

[22] Dostoevsky's moving short story, *An Honest Thief*, depends entirely on the maintenance of the relationship between the thief (who, in a position of trust in the household, stole and pawned a pair of riding-breeches) and the man he robbed. Any display of indignation or assertion of rights would have broken up the right and necessary solidarity between the innocent and the guilty. The beauty of the piece is that the fellow-feeling is preserved right to the end. Not that the theft does not matter: but the 'togetherness' matters more.

The road is wide and straight and bright as crystal, and the sun is at the end of it (p. 384).

No one was more conscious of sin than Dostoevsky and no one was more convinced, at the end, that it is not the last word. And it is on earth that it must be overcome. The intimations of the earthly paradise blend with the visitations of grace; and whether this is Christianity or naturalism ceases to be a question: it is both at the same time. Dostoevsky has succeeded at least in integrating his discarded youth with his mature experiences. The right-wing Christians suspected apostasy, and the left-wing anti-Christians never noticed the change of emphasis. Where Dostoevsky is concerned, even though he sometimes wore them, party labels are best forgotten.

To conclude. In 'Pro and Contra', Ivan has nearly everything his own way. Alyosha is not out-argued: he agrees. There is no justification for torturers – and that is the primary issue. Unless – and here the Christian naturalist remembers his orthodoxy – though no human being has a right to forgive them, they are included in the general forgiveness: 'He gave his innnocent blood for all and everything.' Ivan says, 'I was expecting that. Do you know, I wrote a poem about that a year ago.'[23] And then follows the 'Legend of the Grand Inquisitor'.

III

The transition is a strange one. From the context, one would expect the 'Legend' to illustrate the difficulties of universal forgiveness. And from the prologue, featuring 'The Wanderings of Our Lady through Hell', one would still expect it. But having deftly provided this plausible link, Ivan perplexes us by moving to differing issues altogether: Catholicism and Socialism, miracle, mystery and authority, the Sword of Caesar and the problem of freedom. All these are recurring themes in Dostoevsky, in the novels and the *Diary* alike, but what, it will be asked, have they to do with the case in hand?

Let us see how they arise. The 'Legend' tells how Jesus came

23 P. 259.

back to earth in Seville in the sixteenth century, just after a highly successful *auto-da-fé*. He performs the familiar miracles, adding and subtracting nothing,[24] and receives the familiar adulation. He is apprehended by the gaunt nonagenarian Grand Inquisitor who claps him in prison and then visits him secretly late at night. He explains – and we must remember that it is Ivan who drafts the explanation. Men, he says, are naturally rebels, and rebels cannot be happy. To entrust them with freedom can cause them only misery. But Jesus, when tempted in the wilderness, rejected, for the sake of freedom, the three things they want more than anything in the world – bread, physical immunity, and political power. The Church has impounded this freedom and persuaded its flock that it would be better off with miracles, mystery and authority. It has taken upon itself the burden of the deception, replacing Christ's freedom with its own organization for the sake of the happiness of the ordinary man who cannot cope with freedom of any sort. The original Christ set the standards too high for them: he lived in a spiritual splendour in whose blessings few could share. The returned Christ will do the same; he will destroy the illusions which render happiness possible; he cannot be tolerated. 'Tomorrow I shall burn thee.'

So (brutally abbreviated) speaks Ivan's Grand Inquisitor. In the end he relents: the Christ kisses him on his bloodless lips, and he opens the prison door. But though the kiss glows in his heart, he does not change his opinions. 'Go, and come no more . . . come not at all, never never!' There is still an irreconcilable conflict between Christ and his church.

What does Ivan who created the Grand Inquisitor mean to convey? And what did Dostoevsky who created Ivan mean Ivan to convey?

It is unlike Dostoevsky to make his personages speak out of character; we should expect the 'Legend' to reflect and throw light on Ivan. And one thing at least is clear: the 'Legend' is written with a double mind by a man facing both ways. Intel-

---

[24] That is important: it is the Jesus of the Gospels, just as he was, that is under scrutiny.

lectually, the author is with the Grand Inquisitor; affectively, he is moved by the Christ. By nature Ivan loves life as much as any Karamazov; he perfers 'the sticky little leaves and the blue sky' (p. 242) to 'the order of the universe'. But he has seen what the ordinary anarchist has missed, that the nemesis of rebellion is authoritarianism, and he approves the Grand Inquisitor's reversal of the Christian direction. He is writing in character; as Ivan, he would not employ the machinery of miracles and mystery, and he would not dress up his desperate need for order in ecclesiastical robes; he belongs to the next generation of authoritarians ('my Socialist', Dostoevsky calls him in his correspondence)[25] but the Grand Inquisitor naturally gives a clerical twist to their common convictions, and Dostoevsky the diarist is in the wings proclaiming that Catholicism is about to enter on the Socialist path.[26] But still: he calls for order, to counter his own disorder, thus unwittingly stoking the dialectic whereby the one is converted into the other. Yet Ivan is attracted to the Christ, or he would not have introduced the final kiss, and left the moral deliberately ambiguous. And at no point is it suggested that the Christ is not what the Grand Inquisitor affirms him to be. The magnificent gesture of peace and forgiveness is disturbing and, to a tired sacrificial authoritarian, dangerous.

If his prose poem reveals Ivan, it is in a new light. Ivan in the story is an unbeliever (admittedly, an unsteady one) who starts from 'all is permitted' and finds it wanting. The contrast is between the freedom of *Notes from Underground* and the compulsion of conscience. The contrast in the 'Legend' is between the freedom of Christ and compulsion (however high-minded) of a spiritual autocracy. Freedom and compulsion seem to have changed places, meanings, and values. True, Ivan claims to have written the 'Legend' 'about a year ago' (p. 259), but that is an uncertain alibi; the situation in the 'Legend' is more, not less, complex and sophisticated than Ivan's situation in real life. (Like Dostoevsky, Ivan is more subtle when he writes fiction.) 'All is permitted' has clearly been left behind and replaced by 'all is

[25] To Lyubimov, *Pisma* IV, p. 58.
[26] He was premature but he has yet to be proved wrong.

organized', with the object of averting the unhappiness which 'all is permitted' brings in its train. And atheism, instead of wrecking itself against the meaning of the world, disguises itself and finds a sure refuge in the simulation of that meaning. The reversal is so perplexing that one is tempted to ask whether Dostoevsky did not for once overreach himself and insert in the text a piece of his own which does not quite fit the character to whom it is assigned – a sublime intermezzo, worthy of the opera, but not continuous with it.

This suspicion is strengthened by the loose transition at the beginning of the 'Legend', already noted, and another loose transition at the end of it, when Ivan laughs it off and tells Alyosha not to take it too seriously, disclaims any attempt to correct creation, and reverts to the old phrase 'all is permitted'.[27] Belkin[28] says bluntly: 'He (i.e. Dostoevsky) puts his "Legend" into Ivan's mouth.' On any showing, there is much of Dostoevsky in the 'Legend': the fateful choice between Christ and the world; the double-mindedness of Ivan, which is Dostoevsky's own double-mindedness back to front; the populist prepossessions of the Inquisitor, which Dostoevsky undoubtedly shared, and of which, in Ivan, there are no other signs. All the same, we shall maintain that the 'Legend' is not wholly Dostoevsky, nor the whole of Dostoevsky; not even, or perhaps least of all, of the Dostoevsky who wrote *The Brothers Karamazov*. In the first place, it must be seen in the perspective provided by the rest of the novel. In the second place, it does not at all represent Dostoevsky's own public opinions concerning Christ and the church. Its limitations in both respects are those of Ivan at the time at which he recites it.

1. The 'Legend' occurs in Part Two, Book Five, entitled 'Pro and Contra'; curiously, for it is dominated by Ivan and is nearly all Contra. The difficulties were to be dispersed not by argument, but by depicting a different way of living: one practised in the elder generation by Zosima, and to be practised in the modern style by Alyosha. By the time he wrote *The Brothers Karamazov*

27 *The Brothers Karamazov*, pp. 277–78.
28 In *Tvorchestvo Dostoevskogo*, p. 274.

Dostoevsky had grasped the point which he had constantly been feeling after, and which had constantly eluded him: that Christianity is centred on action. This is what, in the answer, is consistently emphasized. In the whole career of Zosima, there stands out a searching and compelling humility which is very far from non-resistance; and we have already (p. 50 above) quoted his disturbing advice to the self-centred Mrs Khokhlakova on the necessity (and the difficulty) of 'active love'. But that is merely where the signposts begin: the test case is to be Alyosha. It is not without significance that he is represented neither as a thinker nor as a mystic, but as a healthy young man whose Karamazov love of life runs towards action. 'He was honest in nature, desiring the truth, seeking for it and believing it, and seeking to serve it with all the strength of his soul, seeking for immediate action, and ready to sacrifice everything, life itself, for it.' 'A thirst for swift achievement.' Of course he had plenty to learn. Belkin[29] makes much of Dostoevsky's 'author's preface', in which he writes of Alyosha 'the fact is that he was indeed a doer, but an indefinite one who had not become clear to himself'. Naturally, a young man is not utterly fixed in his course from the start unless he is first illiberally indoctrinated; it does not follow that his actions will be futile, only that they will later become more decisive as time goes on. We have already given some preliminary instances. The criticism is intended to suggest that an active temperament will be wasted without a revolutionary goal. It can be said on Dostoevsky's behalf that no external manipulation can remove human misfortune: it is merely transferred from one category to another (e.g. from poverty to despotism): and even if it were removed, is nothing to be done in the interim? The doctrine of Ivan, that happy endings mend no bones, is here applicable, in what Belkin might regard as an anti-social sense.[30]

[29] Ibid. p. 290.

[30] The author's preface is not translated by Garnett and is rarely referred to in British commentaries. It is mainly concerned with the status of Alyosha as a hero. Dostoevsky is worried that he may not be accepted as such, not for the literary reason that he is only on the margin of the plot, but for the more personal reason that he is not 'remarkable'. It is in this context that Dostoevsky writes that as an

To return: Christianity is centred on action and Dostoevsky, at long last, had come to see it. That is where the 'Legend' falls short of his own requirements. For it draws a sharp line between the efficacy of the quest for happiness (through deception) and the inconsequence and strangeness of Christ's intervention: he remains throughout a magnificent intruder. As a clue to Dostoevsky's intention in the novel, the 'Legend' is therefore misleading.

2. If we look outside the novel to Dostoevsky's contemporary expressions of opinion on the same subject, we shall find a similar discrepancy. The 'Legend' tells us that we must choose between Christ and organized religion: an anarchist Christ is confronted by a solidarist church. But that was not Dostoevsky's final position. His social ideal was the sort of solidarity which arises from common participation in a total religious culture. Its basis, as we have seen (pp. 41ff. above) is in *sobornost'* – the whole congregation and the whole church consenting individual by individual to the pervasive will of Christ. The concept is primarily religious, and it enables Dostoevsky to present the following schema: Catholicism, unity without freedom: Protestantism, freedom without unity; Russian Orthodoxy, freedom in unity and unity in freedom.[31] But because his religion was so 'populist' and his 'populism' so religious, he carried the conception of *sobornost'* over into politics. That is why he (so perversely, we are tempted to think) regarded laws and constitutions as *obstacles* to freedom: they short-circuit the necessary consentience.

---

agent Alyosha may seem 'indefinite' and 'unclarified'. But he himself finds him important. He is certainly strange, even an original; but it may happen that such a person, instead of separating and isolating, unites the scattered features of a situation; he 'carries in himself the core of the whole, and the rest of his contemporaries, caught by one wind or another, are temporarily, so to speak, torn loose from him'. It will be noticed that the phrase quoted by Belkin is a concession, and that the rest of the passage puts it in perspective.

In passing, not too much should be made of the phrases 'strange' and 'an original'. They do not nullify the emphasis laid in the text on Alyosha's health and normality. They are as much to say to the average reader: 'Look, you didn't expect to find a novice in your magazine, did you?'

[31] Quoted N. Lossky, *Dostoevsky i ego khristiyanskoye miroponimaniye*, p. 342.

Now the doctrine of *sobornost'* is irreconcilable with the 'Legend'. In the 'Legend' Christ is in tension with the socio-religious unity; under *sobornost'* he is the centre of it. Either the 'Legend' does not disclose an important aspect of Dostoevsky's thought, or it expresses the revolt of Dostoevsky the great artist against Dostoevsky the untrained sociologist. Post-revolutionary Russians and nearly all Westerners incline to the second view. It is here proposed to state the case for the first.

Much of what Dostoevsky says about *sobornost'* is to be found in the *Diary of a Writer*, and it will not impress those who regard the novels as the more revealing. But there are two passages in *The Brothers Karamazov* which may help to throw light on this same central concept. The first, in order of presentation, is Ivan's widely publicized article on the unlikely subject of ecclesiastical courts. The second, which goes to the heart of the matter, is Father Zosima's 'each is responsible for all'.

The article, like everything connected with Ivan, produces in his readers – his readers both *in* the novel, and *of* the novel – a sense of perplexity. Ostensibly, it is a reply to an ecclesiastic who was pleading for the greater independence from the state of ecclesiastical courts. Ivan contends that any such proposal confines the church to a defined position within the state; which is opposed to the all-embracing claims of the church. On the contrary, 'every earthly state should be, in the end, completely transformed into the church, rejecting every purpose incongruous with the aims of the church' (p. 60). It is not likely to happen all at once, and it can happen only in Russia; meanwhile, and elsewhere, the best the church can hope for is conditional freedom under civil law. The mistake of the writer whom Ivan is reviewing is, he thinks, to treat a compromise as a solution. The end to be kept always in sight is the total ecclesiastical society.[32]

When Ivan is persuaded to talk about his article at the 'unfortunate gathering' at the monastery, he stops at this point; the rest of the theme is developed at length by Father Zosima and Father Paisy. At the point where a definitely religious position

---

[32] An illustration is the problem of crime. In the ecclesiastical society the criminal will not be mechanically cut off, but, as religion demands, reintegrated and reformed.

is to be developed passionately and personally, Dostoevsky judges that Ivan is not the man to do it. Yet what Ivan says is a fair if slightly institutionalized version of Dostoevsky's own theme of *sobornost'*. Zosima himself does not criticize its content; instead, he tells Ivan that he does not believe what he has written. Ivan replies: 'Perhaps you are right . . . But I wasn't altogether joking' (p.68). To which the retort is, 'You were not altogether joking. The question is still fretting your heart, and not answered . . . meanwhile, in your despair, you divert yourself with magazine articles.' Ivan as we know is a professing atheist, and here we find him setting out one of Dostoevsky's most cherished convictions. But why not? May not an intelligent atheist come to the conclusion that an ecclesiastical society alone can effect the necessary concentration of material and spiritual forces? That, in fact, is the conclusion of another atheist, the Grand Inquisitor. But it means that Orthodox belief can be simulated by atheists, and how do we then distinguish between atheists and believers? Never did Dostoevsky find a more disconcerting way of 'distributing his voices'.

Thus, paradoxically, looking to the article for enlightenment on the 'Legend', we find that it is both closer to the prose convictions of Dostoevsky and even more subtly exposed to perversion. It omits the disturbing paradox of the 'Legend': Christ. It is true that he may be tucked away behind the socio-religious establishment; but in the 'Legend' he is irruptive and disturbing and at odds with any possible establishment.[33] As far as externals go, the driving force behind *sobornost'* may well be atheism; and that is to repeat, not to correct, the Grand Inquisitor. The article does not appear to help us forward. What does help is Zosima's dissection of Ivan's motivation. We recall that the devil can parody anything; the great thing is to be able to discern the parody from the original. The clue is that Ivan, the man who could 'never learn to love his neighbour' is moved by despair and not by joy. Dostoevsky would have agreed with René Le

[33] There is no escape by distinguishing between the Catholic and the Orthodox Church. The Orthodox Church equally with the Catholic, requires the 'miracle, mystery, authority' which the Christ of the 'Legend' is held to disdain in the name of freedom.

Senne: 'For me, the principal proof of the existence of God is the joy I experience at thinking that God exists.'[34]

The conclusion is welcome: Ivan's article, as Zosima sees, is from the head, but the 'Legend' is from the heart. It is the confession of one who sees through the socio-ecclesiastical pretences, regarding them not only as mandatory but also as unacceptable. Between the two compositions of a versatile author, we must stand by the 'Legend' as his more authoritative expression. The article throws light on the concept of *sobornost'* but it achieves the sense of togetherness at the expense of the sense of spontaneity. No solution will serve Dostoevsky's purposes which does not first distinguish (as in the 'Legend') and then bring together these two essential elements in the life of religion. So, acknowledging what the article can teach us, we pass on to the conversation and recollections of Father Zosima.

From the first, we realize that he is a Christian of a new dispensation. He is compassionate and joyful; not in the least ascetic (to the scandal of more conservative colleagues); as active in good works as his withdrawn profession permits, and commanding Alyosha as his spiritual successor to withdraw from withdrawal altogether; not oblivious of the evil in the world, but utterly convinced that it is a good place to live in.[35] Above all, he commands and exhibits *sobornost'*: not merely emotionally, nor institutionally, but as a personal way of living. We are inclined, as Westerners, to be sceptical of unforced unanimity; it is not an obvious fact of experience, and when cases are examined it often seems to be achieved either by masked force or by unthinking submission. Zosima's answer is that it really happens when each man stops thinking about himself and assumes joint responsibility in all things for every other.

'There is only one means of salvation . . . take yourself and make yourself responsible for all men's lives . . . as soon as you sincerely make yourself responsible for everything and for all men, you will see at once that it is really so, and that you are to blame for everyone and for all things. But throwing your own indolence and impotence on

---

[34] *La découverte de Dieu*, Aubier 1955, p. 18.
[35] Cf. *Diary of a Writer*, p. 985, 'Sin is a transient matter, but Christ is eternal.'

others you will end by sharing the pride of Satan and murmuring against God' (pp. 390-91).

This is not the inspiration of a moment: 'love is dearly bought, it is won slowly, by long labour'. Responsibility means *doing* things which, acting carelessly or on impulse, we should fail to do. It means not only doing things *for* people; that may inflame the sense of humiliation. It means a total identification; an assumption of one's part in the general guilt: not condescendingly, but because, as a fellow-member of the Christian community, you really share in it.[36]

Here, at last, is a solution to Dostoevsky's old problem of personal identity. All his life Dostoevsky was an individualist, quick to take offence, eloquent in self-assertion, loud in his protests against the determinism of scientists and mathematicians ('I spit on $2 + 2 = 4$'; he refused to accept the most ordinary necessities); exquisitely sensitive to the least suspicion of patronage or superiority; and entirely convinced that this natural inclination of his was the root of the general evil. On the other hand he could not accept the collectivist alternative which he presented to himself in the discourse of the Grand Inquisitor; he saw that to be absorbed in a central concern to the point of losing one's identity is to abdicate as a human being. But if one belongs to a concern in which each gives himself, not to the whole but to the other, each admitting his share of the guilt which the more sensitive feel more intensely than others, but from which none can escape, then the person retains his free decision, and yet by that decision is implicated with all. The self-centred freedom of the liberals (and their anarchist descendants) and the deceptive appropriation of their freedom by the Catholic Church (and its Socialist descendants) are alike superseded: and, what is more, they are shown to generate each other, in a succession which looks dialectical but is in fact interminable; the only end to it is to assert what both parties deny (and this is not a synthesis, but a complete re-statement): that personal freedom is not by definition self-seeking (as Dostoevsky, with some justification,

---

[36] Dostoevsky insists that Christians shall not get away with it by selecting the easier cases. Christ's salvation was meant for all.

thought the liberals to believe) and does not, therefore, need to be set aside in a more co-operative order (as Dostoevsky, again with some justification, thought the socialists to believe). The only way out of the impasse is for people to belong together (not merely to co-operate) by their own commitment. And if it is said that this is not practical politics, well, no doubt it isn't; but, as the Ridiculous Man said, if those affected were to develop a new kind of Christian concern, it would all be so utterly natural. On this appeal, which he believed to be consonant with the mental habits of the mass of the Russian people, he pinned all his hopes. If he had been more politically minded, he might have been less confident; if he had been less politically concerned, he would certainly not have conflated the role of the Tsar and the indwelling of the Holy Spirit. Politics is an affair of the middle distance, and it was precisely to the middle distance that Dostoevsky's vision was not adjusted. He was a superb close-range psychological observer, and a disconcerting discerner of unlikely coalitions over the horizon. For both these gifts we must be properly grateful.

It is not, however, in the 'Legend' that the solution emerges. The 'Legend' sets the problem; it does not even attempt to answer it. Ivan was too double-minded for the enterprise; and Dostoevsky himself carried much of Ivan inside him. And perhaps it is permissible to guess that the 'Legend' belongs to his past (*Dostoevsky*'s past) as it is explicitly said to belong to Ivan's. His daughter Lyubov' has put it on record that Ivan was her father's retrospective portrait of himself as a young man. And it is perhaps because the 'Legend' draws so heavily on his past that it is not altogether congruent with his present. He uses it, with great dramatic power, to bring out the contradiction in Ivan from which he felt that he had at long last escaped. The commentators who have related the 'Legend' to the letter to N. A. Fonvizina of 1854 have been right, for the wrong reason. They thought that the 'Legend' expressed a contemporary doubt and that Dostoevsky in 1878 stood in all essentials when he stood in 1854. We suggest that the 'Legend' is the recall, from within a greater assurance, of a state of mind he had lived through when he was more deeply divided: and that he set it down, through the recital of Ivan (which enables him to disclaim responsibility) so that he could finally be quit of it; so that he could lose it and drown it in his recovered faith and hope.

IV

It remains to be asked: even if the solidarity of each with all in Christ is taken into account (and it must be: it is there in *The Brothers Karamazov* as well as in the *Diary of a Writer*), has Ivan's anti-theology been answered? The answer must be, firmly, No. (1) Supposing the desired consummation to have been achieved, does that do anything to wipe out the atrocities that have already occurred? This is the inevitable question bequeathed by Belinsky, and the answer, again, is No. (2) Is the achievement possible within the limits of human egoism? It's all very well for Christ; he was God (Dostoevsky's reflection when Marya died and later voiced in *The Idiot*); for us men there is no end to the dear self, at the best only a diminution. And it is no use to appeal to immortality. True, there may be compensation: but to be moved by that consideration is itself egoism, and in any case Dostoevsky, though profoundly convinced about immortality, did not appeal to it in the Utilitarian manner; he was anti-Utilitarian both here and hereafter.[37]

We have said: identification and sacrifice: that is to say,

---

[37] Father Zosima does try to comfort the bereaved peasant woman by telling her that her dead children are angels in heaven; but Ivan, contemplating his case-histories, would simply reply that there is no excuse for what God allowed to happen on earth, and Dostoevsky has no ready answer. The only possible move is to change the whole frame of reference, and in the end this is what Dostoevsky does. Instead of asking, how can what happens be justified? he asks, taking what happens as the starting point, how can the sting be removed from it? He thus abandons the whole notion of a theodicy. But it can be claimed that theodicy is in a way sub-Christian. The Christian puts all the weight not on the perfection of the world as it stands, but on the putting right of what for whatever reason is far from perfect through the Christian practices of identification and sacrifice. And that is what Dostoevsky in *The Brothers Karamazov* succeeds in showing. For example, Ivan's special case, cruelty to children. Alyosha's answer is not to deplore it as a spectator, but to the extent of his ability, to engage himself with his boys' club so that it will never happen to them; and if everyone were a Christian of his quality it would not happen at all.

imagination and action, both directed against the omnivorous claims of the private self. We have to change both our attitude and our actions. Dostoevsky's conviction at all times was that attitude is central and action consequential. He has little use for the Stoic technique which infiltrated the early church and dominated the Puritan ethic in its later phases, of pressing forward to the action without respect to the attitude. (Neither has the Sermon on the Mount, which traces killing to its source in the feeling of anger.) Zosima observed, 'If you love everything, you will perceive the divine mystery in things' (p. 339). What is denied to our understanding (because it operates as an outside observer) is revealed to love and joy and self-forgetfulness. There really is another mysterious world – God is not simply an ideal – but it takes a worshipper to discover it. As Zosima says:

'God took seeds from different worlds and sowed them on this earth, and his garden grew up and everything came up that could come up, but what grows lives and is alive only through the feeling of its contacts with other mysterious worlds. If that feeling grows weak or is destroyed in you, the heavenly growth will die away in you. Then you will grow indifferent to life and even grow to hate it' (p. 341).

But the new dispensation, planted by God, arises within nature, and, so far, it is there and there only that we have the clue to it. The over-anxious were referred by Christ to the lilies of the field. So Zosima pleads with his friends: 'be glad as children, as the birds of heaven' (p. 340). He had come to it suddenly, the hard way, in the middle of a duel. Having faced his adversary's shot, he had turned to the company with this astonishing address:

'Gentlemen,' I said suddenly, speaking straight from my heart, 'look around you at the gifts of God, the clear sky, the pure air, the tender grass, the birds: nature is beautiful and sinless, and we, only we, are sinful and foolish, and we don't understand that life is heaven, for we have only to understand that and it will at once be fulfilled in all its beauty, we shall embrace each other and weep' (p. 317).

The emphasis is on nature: a theme which has blossomed out from the bad dreams of Stavrogin and the nostalgic cynicism of Versilov, and now, as in the Gospels, figures as the proper preliminary to repentance. It is closer to the abandoned 'Schiller-ism' than some critics realize. It is in fact a return to Dostoevsky's youth—without the duality, and all-importantly, without the tribal conceit of his earlier humanism – at the far end of his metaphysical nightmare. It repeats the Ridiculous Man's asser-tion that if only we understand that life is heaven, so it will be. But it also states the conditions; men must shake off the self-consciousness described by Underground Man as the mark of the age; they must escape from the baneful intervention of their own shadows. This was the sin that by man came into the world; if they can diminish the burden for each other, if they can truly belong to one another, independently yet with their whole being, perhaps, by man, Christ leading, sin might vanish from the world, and be replaced by the spontaneous affections of the age of gold.

But where does God come in? His name certainly comes in, and Dostoevsky pronounces it, as in church, very reverently. But is it more than another way of describing the excellences of nature? From some of the above passages, one could be excused for thinking not. The impression is not wholly dispelled when Dostoevsky goes to the other extreme and writes: 'without faith in the soul and its immortality the existence of man is against nature, unthinkable and intolerable'.[38] There is still no mention of God: immortality is being extolled as a sort of super-fact in its own right. Certainly, it is re-associated with the name of Christ, and it sounds orthodox enough: 'in Christ shall all be made alive'. But 'faith in immortality' (Dostoevsky's phrase) and devotion to Christ, taken together, still do not give us God. Not only nature but super-nature is glorified without mention of God.

At the end of an exhaustive and penetrating review, Pierre Pascal[39] writes: 'As to the existence of God, he admits it, certainly: but what God?' He felt God, he responded to him; for the rest, he was a mystery, dispersed into his manifestations. In D. Grishin's *Aforizmy i vyskazyvaniya F.M. Dostoevskogo*, among the items under the heading of 'religion', all twenty-four

---

[38] *Diary of a Writer*, I, p.3.   [39] *Dostoievski*, p.101.

of them,[40] the name of God appears only twice. There is plenty and to spare about Christ (especially the 'Russian Christ'), orthodoxy, immortality, personal responsibility, and it is possible to surmise that all these are in the divine orbit, but the centre is strangely lacking. It can be found if one looks hard enough, as will be shown below; but on the whole the conclusion to be drawn from the combination of the sincerest piety with the apparent absence of its object is that we are looking for the wrong thing. We are expecting Dostoevsky to recognize God first, and to discern Christ as God afterwards. His way of worship was utterly different. He was not susceptible to the 'wholly other' and still less to the rationalized deity of eighteenth-century modernists. They kept a cosmic God and made light of Christ, and were left with the impossible task of justifying the world as it stands. Dostoevsky's natural approach to God was through his manifestations; at the end of his life, through the joy and gladness of nature, but all through by way of Christ and his gospel. Like Peter, he saw Christ as man transfigured; with Peter he was of those 'who by him do believe in God, who raised him up from the dead, and gave him glory';[41] and he went on to discover the Holy Spirit in the Orthodox Church, not collectively, but displayed in each individual Christian, irrespective of moral standing or merits. If he had not been a Christian, he would have been an atheist: and he thought the atheist nearer to Christ than the indifferent onlooker. If he came to the Christian faith in this way, rather than through God defined without reference to Christ, and especially disfavouring the philosophical father-substitutes, he had some Christian precedent behind him. And perhaps, towards the end, as he made his peace with nature, he understood more clearly than before that 'he that hath seen me hath seen the Father'.

The conclusion is not incompatible with belief in God; it means merely that such belief as Dostoevsky's does not begin with God. This can be shown from the few passages which

[40] Pp. 38–40.
[41] I Peter 1.21. Compare the magnificent sermon on this text by A. D. Lindsay, printed in his *The Nature of Religious Truth*, Hodder and Stoughton 1927, pp. 119ff.

reflect a sense of distance and grandeur. First, Alyosha's mystical climax at which he hears, after the old man's death, the voice of Father Zosima:

'Do not fear him. He is terrible in his greatness, awful in his sublimity, but infinitely merciful. He has made himself like unto us from love, and rejoices with us. He is changing the water with wine, that the gladness of the guests will not be cut short.'

Here the awe and terror enter into the picture, only to be dispersed into joy and love. Undispersed, they would lose their religious significance. It is precisely the dispersion which brings about Alyosha's recovery of faith.

Secondly, Dostoevsky was fascinated by the Book of Job: he records it both in his own person and through the mouth of Father Zosima. Now if ever God was apprehended in his sheer grandeur, it is in that scriptural masterpiece. And Zosima does say, reflecting on it: 'in the face of the earthly truth, the eternal truth is accomplished' (p. 308) - God is not merely present, he overrides. It is not simply that in his overwhelming might God puts one man's suffering in perspective - in fact, this aspect of the story does not occur to Dostoevsky. What God overrides is the assumption common to Job and his so-called comforters, and particularly dear to the Psalmist and the Puritan, that merit and reward belong together. Even if we admit Job 42 as canonical – Dostoevsky had no doubts about it – only those are rewarded who are convinced that their deserts do not count in the sight of God. The story could be read as commending acceptance: 'The Lord hath given and the Lord hath taken away: blessed be the name of the Lord.' This verse is quoted by Zosima;[42] and also, in Russian, *Bog dal i Bog vzyal*, by Stephen Graham, as current among the Russian peasantry before the First World War. But it is only a phase in the development of Job, and what impresses Dostoevsky is not just the acceptance but the mystery it leads

[42] Concerning Zosima, Dostoevsky wrote in a letter: 'Although I myself hold the same opinions as he expresses, yet if I expressed them personally, from myself, I should express them in a different form.' This is a warning that Zosima, as a character in a novel, will use certain language-archaisms (and perhaps concept-archaisms) appropriate to him, and that we must slide in a liberal direction along the language spectrum to elicit what we have called Dostoevsky's 'prose' meaning.

back to: the absence of correlation between the ways of God and the much admired habits of men. God overrides the order and proportion which men prefer to Christian charity. The Creator, as opposed to the craftsman, discards established moulds. There is nothing conservative in this portrait of God, and nothing of the impassively eternal. 'The day of the Lord cometh like a thief in the night', as Paul reminded the unvigilant Thessalonians.

Thirdly, outside the Scriptures, and nearer to the Hellenic traditions inherited by the Orthodox Church, Dostoevsky acknowledged 'higher' ranges of existence, accessible to souls after death and anticipated here and now by those who have adopted the posture of 'active love'. Says Zosima:

'Much on earth is hidden from us, but to make up for that we have been given a precious mystic sense of our living bond with the other world, with the higher heavenly world, and the roots of our thoughts and feelings are not here but in other worlds. That is why the philosophers say that we cannot apprehend the reality of things on earth' (p. 341).

This more conventional Platonic streak in Dostoevsky is not what is most typical, but it is certainly to be found both in the *Diary of a Writer* and *The Brothers Karamazov*. It adds to the variety of his glimpses and confirms the impression that all glimpses, with the exception of God made man, are fugitive and can be expressed only imperfectly in a succession of symbols.

We have noted that Dostoevsky does on occasions speak of God as any non-philosophical believer speaks of him: reverently and fragmentarily, as befits a great mystery, even to the extent of transcending anthropology to do it. But it is within anthropology – his own Christian anthropology – that he presents the fundamental issue: man-God or God-man? The man-God is man translated to godhood by the absence of God: the God-man is God translated to manhood, thus providing evidence of his presence. There is only one case of complete coincidence, Christ: but anyone who is part of him through his church is caught up more or less, and what he is caught up in is not merely natural or human. It is mysterious, opaque to the mere observer but discernible in an unique orientation of human action – what Zosima calls 'active love'. It is in man that God is disclosed. Dostoevsky accepts the traditional attributes as part of his decision for Orthodoxy, but the drive behind the decision is Christ. Better than most of us, Dostoevsky understood the *paradox* of God made man.[43] Nothing could be less likely: there is more resistance to God in man than anywhere in creation. But for that reason nothing could be a greater tribute to his power: if God could be made man he could do anything. Dostoevsky knew it by hard experience. Rejecting the charge of an 'uneducated and reactionary faith in God', he replied:[44] 'in their stupidity they never dreamt of the power of denial that I have lived through' – and reported, we may add, in 'The Legend of the Grand Inquisitor'. That he did live through it is a tribute to his faith, whatever may be said of its shifting foundations. In a disordered period of history, when the feudal order was collapsing, when the new bourgeois order was without restraint or scruple, when the rebellion against them was undisciplined and ill-directed, he saw the worst that man could do, and then he thought of Christ and concluded: 'Sin is the smog, and the smog will disappear when the sun rises in its power. Sin is a transitory matter, but Christ is eternal.'[45] It is on Christ and his dissolution of sin that his theology is concentrated.

We note, then, the clarification through the story of Father Zosima of the Christian intentions of the author, and in particular his emphasis on the beauty and as it were the Christlikeness of nature: but the basis of the novel is still the refutation of Ivan Karamazov by his own *praxis* (I borrow a suitable locution from J.-P. Sartre). It is not a refutation of atheism as such: those who think in these terms are always 'talking about something else'. It would not touch an unscrupulous atheist, or even one of high moral purpose and little sensibility. It is a study of a double-minded contemporary compassionate atheist; a special case, but

---

[43] His recognition of it almost puts him in a line with Kierkegaard, with whose work he was almost certainly unacquainted.

[44] Quoted from the notebooks by Grishin, *Aforizmy i vyskazyvaniya F. M. Dostoevskogo*, p. 40.

[45] Again quoted from the notebooks by Grishin, ibid. p. 40. I translate *smrad* as 'smog' deliberately: its primary meaning is 'bad smell', here combined with 'fog'.

important in the spiritual formation of Dostoevsky, and not untypical at the time: and what more can a novelist do, even one with a passion for problems? To repeat: what convinces Dostoevsky of the truth of Christian teaching is its verification in practice: that is what sustains the otherwordly superstructure and by-passes the theoretical justification which he continues to believe cannot be provided.

The young mentor of Dostoevsky's later years, Vladimir Solovyov, once observed, 'God is in us, therefore he is.'[46] But (1) far more than Solovyov, he took his stand on the presence of God in unlikely places. The presence of God in Alyosha is not surprising; it comes from his heart and is heard on his lips and spills over into his daily conduct, (the *bytovoye blagochestiye* of the Orthodox Church). What is startling to us, but not to Dostoevsky, is the presence of God in Ivan. His special subject was not the success-stories of the saints, but the self-conviction of the unbeliever. God is in him, all right: that is why he breaks down. On the other hand (2) Dostoevsky is less clear than Solovyov that the deity with which we are united, and which acts and reveals itself in us, is something 'distinct and independent' of us.[47] That is why cases like Ivan are so decisive. In Alyosha God is so present that we are not called upon to think of him as distant. In Ivan the failure of coincidence is unmistakable; the overlap of God with Ivan's affairs is such an intrusion that if God is there at all, he must be, in Solovyov's words, 'distinct and independent'. That is the moral that the story carries, even though Dostoevsky does not make the most of it theoretically. That, no doubt, is also why Alyosha is in the sequel to be put under a more continuous strain than the temporary episode of his favourite elder's putrefaction in the novel itself. It is also why Dostoevsky seems at times to be saying that sin is a stage on the road to salvation. He does not mean, as he has sometimes been taken to mean, that it has to be courted in order to be abandoned; he does mean that we shall be involved in it anyway, there is no contracting out, and we shall have to come through to the other side. In the process will be revealed the distance of

[46] *The Justification of the Good*, p. 164.   [47] Ibid.

the God who, if only we give up our self-centred stances, is so readily and so joyfully near to us.

That, then, is how God stands to us; to our self-seeking, or even our self-dependence, present as a menace; to our love and happiness nearer to us than breathing. The immanence of God in all things is the final truth of the matter; to some of the things (or rather people) in whom he is immanent, he is terrifyingly transcendent. It is true that on this showing the transcendence is relative and the immanence is absolute; even when, to the sinner or unbeliever, the immanence appears as transcendence. This is not everyone's theology, but Dostoevsky will throw no one overboard; a God who cannot move among scoundrels and bring them back to his image is to that extent a failure. The dialectic of the 'Legend', and the career of the saintly and utterly uncensorious Zosima, both point in the same direction. Dostoevsky does not talk much about God, because he is absorbed in Christ, and God, too, is absorbed *into* Christ; but in the bad times, when the gap shows, behind the God in the world stands the God who is the sanction of the world, and they cannot be separated. That is one answer to the dualism of the 'Legend', that supreme expression of a lifetime's agony only recently overcome.

Finally, the problem is the 'self'. Everything was conspiring to raise it: the individualism of the rising bourgeoisie, the self-consciousness induced by psychological introspection, the backwash of a romanticism which had beaten in vain against the sea-walls of progress and success. The 'self' was getting out of proportion. It could be met either by suppression from without or dedication from within. The Orthodox ideal of *sobornost'*, of mutual free association in the presence of Christ, provided a social answer. It was reinforced by recent memories of peasants' communes (*mir*: commune or world, as the context takes it): a collectivity not enforced but growing from ageless custom, in which the place of the individual is not to get on at others' expense, but to engage in activities which everyone regards as part of his own. The alternative to *sobornost'* is Western-oriented dissent, which is as self-seeking as what it seeks to displace. In the presence of God, mediated by his church, the self is deflated to normal proportions, its independence is softened into communion without loss of dignity, and its aggressiveness is harnessed to the wills of all. Not collectivity, in the end, but communion; not, therefore, a political recipe, but a pooling of spiritual resources in a common adoration.

Such, as revealed in *The Brothers Karamazov*, and the companion passages of the *Diary*, is the direction of Dostoevsky's pilgrimage; but not the end. There is no end, only an approximation which is always closer and never closed.

V

Announcing to his father his unbelief in God, Ivan Karamazov adds: 'There's no devil either' (p. 139). When he came home after his last interview with Smerdyakov, he suffered a hallucination which might well have caused him to change his mind. The devil was there in person, 'shoddy genteel', as the Irish of that period used to say, a gentleman of fifty-odd, in straightened circumstances, amiable and accommodating, with a tortoise-shell lorgnette on a black ribbon; urbane, ironical and even witty; enjoying his embodied condition and even wishing it could be more permanent; loving the earth where all is 'formulated and geometrical', and dreaming in his more abandoned moments of 'becoming incarnate once for all and irrevocably in the form of some pious merchant's wife weighing eighteen stone' (p. 690). As anyone's conception of the devil throws light on his conception of God, the intrusion of this character calls for interpretation. As the whole episode is more than normally fantastical, the exercise is sufficiently precarious.

In the first place, it is surely significant that the devil has no home – not even a furnace – and depends entirely on casual hospitality. Like any other parasite, he lives on his hosts. He is by definition a hanger-on. This is as it should be: belief in a highly personalized devil usually goes with some form of dualism; and Ivan's agony about the suffering of children would not have driven him into atheism if the responsibility could have been shifted to an independent power of evil. But not only is the devil a dependent, he is a 'double'. Even when most convinced by the apparition, Ivan notes that its problems and stories are his own, projected, and that it stands for everything in him which he would like to repudiate. It is a distanced version of his inadequacies, preying upon and at the same time making use of the qualities he would like to acknowledge. One is reminded of Wasiolek's observation that the devil can turn anything his way. But he is a corrupter, not an imitator: he can only graft himself upon the host whom he inhabits.

This being so, it would not be surprising if the sentiments expressed by Ivan and his 'visitor' somehow came out back to front. For example: the devil takes up Ivan's point about Euclid. Chatting with Alyosha, Ivan had confessed himself Euclidean, unable to fathom non-Euclidean geometry, let alone engage in arguments about the existence of God – 'utterly inappropriate for a mind created with an idea of only three dimensions' (p.247).[48] The 'devil' complains in the same way about his world of 'indeterminate equations'; he is all for solidity and settling down. Which is diabolical: the indeterminacy, or the passion for the solid? Ivan is all for the solid – or is he? Are we now being told that his Euclidean limitations are the self-imposed corrections to a natural anarchism? Ivan has nearly admitted as much by writing 'The Legend of the Grand Inquisitor'. The fact is, the devil can twist him either way; for the devil is both his double and himself. The object of the exercise is to drive him into a corner.[49]

The devil's reputation is that of an 'indispensable minus',

[48] Lobachevsky who first suspected the limitations of Euclidean geometry was a Russian and his views had been available since 1833, and he is certainly alluded to in this passage.

[49] Huston Smith, *The Religions of Man*, Mentor Book, 1958, p.140, writes of the training of acolytes in Zen Buddhism: 'by forcing reason to wrestle with what, from its normal point of view, is flat absurdity, Zen tries to reduce it to the frantic condition of throwing itself against its walls with the desperation of a cornered rat'. The difference is that the Zen training breaks down the structures of reason to make way for a sudden enlightening (or disabusing) intuition. It is a religious exercise. The devil twists Ivan (or Ivan twists himself) interminably, and with no intention but to keep him in perpetual confusion. It is an anti-religious exercise.

promoted by Hegelian logicians to serve the purposes of providence as a 'negative moment'. Without submitting himself to
the enemy to that degree, Ivan's devil none the less congratulates
himself on his essential negativity: without him there would be
no criticism, no newspapers, in fact, no interest of any sort. He
complains that he does not *want* to be *der Geist der stets verneint*
(and here he is completely at one with the public personality of
Ivan); indeed he plays his part in the general good: 'if everything in the universe were sensible, nothing would happen'
(p. 694). There is something here which recalls William Blake,
'the devil is the hero of all good literature': and Blake, in an even
odder way than Dostoevsky, was a good Christian. There is
something too which reflects the darker side of Ivan himself;
and, further back in Dostoevsky's history, *Notes from Underground*. But it is in a new context, which even the devil himself
cannot wholly cancel. That it takes something ineffable and not
quite rational to keep God's business going is part of Dostoevsky's recovered Christian conviction.

That the threads should be thus tangled and confused is not
accidental: it is part of the new diabolic policy. According to the
'latest method', 'I lead you to belief and unbelief by turns, and I
have my motive in it' (p. 697). It might even be 'the salvation of
his soul' – in the first instance, at least through believing in the
devil. His 'visitor' recognizes in Ivan the potential ascetic; that
is to say, Ivan is subconsciously aware of it himself; and that
kind of religion requires a devil to provide the temptations.
What attracts the devil about hermits in the wilderness is
precisely their double-mindedness: 'They can contemplate such
depths of belief and disbelief at the same moment that sometimes . . . they are within a hair's breadth of being turned up-
side down' (p. 698). That is his revised policy for all occasions,
and it is peculiarly delectable to employ it against the accredited
saints. Whether Dostoevsky means us to think that because of
their double-mindedness they are not really saints, or that the
saints are bound to experience in the highest degree the tribula-
tions common to all mortality, it is hard to guess. There is
evidence for both views; on the whole, the increasing emphasis

on joy and happiness in *The Brothers Karamazov* suggests a shift towards the first.

Of the final episode of the 'Dream', the confrontation of Ivan with his early poem on 'The Geological Cataclysm', we have already spoken: as it was clearly an early work, he is reminded of it merely for his discomfort.[50] As we have seen, the recovered golden age is here associated with the worship of the new man-God, under whom, at any rate in the period of transition, 'all is permitted'. It reminds us of what is already sufficiently clear: that Ivan is naturally a believer who will worship man if he cannot worship God. He is Kirillov without his appalling concentration. But what is significant is that all this is revealed at the moment when Ivan is preparing to sacrifice himself for a point of honour. He is disturbed by Alyosha, knocking at the door to report the suicide of Smerdyakov. With his evidence removed, no one is going to believe Ivan's confession; but he will go ahead with it just the same.[51] The part of Ivan not reflected in the devil's recital comes to the fore; at the moment of trial, he testifies by his act to the truth which he theoretically denies.[52] The result of a wholly lucid double-mindedness is his nervous breakdown.

The 'Dream' illuminates Ivan: it is a superb piece of writing, succeeding where *The Double* had failed thirty years earlier, in devising a technique for the description of the divided mind; but it is too tangled to be used with anything but the greatest caution in the study of Dostoevsky's theology. It is further evidence that Ivan is a large part of Dostoevsky's past: in fact, on p. 699, there is a curious oversight which proves it. The devil babbles on to Ivan about a 'romantic strain in you, so derided by Belinsky'. Ivan had not been derided by Belinsky; but Dostoevsky had. For the rest, the identification of the devil with the double highlights the contrary identification of God with consentience. By way of contrast the episode points us to the

---

[50] Though he objects in the same way to being reminded of 'The Legend' (p. 701).

[51] *C'est chevaleresque*, says the devil, in his seedy-gentleman's French.

[52] He could be wrong to associate his dubieties, or even the cult of the man-God, with 'all is permitted', but he at least is convinced he is right.

example of Zosima and the prospects of Alyosha. In fact, his brother's predicament is Alyosha's first test. As Ivan lost consciousness, Alyosha put him to bed, sat with him and understood him. 'God, in whom he disbelieved, and his truth, were gaining mastery over his heart, which still refused to submit' (p. 708). The issue remains open: 'He will rise up in the light of truth, or . . . he'll perish in hate, revenging on himself and everyone else his having served the cause he does not believe in.' But Alyosha prayed for him, as he had worked on him, and when Ivan gave evidence at the trial, though he stammered and blustered, he loyally told what he believed to be the truth. God was working in him, unbelief and all.

And that is where Dostoevsky leaves us. The refutation of the theory is in the practice: in the experience of Zosima, in the promise of Alyosha, and above all in Ivan's testimony at the trial. From their point of vantage, surveying the history of irrationalism in religion from Kierkegaard downwards, some may think he agonized unnecessarily. Indeed, his natural alignment was with Kierkegaard who dismissed in the name of Christianity the 'world-historical' theodicy which Belinsky had attacked in the name of atheism. But something in him demanded of reason, something which he found reason could not supply. He continued to ask for order and justification while making his way to a religion which outran order and dispersed with justification. And some will hold it to his credit that he refused, at great cost to himself, the treacherous dichotomy of God and the world, and utilized, even without the proper theoretical foundations, the one distinction currently available to him: the distinction between theory and practice. Insofar as he took up, in *Crime and Punishment*, the 'conservative' distinction between *razsudok* and *razum*, analysis and good sense, he was on the way to making his point within the ambit of reason. For the most part, he continued to defend religion against reason. Alyosha expresses his final attitude in a conversation with Ivan (p. 242).

'I think everyone should love life above everything in the world.'
'Love life more than the meaning of it?'
'Certainly, love it, regardless of logic as you say, it must be regard-

less of logic, and it's only then one will understand the meaning of it
. . . Half your work is done, Ivan, you love life, now you've only to
try to do the second half and you are saved.'

There *is* a meaning; but one only discernible to those who love
life in the first instance. Truth is a function of joy. But joy itself
is a function of 'active love': active love, though it does not
depend on reason – *razsudok*, nevertheless incapsulates a reason
of its own. It is a sorting out of the human person in which the
initiative of the individual is maintained, and its self-seeking
separateness is overcome. This is presented to us as a sort of
ecclesiastically sanctioned natural goodness backed by national
habit. It could be added that it makes sense – at any rate for those
who love first. That Dostoevsky found it to make *some* kind of
sense appears in Father Paisy's farewell admonition to Alyosha:
'The science of this world . . . has only analysed the parts and
overlooked the whole, and indeed (its) blindness is marvellous.
Yet the whole still stands steadfast before their eyes, the gates of
hell shall not prevail against it' (p. 178). 'The whole': is this a
variation on the post-Hegelian 'concrete universal'?[53] If so, it is
with the reservation that only those who love can see things
whole; and as love is construed as 'active love', we are back
again to the familiar text; 'If any man do his will, he shall know
of the doctrine.' Mere theory, just because it is theory, ends in
atheism, because it analyses and does not see the whole. The
distinction may be too sharp; the disinterested approach to
nature may yield *some* evidences of a greater glory: 'grace',
as the very Western Thomas Aquinas observed, 'does not
abolish nature, but perfects it'. One might wish that Dostoevsky
who saw how knowledge will grow from love had also seen that
love can grow from knowledge. One might wish that he had
lived to read the last sentences of his friend Solovyov's *Justification of the Good*.

It least of all befits believers in the Absolute Good to fear philosophical investigation, as if the moral significance of the world could lose by

---

[53] Dostoevsky once wrote to his brother from Siberia that everything depended
on his reading Hegel's *History of Philosophy*, but he shows no sign of having
digested it and he may not even have received it.

being finally explained, and as though union with God in love, and harmony with his will, could leave us no part in the Divine Intellect. Having justified the Good in moral philosophy, we must, in theoretical philosophy, justify the Good as truth (p. 475).

But if he had thought like that, he would not have been Dostoevsky.

EPILOGUE

It remains to gather together the threads which have guided us through the labyrinth and to survey the scene as a whole.

1. The development of Dostoevsky, literary and personal, was tortuous, retrogressive, but continuous and indomitable, like the growth of a plant hidden by overhanging foliage; making for the light, only to move into more shadow, striking out laterally and again upwards, and finally discovering a promising gap in the thicket towards the sun, just when its vital thrust was beginning to fail. Everything he wrote is unmistakably his own, but there are no set views which can be ascribed to 'Dostoevsky'; everything he set down must be related to a particular phase of his growth or to the characters chosen to express it. Moreover, almost to the end, he was divided against himself. It was inestimably fortunate for us that his bipolar temperament helped him to depict a similar polarity in the social and intellectual situation of Russia in the 1860's.

2. One expression of this 'doubleness', in himself and in his environment, was the dichotomy between faith and reason. He grew up at a time and in a country where there was both 'faith' (among the people) and 'reason' (among rootless intellectuals), and no facilities for interchange or compromise. 'Reason' was presented to him as antithetical to 'faith', and 'faith' as something which could flourish without or even against 'reason'. Again and again he tried to formulate their incommensurability; in novel after novel he tested his 'prose' advances towards God, and

relentlessly found them wanting.[1] In the end, still perched over the cleft between them, he was finding a way not of reconciling them but of combining them in their unreconciliation. He did not deny the conclusions of reason; he even accepted them (Alyosha did not dissent from Ivan's argument); but he found them to be relative in the context of Christian action. The facts are as reason has stated them; but the central issue is: what can be done with them?

3. Reason, as Dostoevsky for the most part understood it, was separatist and analytical; it splits up the totalities in which we live. By contracting the vision, it falsifies. He did not appreciate the artifice whereby, by splitting, it clarifies the totality itself.[2] He did, however, see very clearly that to treat the atomized elements as the real thing was to deform it. Hence his profound distrust of liberal individualism in politics, both in its Utilitarian and in its nihilist form. The error has religious implications; if the individual is intrinsically separate, he is self-dependent – as the bourgeois oncomers put it, with an unconscious atheism, 'self-made'. In fact, for Dostoevsky individualism and atheism went together, not merely historically, but by an inward affinity; they both derive from the analytic outlook which destroys the unity of situations. Dostoevsky's deep antipathies in this region are partly explained by his 'populism': as a one-time Westernizer, with certain persisting Western habits of mind, he distilled from his observation of the 'people', in all humility and with some surprise, the ideal of *sobornost'* – the spontaneous togetherness of a congregation at the moment of worship carried over to everyday living. But they are also explained by his own experience of the all too precious 'I': he treasured it, and hated himself for doing so. His dislike of analytic reason was directed against his own egotism, founded as he believed it to be on a claim to separate identity, and against the public egotisms which he saw

---

[1] In some ways, he seems nearer to the goal in *Crime and Punishment* than in *The Idiot* or *The Possessed*; but only because there the issue is faced less remorselessly. Raskolnikov, we noted, lacks the spiritual stature of Nastasya Filippovna and Stavrogin.

[2] A totality is not a cohesive whole, but a lived situation, the elements of which are more likely than not to be in conflict.

displacing the family-model fabric of a common life. Yet, as so
often, his antithesis is also a compresence: in the working out of
sobornost', the 'I' and the 'whole' are at one; neither loses, and
both gain, from the simultaneous expansion of the other.[3] The
accommodation is never easy or secure; it has continually to be
recaptured from the pressures of the world: but it is among
these pressures that it finds its home. Even when it is ushered
in by a mystical moment, what anchors it, in the end, is its
efficacy in action.

4. It may be objected that goodness, for Dostoevsky, was not
so much a matter of action as of disposition. We are told, for
example, that if only our minds could be changed, our actions,
and the world, would be changed almost automatically.[4]
Certainly, Dostoevsky was not one of those who look for a
gradual salvation through continuous effort. Nevertheless,
Zosima concludes with *active* love, and it is this, in a modest way,
that Alyosha succeeds in putting into practice. However in-
calculable the springs of active love, practice is to be the test of
it. And here we come round to Dostoevsky's version of 'practical
reason' – not the rationalist version of Kant, but one in which
works are shown to be the fruits of faith, and its guarantee. The
contrast between *razsudok* and *razum*, analytic reason and good
sense, noted by the critics apropos of Porfiry Petrovich in *Crime
and Punishment*, if he had developed it, could perhaps have
served him better than he himself realized. The faith displayed in
'active love' is not so far from being 'reasonable'. The drive, of
course, is not intellectual; for Dostoevsky, it might be all the
more reasonable for that.

5. The drift to 'reasonableness' as opposed to 'rationality'
coincides with the recovery of a belief in a better world. We
have noted the young Dostoevsky's engagement with Utopia;
its collapse among the realities of Siberia; and its discreet re-
emergence after his return from Europe in 1871. In *The Idiot* it
looked like a permanent casualty; in *The Possessed* it is to be found

---

[3] A compresence of opposites, remaining opposities, not a Hegelian dialectical
triad.
[4] See *The Dream of a Ridiculous Man*, pp.161ff. above.

only at the far end of a nightmare; but in *The Raw Youth* it gathers strength, and in *The Dream of a Ridiculous Man* and *The Brothers Karamazov* it is actually presented as a long-range possibility – dependent, of course, on the active love of each for all. The proviso makes all the difference; Utopia is now re-integrated in a Christian perspective, at a much deeper level that Dostoevsky could have foreseen in the 1840's. The paradise which the earth can offer is now near at hand, if only our habits can be guided into channels already provided by populist and Orthodox precedent. How difficult, seeing that the 'I' is always with us, distorted and exaggerated in the liberal-anarchist thought-currents of the 1870's! And yet how easy, if only we can let our separateness go and love others as ourselves!

6. The question may be asked: how are we to understand *sobornost'* – the spiritual togetherness of Christians, in which the 'I' is both submerged and enhanced? It could be taken to mean each man doing his own thing in the sight of God along with others each of whom is also doing his own thing, all linked with God and therefore moving in harmony, but not deeply aware of each other. That interpretation fails to bring out what Dos-toevsky was most concerned for. There is no genuine together-ness without active concern: 'each is responsible for all'. It is not enough for the spiritually stronger man to be upstanding: he has to be available, and to give from his spiritual substance, and in such a way that the weaker may receive without being humili-ated. Dostoevsky knew that this was a counsel of perfection, and that the earthly paradise was indeed distant; but at the end he saw how it might come about, and that it was not wholly im-possible.

7. But that is in no way to minimize evil. Evil – not merely wrongdoing, but a metaphysical force with something demonic about it – is a large part of Dostoevsky's world. Fortunately or disastrously, the 'possessed' are self-destructive; fortunately, because it means that they cannot win; disastrously, because their redemption is part of the programme, and the self-destruc-tive desperately resist it. It is the kind of evil which wrecks the cheap theodicies (Ivan Karamazov has rendered them unavail-

able for all time), and which provides the most implacable challenge to the Christian in process. Myshkin failed, because he was too inexperienced, too ideal, too far from the norm. Tikhon failed; he had only one interview and hardly a chance, but he wrecked the chance he had when his insight outran his compassion. Alyosha, programmed to succeed, was young, normal, rooted in a Christian community, and a full member of the sick generation. He points forward to the theological dogma that, to save the world, God himself must be at all points like ourselves: Very God and Very Man.

BIBLIOGRAPHY

1. WRITINGS OF DOSTOEVSKY

Novels and short stories

1846 *Poor Folk*
     The Double
1849 *Netochka Nezanova*
1859 *Uncle's Dream*
1861 *The House of the Dead*
     The Insulted and Injured
1866 *The Gambler*
     Crime and Punishment

1869 *The Idiot*
     The Eternal Husband
1871 *The Possessed*
1875 *The Raw Youth*
1877 *The Dream of a Ridiculous Man*
1880 *The Brothers Karamazov*

English translations

All the above, and other minor short stories, tr. Constance Garnett, Heinemann 1912–1920. *Crime and Punishment, The Idiot, The Devils* (the same work as Garnett's *The Possessed*) and *The Brothers Karamazov*, tr. David Magarshack, Penguin Books 1948 onwards. The three suppressed chapters of *The Possessed* were published as *Stavrogin's Confession*, tr. S. S. Koteliansky and Virginia Woolf, Hogarth Press 1922.

Non-fiction

1862 *Winter Notes on Summer Impressions*
1873, 1876–77, 1880, 1881 *Diary of a Writer*, 2 vols, tr. B. Brasol, Cassell 1951.
Pisma (Letters), 4 vols, ed. A. S. Dolinin, Moscow-Leningrad 1928–59. This is the definitive edition of correspondence. Selections have appeared in English, eg. *Dostoevsky. A Self-portrait*, a selection of

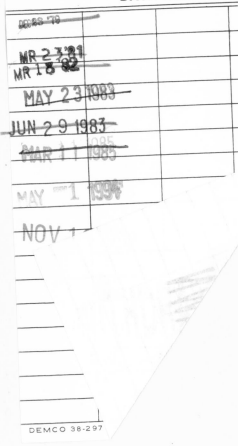
Dostoevsky's letters ed. and tr. by Jessie Coulson, OUP 1962; *Letters of F. M. Dostoevsky to his Family and Friends*, tr. Ethel Colburn Mayne, Chatto & Windus 1917; *New Dostoevsky Letters*, tr. S. S. Koteliansky, Mandrake Press 1929.

Dostoevsky's Occasional Writings, tr. David Magarshack, Vision Press 1964.

II. WRITINGS ABOUT DOSTOEVSKY

In English

Berdyaev, N. A., *Dostoievsky; an Interpretation*, tr. D. Attwater, Sheed & Ward 1934.

Berdyaev, N. A., *The Russian Revolution*, Sheed & Ward 1932.

Carr, E. H., *Dostoevsky, 1821–1881*, Allen & Unwin 1953.

Gide, A., *Dostoevsky*, Dent 1925.

Grishin, D., 'The Beliefs of Dostoevsky', *Twentieth Century*, vol. 17, Melbourne, Autumn 1963, pp. 255ff.

Hingley, R. F., *The Undiscovered Dostoyevsky*, Hamish Hamilton 1962.

Ivanov, V. I., *Freedom and the Tragic Life*, Noonday Press, NY 1957.

Krieger, Murray, *The Tragic Vision*, Holt, Rinehart & Winston, NY 1960.

Lavrin, Janko, *Dostoevsky and his Creation*, Collins 1920.

Mochulsky, K. V., *Dostoevsky: his Life and Work*, Princeton University Press 1967.

Murry, John Middleton, *Fyodor Dostoevsky. A Critical Study*, Secker & Warburg 1923.

Peace, Richard, *Dostoyevsky: an Examination of the Major Novels*, CUP 1971.

Šajković, Miriam T., *F. M. Dostoevsky: His Image of Man*, University of Pennsylvania Press 1962.

Seduro, Vladimir, *Dostoevsky in Russian Literary Criticism, 1846–1956*, OUP 1957.

Simmons, Ernest J., *Dostoevsky: the Making of a Novelist*, OUP 1940; republished by Vintage Books, NY 1962.

Steinberg, A., *Dostoievsky*, Bowes & Bowes 1966.

Steiner, George, *Tolstoy or Dostoevsky?*, Faber 1960.

Wasiolek, Edward, *Dostoevsky: the Major Fiction*, MIT Press, Mass. 1964.

Wellek, R. (ed.), *Dostoevsky. A Collection of Critical Essays*, Prentice Hall, NJ 1962.

Woodhouse, C. M., *Dostoievsky*, Arthur Barker, 2nd ed. 1968.

Yarmolinsky, A., *Dostoevsky: His Works and Days*, Funk & Wagnalls, NY 1971.

Zander, L. A., *Dostoevsky*, SCM Press 1948.

In other languages

Bakhtin, M. M., *Problemy poetiki Dostoevskogo*, Moscow, 2nd ed. 1963.

Bazanov, V. G. and Fridlender, G. M. (eds.), *Dostoevsky i ego Vremya*, Moscow 1971.

Fanger, Donald (ed.), *O Dostoevskom. Stati*, Brown University Press, Providence 1966.

Fridlender, G. M., *Realism Dostoevskogo*, Moscow-Leningrad 1964.

Grishin, D. V., *Aforizmy i vyskazyvaniya F.M. Dostoevskogo*, Melbourne University 1961.

Grishin, D. V., *Dostoevsky-Chelovek, Pisatel' i Mify*, Melbourne University 1971.

Guardini, Romano, *Der Mensch und der Glaube*, Leipzig 1932.

Lossky, N., *Dostoevsky i ego khristiyanskoye miroponimaniye*, Chekhov Publishing House, NY 1953.

Pascal, Pierre, *Dostoievski*, Paris 1969.

Shestov, L. I., *La philosophie de la tragédie. Dostoïewsky et Nietzsche*, Paris 1926.

Stepanov, N. L. (ed. with others), *Tvorchestvo Dostoevskogo*, Moscow 1959.

Rozanov, V. V., *Legenda o Veolikom Inkvizitore F.M. Dostoevskogo*, Berlin 1924.

III. GENERAL

Belinsky, V. I., *Selected Philosophical Works*, Eng. tr., Moscow 1948.

Christoff, Peter K., *An Introduction to Nineteenth-Century Russian Slavophilism; a Study in Ideas*, The Hague 1961.

Chernyshevskii, N. G., *Chto delat'?* (What's to be Done?), tr. B. R. Tucker, Boston 1886.

Edie, James M. (ed. with others), *Russian Philosophy*, 3 vols, Quadrangle Books, Chicago 1965.

Freud, S., 'Dostoevski and Parricide', *The Realist*, vol. I, no. 4, London 1929.

Lewis, C. S., 'Theology and Poetry', *They Asked for a Paper; Papers and Addresses*, ch. 9, Bles 1962.

Sayers, Dorothy, *The Mind of the Maker*, Methuen 1941.

Solovyov, V. S., *The Justification of the Good. An Essay on Moral Philosophy*, Constable 1918.

Zernov, N., *Eastern Christendom*, Weidenfeld & Nicholson 1901.